P.R. Morehouse

U.S. NAVY

Three Squares
&
a Rack

DELTA
Publishing

First Original Edition

© Copyright 2017 by Philip R. Morehouse

ISBN-13: 978-1979918756

ISBN-10: 1979918759

Published by Delta Press LLC

This novel is based on a true story. The names of the characters have been changed for purposes of anonymity.

The USS Fort Mandan LSD-21

The U.S.S. FORT MANDAN (LSD-21) was constructed during the latter stages of World War II, and was commissioned after hostilities had ended. The FORT MANDAN'S keel was laid on January 21, 1945, and the ship was launched June 2, 1945. The ship is named for FORT MANDAN, North Dakota, the home of the Hidasa Indian Tribe on the Missouri River, near where the Lewis and Clark Expedition wintered in 1804-1805.

The ship was officially commissioned October 31, 1945 at the U.S. Navy Yard at Boston, Mass., where it was built. She was originally assigned to the Atlantic 16th Reserve Fleet, but in December, 1945, was reassigned to the Second Fleet for duty with the Service Force, U.S. Atlantic Fleet. The FORT MANDAN was assigned to the Atlantic Reserve Fleet in August, 1947, and was placed out of commission in January, 1948.

As a result of the aggression in Korea, the FORT MANDAN was recommissioned October 23, 1950. In December of that year it reported for duty with the Amphibious Force, U.S. Atlantic Fleet.

The FORT MANDAN participated in the initial NATO maneuvers, Operation Mainbrace, during August and September of 1952. The ship was assigned to the U.S. Sixth Fleet in the Mediterranean from October 1952 through January 1953.

From September to November 1953, the FORT MANDAN took part in Operation SUNEC (Supply North-east Construction) and made calls at ports in Greenland, Labrador, and Newfoundland.

In 1955, the ship made two trips to the Caribbean on amphibious training exercises. In July 1955, the FORT MANDAN again sailed North on Operation SUNEC. Early in September, the FORT MANDAN went through Hudson Strait and spent some time in Western Hudson Bay.

In January and February of 1956, the ship visited Fort Lauderdale, Florida, as a liberty port and later engaged in amphibious exercises off Vieques, followed by liberty in Havana, Cuba. April through mid-August was spent in overhaul at Baltimore, followed by refresher training at Guantanamo Bay, Cuba.

August through October of 1956 found the ship at Fox Basin (North of Hudson Bay). On the way home, between Labrador and Newfoundland, the FORT MANDAN picked up a distress signal from a Canadian motor vessel, and under very severe weather conditions, towed the ship 160 miles down the coast of Newfoundland where a Canadian ice-breaker relieved the FORT MANDAN. For accomplishing this task, the FORT MANDAN was highly commended by the Chief of Naval Operations, the Commander in Chief, U.S. Atlantic Fleet, the Commander, Amphibious Force, U.S. Atlantic Fleet, and other operational and administrative commanders.

During 1957, the FORT MANDAN participated in several Amphibious Operations. Among them was CARIBEX, which was an amphibious landing in the Panama Canal Zone, and MARMID, I and II, which were Midshipmen landing exercises. A summer Naval Reserve cruise to Bermuda was made in August.

The USS Fort Mandan LSD-21

During the period September-November of 1957, the FORT MANDAN was assigned to the Military Sea Transportation Service for Arctic services. The ship accomplished the task of lifting U.S. Army personnel and equipment from Thule, Greenland, and Sondrestromfjord, Greenland to Argentina, Newfoundland and Norfolk, Virginia. After spending a short holiday season at Little Creek, the FORT MANDAN departed for Morehead City, N.C., and Port Everglades, Fla., to load the advance echelon of PHIBTRAEX 1-58, to be lifted to Vieques, P.R., and Roosevelt Roads, P.R. During this cruise, she participated in SPRINGBOARD training exercises and visited the port of San Juan, P.R., for liberty.

The FORT MANDAN returned to the United States via Bermuda where she loaded personnel and equipment of DET H, of Mobile Construction Battalion Six, for transportation to Davisville, R.I. After three days of liberty here, the ship went back to Norfolk to prepare for the second phase of PHIBTRAEX 1-58. She sailed on 5 March 1958 for Vieques, and Roosevelt Roads, where she loaded Marine Air Units for a landing at Onslow Beach, North Carolina.

The FORT MANDAN entered the Norfolk Naval Ship Yard at Portsmouth, Va., for her Biennial overhaul in July 1958. In September, having completed the overhaul, the ship sailed for Guantanamo Bay, Cuba for refresher training.

The FORT MANDAN left for the Med. in early 1959 for a 6 month tour with 6th Fleet. While in liberty in Sete, France the ship was instrumental in extinguishing a large fire on board the gasoline tanker OMBRINA. Since her return in September 1959, she has participated in several landing exercises and has served as recovery ship for Project Mercury's "Monkey into Space" efforts. On 4 October 1960, the FORT MANDAN entered the Norfolk Shipyard at Berkley for a Fram II overhaul.

On February 20, 1962, the FORT MANDAN underwent refresher training at Norfolk, Virginia and then returned to Little Creek to make preparations for another 6 month Mediterranean deployment. Upon her return in October of 1961, the FORT MANDAN was assigned as recovery ship for Project Mercury's "Monkey in Orbit" program. While on this assignment the FORT MANDAN visited Bermuda for the third time. From February 1962-May 1962, the FORT MANDAN was involved in PHIBTRAEX 1-62 in the Caribbean, including visits to San Juan, and the Virgin Islands. Upon its return in May, we spent the summer involved in training Navy, Marine and Army forces in amphibious landings. And then again September 1962, the FORT make a Med cruise which we hope this book will cover in a pictorial fashion.

Picture taken from the USS Fort Mandan LSD-21, Mediterranean Cruise Book 1962 to 1963

The USS Fort Mandan LSD-21

Picture in public domain.

The USS Fort Mandan LSD-21

*Picture in public domain.

Three Squares and a Rack[1], is a true story based on the life Cal Morison; a young, naïve, country boy who leaves the family farm - the only life he has ever known, to join the Navy. His quest is not only just to see the world, but more importantly, to get a higher education, which he knows will later enable him to find a good job. In addition, he also finds, high seas adventure and the love of his life, as he becomes a man.

---

[1] Three Meals and a Bed

Three Squares and a Rack

Table of Contents

Tribute:
This true story has been written as a tribute to Cal's mother who taught her children right from wrong – never to give up and to "treat others as they would like to be treated". The latter being her "Golden Rule".

I also want to thank Cal for allowing me the privilege of writing his story, as his story could be my story and as such, is the story of so many who have lived in abstract poverty; enduring unimaginable hardships. However, in and of these hardships, the family sought to use its lessons as tools to achieve greater successes throughout their lives.

Disclaimer:
The names of the persons and places, in this story, have been changed to provide the guilty anonymity and to honor the innocent. Those who have been a part of Cal's life may see themselves in these pages and perhaps, will remember another time when the world was full of innocence, and the stars were never so bright.

Dear Friends:
Thank you, for enduring my long abscesses while writing this book and for encouraging me in this pursuit.

A Very Special Thanks:
To my editor, Norma Cushner, who lets nothing get by her, and whose efforts have led to the enhanced readability of a story that you will find to be a portrayal of the life of a Navy man during the "60s".

In addition, a special thanks to Lori Snowden, my cover designer, whose work serves as the billboard that attracts my readers to the story within.

Preface:

This true story takes place from 1961 to 1966 during the startup of the Viet Nam War, the Cuban Missile Crisis and Dominican Haiti uprising.

You will feel Cal's emotions as he copes with leaving home, finally breaking free of the hills that had trapped his imagination for so long, his induction into the Navy, the rigors of Boot Camp, Intensive "A" school training, and finally, his becoming a part of the U.S. Navy Fleet. You will be with him as the fleet goes to sea, trains for war and you will learn of Cal's part in those drills. You are there during the Cuban Blockade Missile Crisis and the Dominican Haiti uprising. You will feel the excitement of the crew as they go on liberty in foreign ports, and Cal's working on heavy machinery during a Yard Overhaul in Savanna and finally the overwhelming excitement of returning home after a long absence, to family and friends at the Little Creek Amphibious Base, in Virginia.

As you read this story, you will be walking in Cal's shoes, learning what military life was like at boot camp and on board the naval amphibious ship, the USS Fort Mandan LSD 21 You are with him as he navigates through the straits and narrows of his naval years. You will also get a taste of Cal's personal side; his falling in love, failing, and falling in love again, his transitioning back to civilian life; obtaining his first apartment, learning to live on a budget while balancing his time between his job and that of his fiancée as she studies to be a nurse.

Chapter 1.0

The day Cal Morison left home, was two days after the Christmas of "61". There was a couple of inches of wind-swept snow on the rock hard, frozen ground; the air was crisp and biting and he didn't care, as another adventure was about to begin.

Absently, his mind raced ahead as he waited for the Navy Recruiter's arrival. "It should be any minute now," Cal reasoned, as he paced the living room floor, every so often looking at the old, key wound clock on the wall.

From their country home in upstate NY, of the past 15-years of his life, he'd be taken to Syracuse for processing and swearing in. Then they'd travel on to the Great Lakes Naval Training Center, where he'd enter boot camp. It sounded simple enough, right?

But the reality of the day would end up being far different than what he'd imagined.

While waiting, he quickly ran through a mental list of all the things his brother, Kale, should know when doing his newly acquired chores. Just the thought of his brother skating out of his chores these past years and now, with him having to do all the chores, gave Cal a perverse sense of pleasure. However, after having advised Kale on how to take care of the new, motorized, rotary, horizontal-blade, lawnmower, he was left with a bad feeling in his gut that the mower wouldn't fair well with Kale in charge of its maintenance. Cal felt particularly responsible for it since he'd worked the better part of a summer to pay it off. In the past, he'd used a dull, reel type, push mower to keep the grass under control. When that failed, he'd had fallen back to using a scythe and a pair of foraged grass shears. This was very hard work, resulting in their having only a postage stamp size lawn. However, he had gained a healthy respect for those who worked all day with these types of tools.

Apparently, he was the last man to be pickup, given that the Navy recruiter's car was nearly full when it arrived, save for one space that had been allocated to him.

The recruiter looked extra sharp in his dress blues" and white hat, which was the dress code for performing this "formal duty". His white hat sat slightly cocked, atop a swag of light brown hair, cut short on the sides to Navy specification. His face was square, displaying a bit of determination and yet a certain amount of patience. His blue eyes betrayed a bit of amusement. He was every bit the epitome of professionalism, after all, he was taking the pride of each family away from their homes, to a completely alien environment, and he had all the parent's feelings to contend with and that included belaying any fears for their child's safety. For a time, he'd be their only link to their sons and daughters.

Mom, her graying hair whipping around her face in the icy wind, was bundled in a hand-me-down coat, his sisters; Marie, the oldest, Fanny, outspoken and always in mischief, and younger brother, Kale, all came out to see him off.

He could see the tears in their eyes, and fidgeting hands, but made believe he hadn't. To speak of it would only make him feel even worse than he already did about leaving.

After receiving his final hugs from his Mom and sisters and a last look at his brother's expressionless face, he stepped into the car.

He couldn't help but feel a little bit guilty about his chores falling back on his mother's shoulders, as he knew Kale would continue to skate, as he always had – hopefully she could somehow motivate him to get them done.

Kale, as usual, was hanging behind the others with his hands in his pockets as he stared off into space. Cal knew that he was thinking, "Now that that pain in the ass brother of mine is out of sight, I can get away with anything."

As they left, he turned one last time to see their hands in the air, still waving, as they disappeared from sight. It would be late spring before he'd see them again.

*   *   *

Up the road in the distance, a black car was parked. A man, dressed in black, sat in the car watching the proceedings with great interest. After the recruiter's car left, he put his field glasses down and made some notes on a sheet of paper, which was attached to a sheath of other papers in a manila folder. When he finished writing, he put them away along with the binoculars. Then he turned the car around and drove away in the opposite direction.

*   *   *

Cal knew the days of working in their family garden, then for Parry and Amos on their farms, and later for Len as a handyman and an electrician's helper, were behind him, but not forgotten. All this experience was something to which he'd build upon.

Soon it became uncomfortably warm in the car. He'd become used to living in a cold home and working outdoors winters and so his blood was thicker. He reached over and cracked the window, tilting his head toward the fresh brisk air. The recruiter, noticing, turned the heat down and Cal rolled the window up.

He could tell by the laughter from the others, that they were nervous about what was going to happen next. Each had a story and a reason for going into the service, the going away parties and the life they were leaving behind.

Cal could see that the occupants were all a curious bunch – no two alike, but for their youth. Since his seat was in front, he only glanced at them on occasion. One man was thin with light colored hair – he had a nervous laugh. They called him Jer, no doubt it'd been abbreviated from Jerry. There was also another guy in the back, by the name of Sotak. He was also laughing a lot and talked about a family owned dinner that he helped run. Then there was another; heavier and quieter than the others, who he learned was named Hopko. Hopko mostly listened and watched the scenery passing by their car.

Before he knew it, they'd pulled up in front of the Syracuse Navy Enlistment Center. It was an imposing, formal, cement building, several stories high.

The recruiter, called them all together and explained that they'd be there the rest of the day going through some testing – not to worry, it was not hard and anyone flunking it had to be an idiot.

Cal knew for sure that he didn't want to go first. He'd already learned they'd be getting their physicals. He knew that this included the dreaded blood tests, which evoked unpleasant memories of his early years when he had to go to a clinic twice a year for blood work.

After these tests, they'd be sworn in. Laughingly the Recruiter added with a wink, "*that so far, none of his guys had ever flunked,*" which gave all of them a boost in our confidence.

Earlier, the recruiter had asked him if he had flat feet, wet the bed and some other disparaging questions to which he'd answered resoundingly "no" to all of them. Apparently, if the answer had been "yes" to any of these, he would have been disqualified and sent home.

We were told, that after being sworn in by the (CO) Commanding Officer, we'd have our pictures taken in front of the American and the US Navy Flags. These would later be sent home to their parents or spouses, along with a Navy bumper sticker. Since his family had no car, his mom proudly displayed the sticker in the picture window, so that everyone driving by could see that her oldest son was in the Navy.

However, before he could be sworn in, their review of his medical file revealed that he had a history of Rheumatic Fever. They had to know for sure if he still had any ill affects from it, like a pronounced heart murmur, which would indicate a leaky heart value. With time running out, they rushed him to a heart specialist, where they ran a series of tests. He was immediately told upon arriving, to start doing pushups; ten rapid pushups, then twenty and back to ten, then the doctor listened to his heart and looked at his chest through a Fluoroscope. Next, they had him doing setups and more pushups, after which the doctor listened again. Finally shaking his head in total resignation, he said, empathically, "*that, as far as he was concerned, Cal was healthy and fit for duty,*" and signed off on his paperwork.

Under his breath, Cal said, "*Thank you, God,*" as he breathed a big sigh of relief. He couldn't imagine having to go back home – a reject - a misfit, back to living on the farm - with no future.

Finally, well after dark, they were bused to the airport where they boarded a huge commercial plane bound for Chicago. For him, this was a new experience, as he'd never seen the inside, let alone been on an airplane. Such large planes never landed at their small airport in Binghamton.

Since it was dark, there was little to see outside his window seat, so most of his attention was taken up by what was going on inside the plane. It seemed like they were hardly airborne when the airline hostesses started serving supper on trays along with cold soft drinks. For those who requested it, various types of booze in tiny bottles were dispensed with the same ease as one would ask for candy. This was an experience beyond anything he'd ever seen or heard of. He had no taste for booze but did indulge in as many soft drinks as he could get – no matter the flavor, for him, this was a real treat as they were considered a luxury back home.

About midway into their trip, the guys started getting rowdy; they had had way too much to drink, and as they laughed and talked, their voices were getting louder and less coherent.

Looking around, he noticed that most of the passengers were made up of young men, more than likely from all over New York State. They were boys, soon to become men, fast losing their grip on their adolescences, still desperately grasping at the last of their innocence.

Some of the guys were picking on the airline hostesses – flirting with them and very much pushing the envelope. They were all beautiful young woman. In those days, he'd heard that they had to be single and way above average in the "looks" department, to get the job.

After a time it stopped being funny – some of the guys were getting carried away, and finally one of the passengers stood up. He could have been an officer or a civilian, but whatever he was, he had had enough and chewed them out. After that, it got quiet again. The boys had been looking for that bit of a push back – they needed to know that there were still limitations to what they could do ... there always would be, especially in the military.

He was glad that he was not one of them, though he hadn't done anything to stop it either – so perhaps he was as guilty as they were - "Guilt by Association", a situation that he'd later, unintentionally, come to understand first hand.

Chapter 2.0

It was 2:30 am mid-western time when they landed and emerged from the heated envelope of the plane, to a shocking coldness that was beyond belief. Most of the guys hadn't dressed for the extreme weather, and soon they were all shaking, and their teeth chattering. Someone said that it was thirty below and he could believe it, as he had experienced that kind of cold a few times on their farm.

They stood huddled together for a few minutes, though it seemed like hours, when a green military bus pulled up. They all rushed to the door and crowded into its dark interior, instantly discovering that it wasn't much warmer inside. Their combined breath condensed on the windows quickly icing them over, making them useless for seeing through.

The bus looked as if it might have been an old school bus painted a hideous shade of green. The seats were stiff from the cold and incredibly uncomfortable. It's only saving grace was that it soon warmed up inside and most of the guys dozed off in spite of their discomfort. He secretly hoped these accommodations were not a precursor of things to come.

He was hungry beyond belief since he hadn't eaten since lunch, which was at the start of their airplane trip several hours ago. He doubted very much that they would be fed anytime soon given the time of night and the lack of people around.

After what seemed like hours of thumping and bumping, the bus squealed to a stop. The driver rolled his window down and yelled something to a person standing next to a gate. They later learned that it was the Gate Guard and there were at least two men at every entrance and exit from this and any other US base.

Then they started to roll again. Most everyone had awakened and were exhaling on the windows, trying to remove the stubborn layer of ice so they could catch a glimpse of where we were.

Outside, everything was white. In the darkness, tall, important-looking brick buildings loomed up around us. The bus pulled up to one of these, and they all struggled to right themselves, and exit the bus in spite of their stiff legs. Once off, they huddled alongside the bus in an effort to keep warm.

A rather large man in an unbuttoned, wind whipped, Peacoat, which barely covered his dark blue Navy uniform, came out of the darkness and started screaming at them as if they were to blame for everything that had ever gone wrong in his dominated life.

Cal couldn't believe that any one man could yell so much. In all his life, he had never heard such language or yelling. He told them, at the top of his lungs, that they were no longer PFCs (poor f*$^@* up civilians) but would now be referred to as low, crawling, shit eating, maggots and not to forget it. They were also told that their mommas were no longer here and that they'd better shape up or they'd be shipped back home to suckle with the pigs and several other rather unpleasant things that had to do with animals.

At that moment, he knew he'd made a terrible mistake, and his mind raced to think of a way out of this mess. But ... it was too late. He was trapped in a place and a lifestyle that was as alien to him as the moon was to the astronauts, minus the space suits.

They were ushered into the nearest building with the man still yelling like a scorched cattle herder.

Once inside, he stopped yelling, but continued to scowl and hiss at them. He made a mental note not to drink any milk anywhere near him or it would most assuredly sour and then curdle.

The same man who had screamed at them earlier, lined them all up single file and told them to follow the man ahead of them. They entered a doorway and walked single file past half-awake supply people who threw their allotment of new clothes at them as they passed.

The air was filled with the odor of denim and leather. It reminded him of when he'd bought clothing from the Hugh Sherwood Dry Goods Store in the Point.

Then they were told to stick each of these garments into their sea bag and to keep moving. After it seemed that they could no longer cram even one more item into the bag, they were ushered out onto the cement floor of a huge building. It was referred to as a Drill Hall.

They were told next how and where to stencil their last names on all their clothes. This process entailed using a small Dixie cup filled half way with white paint, a small brush and a piece of plastic with their name cut into it, which had been handed to them.

After painting their name on their clothes, over their shirt pockets and their rear pants pocket, they were instructed to strip every last piece of civilian clothing off their bodies and to drop them into the cardboard box, which they had also picked up on the way into the drill hall.

Next, they were instructed to put every piece of jewelry, other than their wedding rings (for those who were married) into the box.

Pens with box labels were passed out and they were told to put their home address on the label, tear the back off and attach it to the top center of the box.

Then a small box was passed down the line, and all the pens were collected.

There they stood, hundreds, upon hundreds of men, in long lines, ten deep, bare butt naked, with their new clothes piled next to them.

Next, they were told to pick up their boxes, march single file, out a doorway at the far end of the drill hall and down a hall where the boxes were pushed through an opening to another room to be mailed home.

Then, they were told to march on down the hall to the shower located there. He prayed that they wouldn't encounter any women. As they walked over a series of tile pads, liquid disinfectant sprayed upward to delouse them - so they were told. They were instructed after that to take a shower and to form a line outside the room in the same order in which they'd entered. He was sure to keep his distance from the guy in front of him and the one behind. A lot of kidding went on over their precarious situation.

In no time, they were all marched back to the drill hall and ordered to stand over their clothes. He could see right away that they were no longer alone, and he knew that every last man was hoping that we'd be getting dressed, but this was not to be the case – at least not yet.

While they had been showering, a whole staff of Corps-persons had arrived and set up an assembly line for giving shots.

They were shocked to see that there were several women among them, though none caught his eye as being anything to write home about. Row by row, they were marched past the corpsman and given shots in both shoulders; as they took two steps forward and stopped again, two more shots were given and then another two steps, finally ending with one shot in the butt.

The shot in the butt was referred to as a Bicillin L-A shot, a massive, deep intramuscular injection of penicillin, designed to treat many types of severe infections, including strep, rheumatic fever, and syphilis. Since all of those shots occurred at the same location, while bent over holding onto the back of a wooden chair – the floor was soon deep red and sticky from the accumulation of blood. They were all very lame from the Bicillin shot for several days.

Cal wondered if the real intent behind the shot was to keep them from running away.

After getting their shots, they were called to attention and introduced to their CO^2, one, Robert C Palmer. Word soon got around that he was fresh from an Arctic Expedition. They were soon referring to him as "Raincoat Charlie" because no matter how cold it was outside, all he ever wore over his dress blue uniform was a raincoat. He was tall, well over 6-foot, and built like a linebacker for the Chicago Bears. He was even bigger than Cal remembered his grandfather being and, up to this point, he believed him to be the biggest and strongest, toughest man who ever walked the face of the earth. But, after having observed Raincoat Charlie, he knew he was even worse and, they were about to find out just what being driven was all about.

As they were standing at attention, he paced back and forth in front of them. First, he told them that he expected them to be the best company that ever came out of the Great Lakes Naval Training Center; that he'd tell them how it was done once, and after that, you'd get to kiss the deck[3] until you got it right. Next he told them there would be two things they'd never forget to the day they died: your serial number and the name of your CO ... *and ... he was right.*

---

[2] Company Commander
[3] Doing pushups

He also told them that as their training progressed, that they would notice that the guy to the right or left of them would come up missing – that was because they were not good enough to be Navy men. So toe the line or else you too, will be among the missing. As training progressed, he noticed that their ranks were being thinned out as a man he'd seen the night or day before, was no longer with them.

Then he began instructing them about the "*uniform of the day*". They were informed that at the beginning of each day they would be told what the uniform of the day would be (what kind of clothes to put on). For now, since they were "boots" they'd wear a denim long-sleeve shirt, blue jean pants, black stockings and what is lovingly referred to as a pair Boon Dockers, which had to be shined each night to a "spit polished sheen" one that he could see his face in. Also, in the first few weeks of training, their pants were to be folded around their lower leg and tied off at the bottoms with a shoe lace, then tucked into the tops of their socks to indicate that they were "boots." It wouldn't be until they were ready to graduate, that they would be allowed to untie their pant legs and wear the bottoms of their pants outside their socks, over the tops of their Boon Dockers.

*   *   *

In retrospect, the service was an experience like no other he had ever had. It had its good points, and it had its less desirable side. In a lot of ways, it might be comparable to going to college – a college that taught a lot of vocational courses. It was also something else from the first time they shed all their civilian clothes and got their first haircut and put on Navy fatigues; they were all the same. At long last, it wasn't rich kid, poor kid and what your daddy could buy you or the trouble he could get you out of – finally, he had a level playing field - he was an equal, and it felt good. From this playing field, he could launch his new life.

*   *   *

The first part of his Navy experience was the part that no one likes - unless you're a sadist. He would soon come to understand why it's called Boot Camp. After that first night of being humiliated and his body filled with serums for every disease known to man, he finally got to hit the rack to sleep - if you can call it that, as it was only for an hour or two.

He, like all the others in his "company[4]," were exhausted and they all passed out.

*   *   *

They would learn to think and work as a team and not as individuals. Time passed quickly – one day being more or less like the next with the exception of time and length of scheduled classes and their physical workouts. Along with that, there were the occasional surprises which may be extra time off or an unexpected class covering for example, the use of BW[5] gear and being subject to tear gas to emphasis the correct use of the protective clothing,

---

[4] A "company" is made up of 100 to 200 men and a battalion of two to four companies. Three to five battalions, of approximately 1,500 to 4,000 men, comprise a brigade and a division normally has from 50,000 to 100,000 men.

[5] Biological Warfare

mask and gas canisters. These out of the ordinary training time would also include fire fighting and abandoning ship drills. Everything during these exercises was made to feel as if one was actually experiencing the real situation, just as you would aboard a ship during a time of war.

Chapter 3.0

Their wake up call was like nothing he'd ever heard and delivered by a sadist who, no doubt, tortured people in another life. The dead quiet of the morning was shattered with bright lights, yelling and a sound of a GI can[6] be reamed-out with a 16-ounce glass coke bottle. At first, he thought the place was on fire and they had to evacuate right then and there.

They were told that they had 15-minutes to SSS & D[7] and be out on the grinder – whatever that was. It certainly didn't sound very pleasant. Anyone who was thought to be a slacker, the CO kicked in the butt – hence the term "boot camp".

The grinder, they all came to learn, was a large concrete pad covering much of the open area outside theirs and other barracks. This would be where they'd hear their orders for the day and any announcements before going about their business for the day. It was also a place for working out and holding drills. In record time they all "fell in"[8] and their training started as they marched to the Mess Hall[9] – so called as when the ship rolled during the storms, the unsecured trays would slide and fall off

---

[6] Steel garbage can.

[7] Shit, shower, shave and dress

[8] Lined up in several straight lines

[9] The place where meals are served. Called a mess hall do to when the ship rolls during a storm, any unsecured trays would slide off the tables, spilling on the deck, making a 'mess'.

the tables, spilling their contents on the deck[10], making a 'mess'.

As they walked, he could hear the cold snow crunching beneath their collective feet, now housed in stiff, brand new spit-shinned boondockers. He could also feel his starchy, crisp, new blues chafing over his sore rump, as he half limped, half marched his way across the base. Their noses told them long before they got there, that the Mess Hall was just ahead, as they were all snorting like coon hounds on a fresh track, sucking in every wind laden odor.

We were marched to within a few feet of several other Companies who had arrived ahead of ours – how that had been possible, Cal didn't know, as he thought, given the hour, that they would have been there in time to open the place and cook the meal. As they stood in formation, they all started shivering and soon their teeth were clicking from the extreme cold. They could even hear each other's stomachs growling, like a kennel full of dogs. He remembered that many of them hadn't eaten in nearly two days.

Finally, the CO, realizing the situation of his men, told them to all take a half step forward except the first man in each line. As he put it, "close ranks and make your buddy smile". It was a crude way of putting it, but the shift in the formation made them a darn sight warmer.

After what seemed like forever, their turn came to go in. For those who wore glasses, like Cal, they got an immediate coating of ice and couldn't see a thing. Loosening his Peacoat, he followed the man ahead of him and did exactly as he did. Finally, he had a hot metal tray in his hand, then some equally hot silverware. Looking over his glasses, Cal worked his way down the line where he had a large spoonful of runny scrambled eggs slapped into one of the small

---

[10] Floor

compartments in his tray. There was also something that resembled cereal and two slices of toast. He grabbed a hot cup and held it under a spout on a huge, stainless steel rectangular container on legs. When he pushed the oversized handle up, out of a small tube came milk. He soon found out, if you ate fast enough, you could go back for seconds, or at least get more milk.

It seemed like before their butts had hardly hit the seats, the CO was yelling for "Company 3" to dump their trays and to get into formation. So their Company was #3. Soon he learned that they had a sister company which was named Company #8. Their CO was not as hard on them as Raincoat Charlie – he seemed more patient, and his guys actually liked him, where we detested ours. Given what we heard, their CO actually felt sorry for us.

Every day pretty much started out the same: up long before daylight, SSS, go to quarters and stand in formation, listen to the briefing, which included information about the uniform of the day and any special orders; do a brief work out and then march in temperatures so cold it burned the inside of their noses and the moisture from their breath froze on the front of their peacoat collars, as they marched.

Raincoat Charlie thought it was pretty smart to march them through snow drifts and around the grinder in below zero temperatures. He reasoned that it would toughen them up, though they all personally suspected he was on a psycho, power trip and got some perverse pleasure out of inflicting pain. Someone higher up must have seen them out there and said something to him because all of a sudden they were marching inside the drill hall, instead of outdoors. They were also doing more exercises each day and coming in earlier. More often than not, they were there first and still there after everyone else had left.

Inspections are the norm when in boot camp. There are inspections for everything, almost from the first day of boot camp.

The first inspection was the PI[11], it occurred every morning at quarters, like clockwork. It consisted of standing in formation, looking straight ahead and not moving a muscle anywhere in your body with your thumb stuck into the front of your tee shirt and then inverting it after the CO shouted, "present for PI". The idea was to see if the fluffy white seam was fluffy and white. If it was gray, God help you. Pushups would be metered out – perhaps only 20 if he was in a hurry and, on some occasions, 100 – rain or shine. They also inspected the shine on their shoes and the inside rim of their white hats to ensure that it was clean. Their bunks got inspected, along with the lockers and bathrooms. The bunks had to have been made with square corners[12] and the sheets bowstring tight in both directions – no wrinkles were allowed. If it was possible to be inspected, it got inspected.

It felt good to be part of a team, a team where they were all treated with respect. It was all about what you could do and what kind of a person you were. They were told to use last names and to remember their serial number, as it would become the only number in their lives that really mattered. Without it, you don't eat, and you don't get paid.

Their initial quarters was at Camp Moffett. Camp Moffett was built after World War I and enlarged prior and during World War II. It contained hundreds of long, multi-storied, rickety wood, clapboard, uninsulated buildings. The clapboard exteriors always looked like they were in need of paint. Each building was a carbon copy of the next, standing in

---

[11] Personal Inspection
[12] Hospital folded corners

endless bleak lines in every direction one could see. The only thing that marked any difference from one to the next, was the name of each street, and the number on the flag post out front.

It was in these meager surroundings that they spent their first extremely cold weeks, listening to the wind beat on the building. At times it caused the windows to rattle like castanets at a Mexican wedding.

That particular year, he later learned was a record-breaking, cold winter at Great Lakes. About four or five weeks into the training, he came down with pneumonia. He was determined to tough it out, as he knew that to go to sickbay would mean missing drills or classes and if you missed more than three days, they'd put you "back" a week, and that meant not graduating with your company. There was no way he was going to miss out on graduating with his company. So he lay in his bunk wheezing and trying to cover up - his bed shaking with each gut wrenching cough. One morning, he woke up weak and dizzy, the bed was soaking wet, so he quickly stripped the sheets and put new ones on before the CO came in and ran an inspection. He was lucky, as there appeared to be no inspection that day or the CO would most assuredly have picked up on the wet sheets in his ditty bag. That evening, he washed them out by hand and hung them in the hot room. In the middle of the night, he took them down and folded them, thereby replacing the one he'd put on his rack. He was terrified that he'd be caught.

With the fever having broken, he mended quickly and went on to graduate. During their weeks of training, they all became one in thought and deed, strong and sharp, and a formidable sight when in parade. All the extra hours of training had set them apart as a superior company.

Space had apparently opened up at Camp Porter and suddenly they were moving lock, stock, and barrel to their new quarters over on the other side of the base.

These accommodations were as new as the other was old. The place was trimmed in chrome and gleamed in the sunlight that came through the windows that circled their area. It was a three-story white brick, mirrored with banks of windows. It reminded him a lot of a huge college dorm; only each room housed a whole company of men. However, they had more room around their bunks, and there was an office and separate sleeping quarters for the RCPO (Recruit Chief Petty Officer) and of course the Company Commander, whenever he chose to stay over. The area that housed the RCPO and Company Commander's office was referred to as "God's Country" as it would be aboard a ship.

One day the CO asked for volunteers for the Drill Team and Cal raised his hand – anything had to be better than being under this guy's thumb. This activity would allow him to associate with a "*normal*" bunch of guys.

As time passed, he enjoyed marching with the drill team, and he learned to do some really incredible things with his piece[13], like spinning it around and throwing it into the air and catching it as it fell while marching. To make it even more impressive, the bayonet was chrome plated as was the rifle barrel. One miss step and you or someone marching near you could be stuck with it.

Later, when the CO asked for volunteers for The US Navy Command Band, he again raised his hand. He had experience playing in the Junior and Senior high school band and played the French Horn. This

---

[13] .30-06 Rifle, gas operated, rotating bolt, 40 to 50 rounds/min, velocity 2,800 ft/s, 500 effective yards, weight 9.5 lbs.

activity got him out of more stuff and even off the base. Suddenly he found himself competing in marching competitions all over the state. Right away, they placed FIRST at Benton Harbor and went on to do the same at other events in other places.

When they weren't marching, going to school or performing some other form of training, they were cleaning the "space"[14] or doing laundry. There was very little "down time", and when it did occur, they used it to write letters home and to catch some ZZZZZs[15] which usually meant napping on the deck[16] so as not to wrinkle our bunk[17].

Sunday was their only down day, if you could call it that. He found that by going to church, he could avoid any surprise, extra duty. You never knew when the CO might grab you for one thing or another. He also found that he could slide down behind someone bigger and cop a few winks.

Once in a while he would catch a nighttime watch – they were boring and consisted of walking around the floor of their company while everyone else slept. They were told that should they encounter any "outsider", to challenge them and ask for the "Password of the Day" and to state their business. Without the password, they'd be refused entry to the building. It only occurred once, and it was an officer – one of the guys had caught him entering, and he didn't know the Password and was kept from entering. The poor boot was visibly shaken, thinking that his days in the Navy were over and he'd be put in the brig for sure. Instead, he was publicly honored for his alertness and for protecting the base.

---

[14] The area where they lived
[15] Napped on the deck
[16] Floor
[17] Bed

Thankfully, their watches were for only four hours, and then it became someone else's turn to challenge and protect.

We learned a lot while we were there, and things started to develop into a rhythm. Most of them lost track of time as their days became weeks and the weeks melted into months.

We learned how to do our laundry, and hang it in the drying room or outside with "clothes-stops"[18] when it became warm enough. Cal thought this was an exercise in tradition, more than convenience. Within the center of the building was a courtyard that contained several rows of steel poles with clotheslines running between them. The area was at ground level and opened skyward for the distance of three stories. It measured about 50-foot by 50-foot. Due to the extremely cold weather, they were allowed to use an inside drying room. It also contained rows of lines and was so hot that no one could stay there very long without being soaked with perspiration.

Folding clothes the Navy way was also something we all learn and fast – or we'd spend a lot of time doing pushups. Once you learned this method, you never forgot and to this day, Cal still folds his clothes in this manner.

To reinforce cleanliness and doing things the Navy way, there were frequent surprise inspections and woobe-it to anyone whom they caught with so much a wrinkle in a bed sheet, uneven rows of skivvies in his drawer or a column of socks that didn't stand square in his locker. Pushups and standing watch in a distant corner of barracks with his nose touching the corner and feet two foot from the wall, were meted out with sadistic pleasure.

---

[18] Used in the Navy instead of clothespins. The clothes stops were short pieces of string with which they secured their laundry to the clothesline.

If there was a hard way to do anything, the Navy knew what it is, and that's the way they want you to do it too. Even the brushes they used to clean the floor and the endless washroom sinks, were extremely small and looked a whole lot like toothbrushes. Each of them got to know every square inch of the place - intimately.

Chapter 4.0

While they were going through their boot camp training, a strange thing happened. They were told that their company, because of their fitness, would train with another "new company". That it was a test to determine which of the two forms of training was the most effective.

The scuttlebutt was that this other company had been flown in from a Marine training facility that was being used to train a special combat unit and would be housed in their building. *This information was withheld from them by their CO, and we didn't learn about it until much later.* All they were told was that they would be training together and learning things not normally taught to sailors. They emphasized that this was an experiment and not to talk about it to any other camp personnel. Whenever they worked out together, they always had the whole workout area to themselves. Usually, it was filled with other companies. This new experimental company appeared to look like them; same blue jeans and shirts, all neatly tied off and tucked in. As usual, they started out with several sets of pushups, then jumping jacks and sit-ups. They seemed to be tied with the other company – perhaps even a little better; crisper and quicker. He wondered if their CO knew about this ahead of time and that was why he'd drilled them extra hard. Apparently, it had worked because, as the day wore on, they started to pull ahead of the others and their guys were dropping out one by one.

After shaking it[19] out and running around the drill hall a couple of times, they were ordered to fall in. Then several guys from the other company were called out, and started teaching them hand-to-hand combat techniques with and without a Piece or side arm. It was not long before both companies were performing these techniques to the approval of both CO's.

They also started practicing on the firing range. With his experience on the farm shooting woodchucks from various distances, he had the edge over most of the other recruits who apparently were all city boys. His shooting ability became apparent as soon as he went to the line the first time and scored all perfect rounds. The line commander asked him if he grew up on a farm. He replied, "Yes, Sir" with pride in his voice.

"It shows son, as you're a crack shot – you might want to consider "switching over" and becoming a Specialist – he told Cal that he could make it happen and we'll make you a sniper in no time."

Cal just nodded his head and smiled. Later his CO called Cal into his office and told him that he had an opportunity to switch to a Special Forces type of training – they want to make a sniper out of you, he said somewhat sarcastically.

Seeing Cal's hesitation, he told him to think about it and let him know his decision tomorrow at quarters. Cal thought about it all night, and the next morning, he told his CO that he wanted to stay with his company and in the Navy.

A month later, the "Specialist" company left in the middle of the night. Again, Cal thought it was strange – whatever the experiment was, it appeared

---

[19] Vigorous workout of the body by jumping up and down while waving your arms in various directions – wards off cramps

to be over, and they were all told again, not to mention it to anyone – ever.

To this day, occasionally Cal still thinks about it and wonders what the outcome of the test had been. One day recently while this story was being written, he "Googled" his old company, looking for any information on it, but hard as he looked, there was no evidence that there ever had been a company 3 or 8. It was as if both companies were scrubbed from the face of the earth. Whatever the secret was, it had been erased.

A few days went by, and he was singled out by his CO and asked if he was interested in joining a group to be tested for diver training.

He was surprised, and shrugging his shoulders, replying, "Why not?"

A few days later, he was sent to another place on the base. Transportation had been provided, and he was told to take his pants out of his stockings – that, as long as he was a part of this training, he was freed from the "boot camp regimen". This was the first clue that he was involved in something very different from the norm.

Upon arriving, he was checked through security. His finger prints were checked against those that were on file. He was frisked, presumably for some type of weapon, but in his case, that would be ridicules given where he'd been training.

After being frisked, he joined five other men, all looking extremely fit and dressed in boot camp type clothing.

A man with a commanding presence, wearing a camouflage uniform, came through a door to the far end of the room. The room reminded Cal of a simulated ship's engine room, but that was where the resemblance ended, as this space had an extremely high ceiling with frosted-over sky lights.

In the middle of the room was a huge tank that looked vaguely like a submarine, except that it had several thick, viewing ports and one large access hatch in the end.

They were ordered by the man in a camouflage, whom he thought was a diver, to line up and stand at attention. He then proceeded to brief them.

As he suspected, the object in the room was a Hyperbaric oxygen tank[20]. The instructor explained that it provided an atmosphere that duplicated deep-sea diving and it was and could be used as a decompression chamber to treat a diver for the "bends," also known as Decompression Sickness should he need it. He briefly explained Boyles Law, in which depth was measured by "atmospheres." Since they were going down to 100 ft for O2 testing, they would be at a depth of 4-atmospheres.

The instructor also told them that there was nothing to fear, that at the worst, they might experience a little discomfort in their sinus, a momentary pain and, in some cases, a nose or ear bleed. The upside of this testing would mean no more sinus problems.

To Cal's knowledge, he'd never had any sinus problems, so this should be a breeze. He learned that they would be tested, two by two and, as the instructor said it, he pointed at him and the guy standing next to him and said, "you two will be first".

He felt nervous and excited at the same time, as he followed the instructor over to the Diving Chamber's entrance.

"I'll be at the controls and in touch with you by voice, the second that you feel you can't tolerate the

---

[20] *Diving Chamber*

test any further, let me know, and we'll bring you back up and, of course, you'll be dropped from the training program.

"Wow," he thought, this is happening.

Once in the chamber, both Ripley and he sat on seats that were structurally part of the chamber. He noted the table between them and a deck of cards; no doubt put there to while away the time. The interior was painted white; deck, bulk heads, cabling, piping – everything. He noticed the glass-covered, port holes were now lined with the faces of the others.

Cal heard the instructor's voice as he asked if they could hear him, and they both shouted, "YES."

Then the door slammed shut, insulating them from the outside world and all its sounds. It was as if they were diving into the deep – the sound of air entering the chamber and a moment of vertigo added to the realism.

They settled into playing a game of hearts – every so often the instructor would ask them a series of questions and tell them their progress. It didn't take long to get to 50-feet and, as they approached 100, their voices sounded like Donald Duck. All of a sudden, he felt a sharp pain rip through his head from front to back. He knew that it was his sinus adjusting to the pressure. Then Ripley started bleeding from his nose and one ear. It was obvious that he was in a lot of pain. Cal yelled out at the instructor that Ripley had just had an attack.

"Well, you're at 100-feet," the instructor said, "Ripley can you stand the pain for five minutes?

Ripley numbly nodded, "Yes."

Cal knew that Ripley didn't want to flunk their first test. He also hoped that the damage to his ear and sinuses wasn't anything permanent.

Once the test was over, and the others had completed it, they were informed that they would be tested in a hard-hat suit[21].

The following day they reported back to the diver training facility and were taken to a room that was much like the last, only with an overhead track, a deep water tank that appeared to be bottomless, as an iron ladder running down one side, disappeared into its illuminated depths.

He noticed that Ripley was missing from their lineup, now they were down to five trainees.

After they were instructed about the workings of the hard-hat diving suit, he was again chosen to go first, and he couldn't help but wonder about that, since he'd been chosen first for the decompression tank.

The Diving Helmet contained a transceiver for communications, a series of window, like ports of which only the front and two side ones offered visibility. There were two cocks; one controlled the incoming air[22] and one the out going[23]. All of this was supported atop the Breast Plate, which connected the Diving Helmet to the diving suit via a series of studs and wing nuts.

He was helped into his suit by the others, which were referred to as Tenders. First, he stepped into the suit, pushing his feet down into what felt like

---

[21] Standard Diving Dress: is a type of diving suit that was formerly used for all underwater work that required more than breath-hold duration, which included marine salvage, civil engineering, pearl shell diving and other commercial diving work, and similar naval diving applications. Standard diving dress has largely been superseded by lighter and more comfortable equipment. For more information, consult https://en.wikipedia.org/wiki/Standard_diving_dress from which this excerpt was taken.

[22] *Spit Cock*

[23] *Escape Regulator*

over-sized lead boots[24] then the suit was pulled up along his body until his arms could force his hands and wrist through the watertight wrist seals. His last minute instructions were to breathe normally and how to adjust his escape regulator.

Once down on the bottom, his job was to locate the bolt, put all the washers onto it, that fit and to find the correct nut that also fit. Once completed, to bring it back up to the surface and hand it over to the instructor for evaluation. If it had the correct number of washers on it and the nut was thoroughly secured, he'd pass the test.

Next, the hard hat was placed over his head and bolted fast. He could distinctly hear the air rushing through the openings and into the helmet. The smell was a mixture of sweat, neoprene and stale air.

He quickly adjusted the escape regulator in a manner that kept the suit from filling with air. Once the air had been adjusted, he was slowly lowered into the tank. As the water closed in over his head, he was momentarily startled – feeling slightly claustrophobic.

The instructor, immediately understanding his situation, calmly told him that he was doing just fine. There were no bubbles to indicate any leaks and that the air pressure in his suit was perfect. If he were ready, they would proceed to lower him.

Holding his thumb in the air, and saying okay in his strongest voice, he felt the winch release its brake, and he started his descent. He absently counted the rungs on the steel ladder beside him, and at 90, he realized that he was at 90 plus feet and even with the lights on, it was getting very murky.

---

[24] Heavy weight diving shoes – approx 40 lbs a pair

Suddenly, he felt his feet touch the bottom, and as they did, he told them that he was down and immediately the downward motion stopped.

As he looked around to ordinate himself, he sighted the bolt but knew he could not reach it. So he said, "give me another ten feet, which they did. Clumsily, he walked toward the bolt. The best way to walk in a suit like this was to use exaggerated steps as if he was some huge robot. Once he was over it, he bent and picked it up. "So far, so good," he thought - now to locate the washers and nut.

Since there appeared to be all sorts of nuts and washers strewn all over the place, he mentally created a grid to work from. Slowly, he circled the circumference of the tank, checking nuts and washers as he went - if they fit, he put them on the bolt, if not, he discarded them in piles, so he wouldn't waste his time rechecking them again on his next trip around the chamber. This he kept doing until he had checked all the washers and nuts, ending up with all the washers he could find that fit and the one nut, which he had located early on.

Upon finishing, he called out to his tenders above to haul him up. The voice of his instructor came over the intercom, telling him to be sure that all the washers that didn't fit, were evenly disturbed around the tank's floor. He had apparently noted how he had organized his search.

After making a couple of turns around the bottom and kicking all the little piles into oblivion, he said, "okay, I finished my housekeeping, how about pulling me up".

He immediately felt the cable tightening, and his feet suddenly felt a whole lot lighter, as he left the bottom of the tank behind.

Even though the suit was pressurized, they stopped a couple of times and waited several minutes before resuming his assent. During this time, he rotated his arms and moved his legs up and down as if he was climbing stairs. He knew that would excise his muscles, helping to force any residual air bubbles out of his veins and arteries.

Finally, his diving helmet broke the surface, and the light came flooding in and onto his face. It was like being born again. Soon he was standing on the cement, and many hands were busy taking his Diving Helmet off. He dislodged his arms from the seal and stepped out of the suit.

When asked, "if he would rate the experience as being at the top of his "to do list," He quickly replied, "YES, I'd love to do it again for real."

In the meantime, boot camp training continued around these classes, which were held a few hours, one day out of each remaining week of boot camp up to graduation. When he finished contingency diver training during boot camp, he and one other guy were all that was left of the original six.

Once, while they were drilling outdoors, they were marching within seeing distance of the Transit Drop-off station. The "Loop" as it was referred to, ran between Milwaukee and Chicago. Usually, the platform was empty, but this time there were a dozen or so young women standing under its railroad roof, watching them. Their CO threatened them with extra duty if they so much as broke step. As they marched by, he caught them, out of the corner of his eye, waving at them and he thought that every single man wished he was over there, able to talk to them. They all ached for female companionship and those with families, wished that they could be with their wives, fiancées or girlfriends. He had neither, but that didn't stop him from wishing.

In retrospect, the first few weeks of boot camp were extremely difficult because no one knew what to expect. Each day had a certain routine, but then there was always the unexpected things that pop up. For example, one day they might be in a class learning the different types of seafaring knots and their use; the next, learning how to put out a fire on board a ship.

In their classes on fire fighting and biological warfare, they used tear gas as a biological agent as they ran through their drills. Then the following day, they would be out on the grinder doing a tug of war contest with their sister company to win the "A" flag (Athletic Flag). They had won all of them, except the "A" and try as they would; they couldn't win it. He knew that it all but killed their CO, to not have won that last one. It would have meant that they were a full "Color Company", a very prestigious accomplishment within the Battalion.

Finally, they had all reached the half way point of their training and were granted Cinderella Liberty, which is, as the name implies, that they had to return before midnight or be in a lot of trouble. Most of the guys headed for the bars to drink and mess around; He headed for the Y, got a room, laid down and slept most of the day.

With his need for rest satisfied, he left and took in some of the Chicago sights – truly it is the windy city. He hadn't realized how so, until leaving the protection of the skyscrapers and stepping out into the open, unprotected street corner and nearly being blown into traffic.

There was little that he saw near the "Loop" that was worth writing home about. It was dirty, noisy and full of seedy, shabby bars. Since he was pulling boot camp in the middle of winter, he realized that one couldn't expect to see the city in its top form. However, not seeing anything that caught his interest, he headed back to the base.

Finally, their time in boot camp was drawing to an end. Their test results would determine if they would go to one of dozens of "A" schools or out to the fleet. Test day came, and they spent all day taking exams. The next day, those who were able to apply to an "A" school, were taken to one side and, one by one, they were counseled on the pros and cons of each type of training. Cal picked his – ET (Electronic Technician) school - though that would suddenly change, quite unexpectedly.

A few days went by, and finally, it was time to graduate. The day was warm, but not warm enough to have the ceremony outdoors, so they used one of the largest drill halls on the base. It was a great day, marking the end of a long and difficult basic training schedule.

From the time he got off the bus until he graduated, would be over 18-weeks, the longest boot camp tour on record. Boot camp has since been dramatically shortened and is much less difficult.

Chapter 5.0

The last few days of Boot camp were far different than the many weeks leading up to it. They were now the seniors - the graduates. They were top dogs on the base as far as the other "boots" were concerned. They got to wear their pant cuffs outside of their socks - before they had no insignia on their shirts or coats - now they did. When they walked by other "Boots" (before they had to run everywhere they went) they were now being saluted by them - they didn't know any better as they were only E2s. In a way, he felt sorry for them, they were just starting out with their training, and he was done.

It felt good to be part of a group - to belong - to be wanted. They were like one big family, they had seen the worst of each other and the best, and they accepted each other for what they were and what they could contribute. They still went by last names, as very few of them knew anyone's first name unless they were close friends - that was just the way it was – rules to live and die by.

Finally, after waiting breathlessly for a few days, their orders came through. The excitement was palpable, like electricity that sparked and jumped from man to man. Previously, they'd all filled out "Dream Sheets". This listed the locations of 3-bases they wanted, with the one they wanted the most being first. Some guys were shouting, others swearing – mostly they all got what they wanted. He got orders for school; he was to start "A" school the 1st week of May. That meant he'd be coming back to the training center, but this time it would be different, he'd be free to go wherever he wanted, on or off the base. He was all set to go to ET (Electronics Technical Training) school when one of the tests – a color test revealed that he had a color issue with reds, greens, and browns. This had surprised him, as no one had ever checked his color vision before.

His advisor said that there were other choices, but he hardly heard him through his disappointment. He was devastated, which was an understatement as it really didn't adequately describe the depths to which his feelings had fallen. His heart was in the crapper, and his head started to spin. Now, what was he going to do? His enlistment in the Navy was predicated on getting an education. There was no way he could afford to go to college on the "outside."

Again, he could hear his advisor's voice. He was suggesting other alternatives. He could become either a Boiler man or Machinist Mate, neither required any type of color proficiency, he explained.

Frankly, neither one sounded very exciting. Becoming a Machinist Mate sounded like someone who stood in front of a lathe or drill press all day, and a Boiler man must be someone who shoveled coal into a boiler all day.

However, he quickly learned from his advisor, that for the most part, he was wrong. As he listened, he went on to explain that a Boiler man worked where it was super hot due to the oil fired boilers. He had to keep them in repair, clean the space and bilges.

Right away he knew that he wanted no part of being a boiler man or BT as they were called. The advisor went on to explain the duties of a Machinist Mate that they ran and maintained the ship's evaporators, generators, air compressors, refrigeration (reefer) units and lots more. He knew that these skills would be valuable in civilian life and would help him find a good job after he was honorably discharged from the Navy.

Besides filling out their Dream Sheet[25] for schools and the location of their next bases, they were also allowed to put in for two weeks leave before starting their next training phase. Cal had been missing his family and wanting to get home to see them as quickly as possible, so he opted to pay a little more and fly, though he soon learned that flying military standby was not only faster but less expensive than taking the train.

Other than flying out for boot camp, this would be the first time he'd ever flown completely on his own and was completely ready for the adventure.

The day finally arrived and all of the guys from Binghamton piled into the bus with their sea bags packed and headed for Chicago's O'Hara Airport. Even though spring had arrived, the wind was still raw, but they were used to it after weeks of drilling in the snow and standing in line waiting to eat before dawn in sub zero temperatures – if anything, he had learned patience.

Shortly, they were on the plane, seated and waiting for takeoff. Even though they had all flown out to Chicago from Syracuse before arriving at the base, it had been dark. Now in the daylight, it was as if he was truly experiencing it all for the first time. From the huge under carriage to the slick, streamlined interior, it was a machine built to move quickly. Cal had asked for a window seat and had gotten it. He was able to look outside and enjoy every moment of flying.

---

[25] In most cases, you fill out a form, known as a "dream sheet" to list your assignment preferences.

Nervously, he divided his time looking out the window with that of watching everything in the interior – he didn't want to miss a thing.

Inside the plane, the pretty, pert, airline hostesses were checking everything before takeoff and the other guys missed no opportunity to flirt with them. He knew that each hostess was single, and they all were very good looking and friendly to a fault. In no time, several of the guys were talking to them on a first name basis and had their phone numbers. He was not that full of himself and was content to just watch the people on the plane and the ground crew as they rushed about outside preparing the plane for takeoff.

Finally, the fuel lines, cables and baggage carts were removed, and the chalks[26] were kicked out from the wheels and dragged to one side.

A man with two flashlights ran out and started signaling the tow truck driver, and the plane started to move. It was an awesome feeling being so high up and, feeling the movement, and he seemed somehow detached from the reality of the moment. After a few minutes, they stopped, and there was a noticeable wait before the plane started to move again.

From inside the cabin, he heard the shrill, high-pitch whine of turbines. Then, as the plane eased forward, he could feel the pilot applying his brakes and then releasing them. They taxied along the oversized strips of concrete resembling streets, only much wider. They went first this way and then the other – frankly, he didn't know how the pilot knew where they were going, it was all a maze to him. Finally, the plane turned and stopped once again and sat still for a moment.

Suddenly the turbines started to whine, and long yellow flames shot out the rear of each engine. He

---

[26] Blocks used to keep the wheels from turning.

knew that, at any moment, something profound was about to happen. Then he felt the brakes release, and the plane lurched forward, gaining speed with each second. In a matter of minutes, they were racing down the runway, no longer feeling the indentations in the cement. He had never traveled this fast in his life, not even when he was riding with his Uncle in his new Desoto. As suddenly as they had started to move, the plane broke lose from the runway and was airborne.

His heart was in his throat, what an exhilarating feeling, as the plane pushed its nose high into the sky and the engines opened up even further. As they were accelerating, he could feel a great pressure pushing him back in the seat so hard that he could scarcely raise his head. After a few moments, as he watched the ground disappear beneath them, the high-pitch whine of the engines disappeared, and the plane became so quiet it was as if he had entered some kind of alternate universe where sound and presence were no longer tangible. It was as if they were suspended in space – not moving – barely existing. They must have gained altitude as he could see the clouds floating by beneath them. *Surely they must be flying through heaven*, he thought.

With the "Fasten Seatbelt" and "No Smoking" signs turned off, several people got up and walked toward the Rest Rooms. The spell was broken – another reality was upon him.

From the smell and sounds of stainless steel clinking from somewhere behind him, Cal knew they were about to be fed. This would be another new experience. He didn't have long to wait, as a stainless steel cart emerged from behind some curtains and was pushed down the aisle. Every few feet it would stop, and the hostess would hand out a tray Along with the food, mixed drinks were being snapped up by most of the passengers along with soft drinks. He opted for a Coke. The food was sparse, but good he thought. It was a toss up which was better, the boot camp food or the airline food. He remembered having had mashed potatoes, a slice of beef with gravy over it and string beans, along with a small piece of yellow cake for dessert. He ate it all but noticed that the others left part of their food and complained among themselves about its quality. He absently thought, "*if they had grown up the way he had, they would have eaten every crumb and smacked their lips for more.*" He was ashamed for them.

He had hardly finished when one of the airline stewardesses came by and picked up his tray. As she did, she smiled. She was pretty, and he was taken with her – he had noticed her earlier when all the other guys had been hitting on her. She had politely brushed them off and went about her job, paying them scant attention. But when serving him, she had smiled, and he smiled back. Later, she had stopped to ask him if he needed another drink and, at the same time, checked to see that his seat belt was properly fastened. Each time they had exchanged smiles, and she had hurriedly gone about her business. He had mixed emotions on asking her for her phone number – "*what were the chances?*" he argued with himself, of his ever seeing her again – they traveled in different circles, - their chances of ever meeting again were slim to none, particularly since he hardly ever flew. In no time, he had talked himself out of asking – besides, he had a lot of other things on his mind, like how he was going to get from their little airport back to his home. It was quite a distance, and he had no car. He also remembered that most of the time, the "Point" didn't have any cab service. He guessed he'd have to call Len and see if he could come down to Binghamton and get him, if not, he'd have to thumb his way home with his sea bag slung over his shoulder.

Suddenly the "Seat Belt" sign came on, and he could hear a chorus of clicks. The pilot's voice barked through the speakers like God handing down the Ten Commandments, as he announced that they were about to land in New York.

He watched in amazement as they broke through the clouds. Below were blocks and blocks of buildings lining street after street as far as the eye could see in every direction. What a maze – "God, how can anyone live like that?" He asked himself.

In a matter of minutes they flew across some water and out over the harbor, he caught a fleeting glimpse of the Statue of Liberty with her torch held high, just like in the pictures he'd seen in Life Magazine, at home. Just looking at the statue gave him a big lump in his throat and made him proud to be an American.

There was a jolt announcing that they had touched down – that magical moment in the clouds had vanished as they were now again part of the earth – its captive. After taxiing this way and that, they finally stopped, the "Seat Belt" sign was turned off, and the clicking of seat belts being unhooked could be heard all around him.

After several moments of gathering their stuff from the overhead lockers, they filed toward the back door. The airline stewardesses were all lined up shaking their hands as they left. This was totally unexpected as he thought he'd seen the last of his. As he filed by her, she took his hand in both of hers. Was it his imagination or did she hold it a little longer than the rest and was her smile warmer than before as her eyes fairly twinkled when he looked down into them. He was forced to catch his breath – then he felt some pressure from the person behind him, no doubt anxious to be on their way. Their hands parted, and their eyes lingered for a moment longer, as they moved apart. It was then that he felt the small piece of paper in his hand and looked to see what it was as he felt his way out of the plane. It contained a name and phone number. He was stunned – why me? What did he have to offer such a sophisticated, beautiful girl? It had to be a mistake. The thought of calling her caused his stomach to knot up and his head to spin. What would he say - no, it was impossible, he had to stay focused. He had to get home to see his family. He was worried about them – how had they faired since his departure.

Cal never saw his "sky angel" again. He sometimes wonders about all the people he has met over his life, even remotely and wonders what has become of them.

The connection to a much smaller commuter plane was made easier because there were other guys traveling to the same destination who seemed much more travel wise than himself, so Cal followed their lead. Soon they were boarded, strapped in and ready to take off.

The trip home was bumpy and not nearly as nice as the larger plane, but they didn't care. After what they'd endured in boot camp, this was a cake walk.

Even before they'd landed, Sotak told him to be sure and call him; his folks were planning a big party, and all his friends were invited. As he handed Cal his phone number, Cal nodded, "sounds like fun," he said – "thanks," and gave him his number. This was the first time he'd ever been invited to a party by someone who was not a member of his family - it felt good to be accepted by his peers. Then another guy gave him his number and told him to stay in touch. He was moved that they were willing to share their time with him when they didn't even know him ... not really. He knew that it was all because he was now a part of a very large fraternity of brothers – the military.

He wondered what they would have thought, had they known his secret. By now he had reasoned out more about it, and even though he was not guilty of having done anything wrong, he still felt ashamed. For a time he'd forgotten about it as he had been swept up in his new life where they were all equals in a new life and adventure.

When Cal walked through the old kitchen screen door and looked around, nothing seemed to have changed. He slowly released the door so it wouldn't bang, giving his arrival away. His mother had her back to him and had just finished washing dishes, as he saw her wringing out the dish cloth and hang it over the spigot to dry.

The kitchen smelled of fresh bread and biscuits, an ever present smell that he remembered growing up. He could hear the voices of his sisters and brother coming from somewhere upstairs, and then he saw his mother turn, and her tired, weary look disappeared when she saw him standing in the doorway. He'd never forget that look and, even to this day when remembering it, a lump forms in his throat.

Her face lit up like the 4th of July, as she dropped the dish towel on the counter and hurried toward him – hugging him as if she never wanted to let go. He liked surprising people by just showing up, and he would do it several more times during his tour of duty – *it had only back fired on him twice, that he could remember.*

Most of the day was spent answering questions, many defied answering in a way that they'd understand, so he was vague, only saying what he had to, to get past the question. He had quickly discovered that he couldn't even begin to tell them what training was like or what they did day to day –

they wouldn't have understood. After all, it was as if he'd just stepped out of another world, one which they'd never know or understand. You had to be there; you had to go through the training experience to appreciate what they'd all become. Even though he loved them, they no longer spoke the same language, and he felt himself being drawn back to his brothers – his new family.

Later, he made the call and, in a few hours, he was among them, meeting their families – so different from his, yet so alike in many ways. They seemed to be more tolerant of their ways and not judgmental of a Freudian slip of the tongue every now and then. They were all men now and therefore allowed to enjoy a few excesses, and no one was going to tell them they shouldn't be doing this or that or scold them for cutting lose. They seemed to understand and it was okay.

One of his friend's parents owned a Restaurant called the Oasis; it was located on Clinton Street. His name was Sotak, and then there was Hopko, who had been their RCPO and Jerry Kosick and others who'd been through it and understood. They all had a few beers, played pool and danced with the girls from the "village". He didn't remember much about the next few days. He slept, ate and slept some more – after a couple of days of partying, he felt guilty about deserting his family and had one of the guys cart him home. They all promised to stay in touch, but that was the last time Cal saw any of them. They had their own lives – new experiences found while traveling along other roads.

Long before he was due to go back, he found himself looking forward to moving on. He knew that over those hills were new experiences, new people to meet and places to see and he longed to be on his way. He was packed, and his paperwork was in order. One of the guys picked him up, as his family still had no transportation. He made a mental note to save up for a car; he'd never again come home without having "wheels".

*   *   *

In the distance, a man in black was sitting in the back seat of a black car and watching the house far below through his binoculars. He smiled slightly, made some notes on a piece of paper, then closed the manila folder, putting it in his brief case along with the binoculars. Then he signaled the driver to follow the car that had just left the house.

*   *   *

The roar of the plane's engines was music to Cal's ears. Mentally, he was miles ahead of it. He had landed in Chicago and was on his way back to the base for "A" school training.

After Cal was out of the service, he looked up Jerry. He was a plumber as had been his dad, and Cal soon discovered they had little in common beyond the service. Jerry was married and very busy with his work and family, so he shook his hand, wished him well, and was again on his way to - where, Cal didn't know.

Cal had learned another lesson about time - you can never go back. Friends in school are not necessarily friends once you've graduated. Cal found this out when he went to visit his old high school buddy, Will Fern. You would have thought they were from different planets. He could immediately feel

Will's hostility in the way he deflected his gaze and his silence when asked a direct question. Perhaps it was jealousy because he had stayed home and worked in a machine shop, as his father had done before him. Cal had been free to travel and do things that Will couldn't. Life's experiences, tend to separate and turn friends into strangers – tearing away the bridge built on the memories they'd once shared. All too often family and old friends can not relate to where you've been and the new experiences you've had, forcing you to move on, while looking for a connection, or some meaning to your life.

Back at the base, where it had been so cold the past winter, spring had somehow found its way there. The grass was green; the breezes were warm. The return trip was the reverse of the one out, only his special hostess that he had met earlier, was not one of the crew. He got up the nerve to ask one of the hostesses if she knew her and she nodded and smiled in acknowledgment, saying she was on another flight out. In a way he envied them, traveling to new places and meeting so many different people. They too were a fraternity of sisters who seemed to know each other in this high flying, fast moving, business of air travel. They also shared a unique bond of experiences and history that no one else outside the business could understand; the same as he and his friends in their world. Sure it was fun to share stories and to laugh about their different experiences, but they would never truly be a part of each other's group.

At first, even though he longed to savor new experiences, he was apprehensive about going back – his memories of boot camp were still fresh in his mind, and he had no intentions of repeating that time in his life. However, Cal remembered several different people who reassured him that the rest of his time in the Navy would never be as arduous as boot camp. Armed with this memory, he entered the training area of the base. He soon found that it was as different as night and day to anything having to do with boot camp. Even so, old habits die-hard, and he still jumped out of his skin every time he saw anything that looked like an officer and, he still had the urge to run everywhere he went. He defended the practice as being a good way to keep fit, but soon learned that no one runs anywhere on the Navy "A" School Campus - it just wasn't cool. So that habit, like so many others, died a quick and just death.

Chapter 6.0

L ife was different in lots of ways on the "A" school part of the base. One of the things he quickly learned was that there were lots of women on the base called "Waves". They were the equivalent to the males being called Sailors. This was not the case in boot camp as there were no Waves or women, except for the medical staff. He had discovered this when he'd stopped by to have his teeth checked. There was a woman in uniform at the front desk, and as he moved around the base, he observed others on their way here or there in their Wave uniforms. He wondered absently, where they had their boot camp.

One day while walking with some of his friends, he casually asked where the Waves stayed. Without missing a step, one of them raised his arm and pointed across the huge grassy medium that was between their quarters and a row of buildings on the other side. The grassy area was a couple of football fields in size and was referred to as "No Man's Land".

Then he found himself casually asking, "and how does one get to meet one for a date"? To wit, his more informed pal said, "just walk over to any of the buildings and ask the girl at the front desk if there's anyone who would like the pleasure of going out with you on a date.

"Easy as that", he echoed.

"Yep", he said, "but it's sort of like pot luck, as you might get a few frogs before you get a princess", he added with a chuckle, "but if at first if you don't succeed, try, try ...."

"Yeah," ... "try again", he replied, as they both laughed.

He stored that piece of information away for future use - perhaps he'd pay them a visit this coming Friday. That'd give him time to gather some much-needed courage. He was still not as brave of heart as his contemporaries, but he was getting there.

The first day of "A" school, they were all lined up single file facing the CO who ran the training program for the base. He welcomed them to the program and briefly covered the rules of their training and subsequent assignment. Then he instructed them to look to their left and then to the right and then back at him. He told them something that Cal would never forget – that those people on each side of them wouldn't finish the training – that it was that hard. Two out of three people will flunk out of this course. If you don't feel that you're up to it, leave now. Then after a pause in which no one moved - he dismissed them.

Cal was stunned. Was he really up to it - he had to be, his future depended on it.

School started at 0800 hours each day and ended at 1700 hours with a break midday for an hour lunch. They had Saturdays and Sundays off. He made it a rule to get his studying and homework done after supper each day. There would be no slacking off – he had to pass this course. Everything was riding on it!

Friday arrived, and he hurried through his homework, this was the day he'd walk across No Man's Land and up to one of those buildings and ask someone out.

He grabbed an ice cold RC from the machine in the hallway and downed it in a couple of gulps. They were quartered on the second floor in a wooden barracks that was one of many buildings in the area.

Theirs smelled of old wood, dust, heat, and sweat. Thankfully, they were air-conditioned, so he never felt any discomfort.

*   *   *

About halfway through their training, those that were left in the program were transferred to a newer building that offered cubical-like rooms for studying and sleeping. The enhanced accommodations, having desks, cushioned chairs and desk lights for each of the two occupants, were more conducive to studying. Also, instead of lockers, they each had a dresser in which to put their clothes and a closet for hanging pants and shirts. Twin size beds, which they made before leaving in the morning, were situated on both sides of the room. A double window afforded them light during the day, and helped prevent spatial deprivation.

They never stood inspection, and there were no watches; all they did was report to school, attend class and pass their tests. If you failed, you were shipped out to the fleet ASAP - they didn't have time or money to waste on you. However, for the people who were achieving, every possible convenience was afforded them.

There were guys in the various barracks lining their street, taking courses in everything from Signalman to Corpsman courses. He fell in with a bunch of Snipes[27]. After hours they'd wear civilian clothes; but, as yet, he hadn't bought any, and proceeded to put on a clean, freshly pressed, set of whites that were dry-cleaned for him – he no longer

---

[27] Machinist Mates, Boiler man, and Engineman – essentially below decks engineers

had to do his laundry. After shaving and combing his hair, he was set to go.

Taking a deep breath, he took the stairs two at a time and flew out the door into the sunlight. It felt good, and he felt good. In a matter of minutes, he had walked the distance across No Man's Land to the Wave's side of the base.

All the buildings were like their old ones; each looked the same as the one next to it. Cal walked by a couple of buildings trying to decide which one to turn into and, as he did, he heard a slight sound above him. It was subtle, like a nervous snicker, followed by a shish sound. He turned his head ever so slightly so he could see where it came from and, out of the corner of his eye, glimpsed several girls with their heads out the window watching him walking down below. A couple of them looked pretty cute, so he turned in at their building.

The walkway was concrete and, even though it couldn't have been more than twenty feet or so, it seemed like a mile. Cal's legs felt rubbery as he went up the wooden stairs worn deeply by thousands of feet over the years. The large white door yielded to his touch, and he found himself suddenly in the lobby.

The interior was gloomy, and there was a slight odor of perfume mingling with the smell of aged wood and dust, much like his earlier quarters. Besides a US flag, a small, beat up wooden desk, a couple of heavy-looking wooden chairs, and a picture of the President of the United States on the dingy wall with an RC Coke machine under it, there was little else to announce that it was a lobby to the building.

A slight movement behind the desk caught his attention, as the young girl looked up and asked him to state his business.

She was neither friendly nor hostile; her attitude was as benign as a robot. Cal couldn't read her, which surprised him, so he answered her question directly rather than trying to attempt any kind of humor.

He was here to see if any of the waves would like to go out to a show, he told her.

In answer, she merely turned and yelled, "Anyone up there want to go out to see a flick[28]?

There was a commotion of someone's feet hitting the floor and hurried steps, followed by a voice, "I'm coming".

To this day, he didn't know how they decided who would go out with whom or if they had their names on a list and whoever's name came up next, got the next guy that showed up. He suspected it was the latter.

He heard hurried steps coming down the stairs – she was neither a beauty queen, nor so homely that you'd have to tie a dog to her belt so it wouldn't run away. She was a petite 5-5. Her dark brown hair was cut in the usual short pixie cut that most of the girls wore while in the military, and it suited her. He also noticed that her eyes were brown like his and seemed to be hiding a bit of mischief.

She smiled, and he smiled back and said, "Hi", I'm Cal Morison.

She immediately said, "Penny Whitney".

They walked side by side out the door and followed the sidewalk to that part of the base that had a soda bar, Movie Theater, bowling alleys, ENCO Club and base church. It was a bit of the civilian way of life – a place where you could relax and be yourself.

As they walked, she said, "where to".

"Flick", he replied nonchalantly. "Don't mind do you?" he asked, as an afterthought.

---

[28] Movie

"Nope", she replied as she kept up with his brisk pace, despite her much shorter legs.

Glancing in her direction, he noticed that she was smiling mischievously. He refrained from commenting, as he thought perhaps she was just glad to be out of her building for a while.

As they walked along, their rigidity wore off and soon they were talking back and forth like old friends. She was easy company, and they got along well; beyond that, he had no feelings one-way or the other about her. She was just a pal, who happened to be a girl.

She seemed to enjoy seeing the flicks. They were cheap at a quarter each, and they provided an escape from the realities of base boredom and his studies. It was also a pastime that had not been afforded him while growing up, as they had no car to get to the movies in the Point and no money to waste on tickets.

As they went out together more often, he expanded his repartee from just watching movies, to bowling, and they always stopped for a root beer float – these activities were his all-time favorites, and she also was enjoying herself, frequently laughing at his antics.

He found himself stopping by on most every Friday, Saturday and Sunday. She was easy to be with and for some reason they started holding hands. Even so, one Friday afternoon the opportunity came up to go with some of the guys in his division to a party off base.

He knew that these guys were considered to be extremely successful at meeting beautiful girls and were regulars at all the college parties. There were always girls coming on base and picking them up in sports cars and, out of the blue, they'd asked him if he had some spare time to join them. He couldn't believe his ears.

Nodding, he said, "Yeah, no problem".

Then they asked him if he had any civilian clothes because the girls didn't want to be seen with "base guys" – they'd catch a lot of static from their folks and friends.

His face dropped a mile as he said, "no".

One of the guys said, "no problem, you're my size, and I've got an extra pair of pants and a shirt you can borrow".

In no time, a convertible pulled up and they were off with three of the best looking girls he'd seen in a long time. Two of them were blondes, and he was paired with a redhead. They all wore painted on minis. Apparently, the other two guys knew the girls as they made small talk while one of the blondes drove them into the hills of Lake Forest and out to a cottage. He had visions that they would be drinking and partying all night.

They arrived in a surprisingly short time and piled out of the car and into a log cabin, sitting all by itself in the depths of the woods.

One of the girls turned the music on and started to twist and turn to a new song by an artist called Chubby Checker. He knew that the song and dance were the rage and soon his two friends were dancing like they had choreographed the steps. He was at a loss as to how to do it. His date, realizing his dilemma, took him by the hand leading him toward the back of the house and into one of the bedrooms. He had a fleeting impression that they may not be there to talk about the weather. Still holding his hand, she led him toward the bathroom where she yanked a long towel off the rack. He couldn't imagine what she was going to do next.

She quickly led him to the middle of the bedroom floor while he wondered what kinky thing he'd be learning this night. He was all eyes as she threw the towel around her backsides and said, "watch".

As he watched, she moved her hands in and out like a prize fighter shadow boxing and, at the same time, swiveled her tail provocatively against the towel. She said, "make believe you're drying your backsides and you'll get it".

In no time he was twisting with the best of them, up and down and all around as the man was saying in the song.

He was rather proud of himself as he moved as well as anyone there – maybe even better. He was really getting into it when one of the girls signaled that they had to be heading out.

The evening was shot, and she had to be getting back into town before her folks got home. They made the trip back to the base in record time and were dumped off rather unceremoniously at the curb in front of their buildings.

According to the other two guys, he'd been cool, the girls had all liked him. So Cal had high hopes that he'd be seeing more of them. But, as it turned out, just as quickly as they'd come into his life, they were gone and he was on to other things.

Classes were drawing to an end and they were all cramming for their tests. A lot was at stake: his advancement, his next base, and most of all, a raise in rank and pay if he passed. He crammed and crammed until he could answer every question. The day came and they were all waiting to start with their black ballpoint pens poised above the test booklet.

The instructor opened by saying how pleased he was to see that a record number of men had made it to this point and that if they passed this test, they would be a credit to the uniform and the base training facility. He also went on to say how their education had cost the US Government 100k per man and was equal to that of any four-year engineering school in the country. He felt honored to be there, particularly after hearing that.

The bell rang, and they all wrote their names and service numbers on the test cover, then flipped to the first page. Several hours later, the bell rang again, and they all put their black ballpoint pens down. They rose as one, filed up to the instructor's desk and handed him their tests on the way out.

He had a good feeling about the test. He had studied virtually everything that was on the test and had picked the answer that jumped out at him in every instance - now the hard part ... waiting.

As it turned out, there wouldn't be much of a wait. By the next morning, the grades were posted and their orders cut. He worked his way up through the other guys to the postings and looked for his serial number. To the right of it, he saw that he'd passed by quite a large margin – nearly a perfect score - 3.9 out of a possible 4.0. In effect, he had nearly ACED the test. He noted as he looked down the long list of grades, that he'd graduate at the top of his 200-person class and would go into the fleet as an E4. This was, without a doubt, the high point of his life and he had to share it with someone. Since it was the weekend, he hurriedly got ready to see Penny. He knew she'd be excited for him. As soon as he showered, shaved and changed, he partially sprinted over to her barracks.

She'd received his message and was already waiting in the lobby for him. As they walked along toward the bowling alley, he told her he had some great news – he'd passed the Machinist Mate test, scoring a 3.9 and had been elevated to the rank of MM E4, effective immediately. She was ecstatic for him and was jumping up and down with excitement. In passing, as they were again walking along, he added that he'd received his orders and would be shipping out Monday for Norfolk.

Suddenly, she grew very quiet, and he noticed she was no longer walking beside him. Turning, he saw that she had stopped dead in her tracks and had burst into tears; both hands were trying to stem the flow as she stood shaking all over, and turning in circles in the middle of the sidewalk.

His mind rushed back over what he'd said, trying to figure out what he'd said to hurt her feelings. He couldn't think of a thing. He was perplexed. He felt helpless – He had no idea what he should say or do. He asked rather lamely, "What is it? - Are you okay? - What's wrong?"

She just shook her head, swabbed her eyes with a Kleenex that had suddenly appeared from her purse, and replied, "It's nothing. Girls sometimes just cry when the mood strikes them," she bravely smiled.

Her slightly damp hand found his, and it seemed like she was squeezing it much harder than before. After they'd walked for a time, she asked if he'd stop by before leaving and he said, "Okay".

The bowling and later the ice-cream float did not live up to all the ones they'd had before – he sensed that something was different about her; she didn't laugh at his attempt at humor. She seemed moody and not connected. It was almost as if she was waiting for him to say something, or do something and he didn't know what she wanted from him.

As usual, he walked her back to her door – he always tried to remember his social graces as his Mom had taught him.

Again she turned toward him, looking into his eyes as if waiting for something....

He gave her hand an extra squeeze and thanked her for going out with him, then turned and left as he'd done on all the other occasions. His mind was already rushing ahead at top speed to the things he wanted to do before leaving.

Saturday, he sent her a note saying he wouldn't be seeing her that day as he had to take care of some last minute paper work before shipping out. He was still mystified about what her problem had been.

He was still thinking about it when his eyes settled on one of the guys that was considered by the others as being "*a man about town*". He was sitting nearby, listening to the radio and, every so often, he'd get up and practice some dance steps. He was one of the guys that had invited Cal to go with them the night he'd learned to do the twist. He told him what had happened from beginning to end and, after finishing, the guy said, "Why, you lady killer – she loves you, you fool. Have you been bedding her? It would explain why she's crazy about you".

Cal shook his head, "No".

"Well, I got to tell you, she'd do anything for you man – do you know what I'm telling you? When a woman loves a man, they want to love you all the way – she needs you, cause that's all she's going to have once you're gone, and she knows it," as he went on talking to him like "Father Time".

Could he be right? If so, just knowing this was overwhelming. He had no idea that she'd fallen for him. Now he was scared to death to see her again, knowing what she was expecting of him. It all made sense now, about why she'd been acting funny. He knew that he didn't feel that way about her and he certainly didn't want to have "relations" with her just because she needed him to. His mother had raised him to "save himself" until he was married - that it would be something special between his wife and himself. The concept of saving himself seemed trite in this day and age, particularity if you were a serviceman.

Should one of the men on shipboard, ever find out that one of their shipmates was a virgin, they'd harass the poor guy unmercifully. So he made sure he had a good story to tell to keep them off his back.

The topic of sex and, for that matter, anything to do with sex occupied most of the guy's conversations morning, noon and night. It was a driving force, consuming and preoccupying their every thought. The only other topics most of the men could or would talk about were sports and cars. He knew something about cars, virtually nothing about sports, nor did he care to. This was probably due to spending his early years on the farm – too busy to go out for a team, subsequently, always being picked last for any team. He still could remember standing all alone, waiting and suffering through the humiliation of rejection. Consequently, he had virtually nothing in common with his fellow sailors and he mostly kept to himself, reading books or writing letters.

Again his thoughts turned to Penny and his dilemma – he knew that he should face her and tell her Goodbye and wish her well before he left.

Chapter 7.0

He spent most of the evening packing and checking out[29]. He'd heard that they were shipping out at dawn – Cal knew then that there was no way he'd have time to see Penny one more time. Secretly, he was relieved that he didn't have time for a face-to-face with her and in another moment, he felt he owed her something more than just disappearing. So he quickly scrawled her a note, thanking her for being his friend and for the good times; for laughing at his jokes and most of all for listening - that he would never forget her. He wished her the best in her Navy career and hoped that someday, she'd find that one special guy - the one that she deserved above all others. He also added that he had found out, unexpectedly, that he had to leave early the next morning for his flight. It was the truth, so he felt vindicated about leaving in this manner.

He was awake long before dawn; his bed stripped, showered, shaved and dressed to travel. He signed out for the last time and, without looking back, climbed aboard the base bus, threw his sea bag into the seat beside him and kicked back. As the saying goes, he was free, white and had money in his pocket. And now he was on the move – just the way

---

[29] "Checking out, is required of everyone changing duty stations. The person must check in with each support department and sign out, thereby allowing notification of being officially separation from that department and their paperwork being sent to their new duty station support people.

he liked it. No strings to hold him back, no responsibilities - or at least none for the next two weeks.

As luck would have it, his old friend from boot camp and "A" school, Devery, was on the same bus and so he got up and moved to Cal's seat and immediately started making plans for a good time in New York City. Whenever Devery got excited about something, his voice picked up a bit of an Irish accent of sorts and now was no different.

Daylight was breaking as they got to the airport. The sun was well up, shining over the distant trees that lined the airport property, when they boarded the plane and headed east. In just a few hours, he'd be back home.

Cal thought about how surprised and proud his mom would be of him. He never tired of surprising her.

The plane soon landed at New York's Idlewild Airport, now called JFK. From there, Devery and he caught a shuttle into the city.

Devery was from South Hold, Long Island. He was tall, well over 6-4, splendidly built, with a quick smile and a happy-go-lucky way about him. They had become friends in boot camp and had hung out on occasion in "A" school. Devery was always talking about New York City and what a wondrous place it was. He was determined to show him around and, in particular, Time Square. In fact, that was nearly all he talked about, and shared with him, what he called a Boilermaker. He wasn't a drinker, so had never had one before.

As they walked along, Devery told him that picking up women, any women, in NY was as easy as ... well, just asking. The idea of this seemed to be so far out of his realm of possibilities that it didn't even seem remotely possible. However, Cal decided to call Devery on it – so he bet him that he didn't have the nerve to do it, much less to succeed. He knew that Devery was a sucker for a challenge and would do almost anything to prove that, not only could he rise to the situation, but succeed too. He was a big believer in asking and receiving. As cocky as he was, he tilted his head and said, "okay, you're on, call it". Cal noticed a very attractive, young women in the distance with a nice set of legs coming their way and said, "that one". Devery whispered between clenched teeth, *"that's not a broad, it's a dyke"*. Cal's eyes almost fell out of his head as *"it"* walked past – it was beyond belief – he couldn't tell the difference. To his knowledge there were no such people like that back in the Point where he'd grown up.

"How do you know?" he challenged Devery, thinking that old Devery was just putting him on, so as to get out of their bet.

"His boobs weren't bouncing and he had an Adam's apple," Devery said nonchalantly as he flashed him that man of the world smile.

Cal fast reversed his memory to try and remember what he'd seen in that department, but all he remembered was the blond hair and long legs. He guessed, he'd have to take Devery's word for it.

Soon, among the hundreds of people coming toward them, he noted another young girl. She was a drop dead, great looking young women, obviously a manager or something, given she was dressed in a form fitting tailored suit and he noticed through her white tailored blouse that her boobs were moving in perfect rhythm as she walked. She was so fine looking that Cal probably would never have even approached her for a date, let alone dared to ask her to go to bed with him. He was sure that Devery had met his match; so he nodded toward her as he hissed, *"ask her"*.

He stood back, sure that he'd win this one hands down.

Without so much as missing a beat, Devery approached and stopped her, asking if she was interested in doing the both of them.

Cal's mouth fell so far open, it must have hit the pavement, cracking the cement. He suddenly felt like sinking into the ground – this was not really happening, his senses shouted.

She calmly looked them both over as she walked around them and smiled, then looked at her watch and made a clicking sound that indicated she was disappointed that she didn't have the time right now – "maybe another time," she said as she frowned and continued on her way. He watched her wistfully as her hips and legs seemed to say, *"Too bad ... how sad"*, and then she was gone in a sea of humanity - just another blur moving along the long cold sidewalks of New York City.

Devery just laughed as he said, "see, nothing to it"; he bet the next one would say yes. Want to try again, he asked, his eyes dancing with mischief?

Devery had made a believer out of him, but he was not interested in getting laid, only in getting on his bus and getting home.

Quickly, so as to get his mind off their contest, he said, "I thought you were going to show me Time Square".

"Right you are my laddie," Devery laughed, "and that I shall".

So Devery proceeded to show him around Time Square, pointing out this building and that one. He also told Cal the names of the buildings and who lived there or shopped here and, after a time, he led him to a basement bar.

He had been surprised that Devery knew so much about New York, even beyond the obvious details.

As they entered the bar, he was stuck by how dark inside it was, save for a few light bulbs hanging from the fly stained, porcelain fixtures, attached to the ceiling and over the bar. An overhead fan spun slowly doing little to eradicate the smoke laden air, which permeated the gloom. Bright colored neon lights flickered fitfully around the mirror behind the bar offering a sort of psychedelic illumination of the patrons - what few there were at this hour of the day. He knew somehow that as five o'clock approached, business would pick up, until they closed. The bar was right in the middle of the business district.

He remembered that he hadn't eaten in over 14-hours, and the thought of drinking alcoholic drinks didn't appeal to him – but he had promised Devery that he would partake of at least one Boiler Maker, so he watched as the bartender poured a shot of liquor into a shot glass and a beer into a beer glass.

Devery made a major production out of how such a drink should to be partaken. First, you threw the shot down, and then immediately chased it with a beer. This scenario he carried off with great aplomb and then motioned for Cal to follow suit. He did, though not without starting to cough as the whiskey let itself down his esophagus. The beer helped to calm the effects of the whiskey, and before he could recover, Devery had paid for a second and in no time it was waiting beside his still unfinished beer. Again, Devery cajoled and begged him to have another ... "for old time sake", he lamented, his eyes staring upward as if speaking to someone in heaven.

Cal was starting to feel a little annoyed at Devery for pushing him to drink on an empty stomach, knowing full well that the effects of drinking like this would render him quite incapable of finding his way to the bus station. He made a deal with Devery: he'd take the drink if Devery promised to see that he got to Port Authority ... and in the right line for his bus. He heartily agreed and Cal took the drink.

He managed to get to the doorway and up the stairs to street level before he started feeling terribly dizzy. He told Devery to take him to his bus now – otherwise, he was going to have to carry him. Devery nodded and took off, with him in hot pursuit. Devery's long legs made short work of what his shorter legs had to work twice as hard to accomplish. The sea bag hanging over Cal's shoulder served as a rudder to keep him upright and walking relatively straight. Cal kept Devery's foggy figure in sight which came into focus when he closed one of his eyes.

They wound around the sea of people and finally headed into a large building that didn't look any different from any of the others until they walked through the back doors. There, before him, was row upon row of trains. After walking by a slew of them, they arrived at the Greyhound terminal on a higher level. Devery looked at his ticket and pointed to an overhead sign and said, "stand here until the line forms and follow it out to the bus, that will be going to Binghamton".

Cal did exactly that for the next three hours, not moving a muscle. He spread his legs apart and leaned up against his upright sea bag, using it for support. In this manner, a three point stance was established for stability. Then he locked his legs so he wouldn't succumb to the world spinning around him. It was as if he was inside one of those globes that you shake up and the snow flies around and around until it finally settles on the objects in the globe. Cal was sure he was in some kind of vacuum where everything was going around and around, but he was unaffected by it. He couldn't hear it, he couldn't feel it – it was all a haze of subtle colors and muted sounds.

After what seemed like forever, a line formed behind him and Cal knew it must be getting close to boarding time. After another long wait the bus driver motioned him to come forward and, grabbing his bag, Cal, with great determination, launched himself in his direction. As the driver looked at his ticket, Cal told him that he would be in the back seat sleeping - to wake him when they got to Binghamton. The driver nodded knowingly as Cal moved on with his sea bag over his shoulder, hitting every seat as he passed. Arriving none too soon at the back seat, he threw his bag over his shoulder onto the seat and sprawled across the bag and seat, falling instantly asleep. The bus could have gone to Timbuktu and back, and he would have never known.

The next thing Cal knew, he was being shaken by the driver – he turned and left the instant Cal opened his eyes. Cal quickly got up and swung his sea bag over his shoulder, noting on the way out that all the other passengers had already exited the bus.

It was still dark and very damp outside as he stepped off the bus. His mind went back to all the times his family had come into Binghamton arriving at this very bus station. For them, it had been one of their twice a year trips to the Rheumatic Fever Clinic at General Hospital to have their EKGs, blood work, chest X-Rays, hearts listened to, and a number of other tests run. It took nearly all day. Within the remaining time, mother worked in the dentist, eye doctor, shoe and clothing stores and if it was Christmas - the Elks Club. They'd hand out free gifts and food for the poor kids.

At that time in their lives, they hadn't, as yet, realized they were only getting these handouts because they were on Welfare. It was a big deal to them, and they looked forward to it almost as much as stopping at Neisner's and having a hot meal along with a frozen mug of Hire's Root Beer. He could still see the huge keg on the counter that said Hire's Root Beer on it.

The Greyhound station smelled of diesel fumes, cigarette and cigar smoke. Over the years the art deco look that permeated the place was showing extreme wear. The cement had been worn smooth from the feet of millions of people. It was stained with oil, fuel, drink and littered with squished cigarette butts everywhere. The paint had long ago worn from a bright gray to a smoky, cobweb, soot smudged shell that gave the area a feeling of having long ago lost itself somewhere in time.

Once inside, the high, silver-colored lights cast a yellow illumination over the hard, long benches, gray metal rental lockers and the soot stained, yellow walls that seemed to stretch upward to the sky. There were two ticket counters - one was always open to serve the public. Along the wall in the back of the main room was a row of phones in small dark booths, in all stages of disrepair. Most lacked a phone book, and those that were still there were missing huge sections. Looking at the large clock on the far end of the station hall, high up on the wall, he guessed that it would still be several hours before the bus station's cafeteria would open and the city buses would start running so, throwing his sea bag over his shoulder, he started the long walk from Binghamton to Johnson City.

Cal knew from the letters his Mom wrote, that she and his sister had an apartment in JC within walking distance to work. If he got there soon enough, he'd catch them before they left for work.

As he walked, he failed to notice a black limo parked along the street.

It had been deliberately parked where the overhead street lights wouldn't shine on it. Inside was a man dressed in black; he'd been notified that his target was back in town and where he was located. Again, he made some notes as he observed him and then he took a picture of him with a very special camera, as he had been ordered to do. Again he put his things in the briefcase and signaled his driver to drive on ahead a short distance and again park as he had done before. In this manner, they followed the young sailor across town. He was interested in learning where he was going, suspecting that he was headed to his mother's.

The walk across town was invigorating, he was used to long hikes and was in top physical condition. He shifted his sea bag from one shoulder to the other periodically as the city blocks passed one after the other beneath his feet. The only thing that interrupted the tranquility of his walk was an occasional patrol car. They'd wave at him and keep going. Finally, he made it to where his Mom and Marie lived and paused out front. He was not familiar with this place, they had moved again and he was not sure which apartment they were in. Knowing how careful his mother was about getting her mail, he knew if he found the mail boxes, he'd know the apartment as they were all labeled by apartment number. Locating the mail boxes, beaten and rusted looking, he recognized his mother's smooth cursive handwriting and looked at the apartment number. In a matter of minutes, he was knocking on an unfamiliar door, but as he listened, he recognized the voices that leaked through the door – it was evident that they were getting ready for work.

From the other side of the door, he heard a muffled, "Yes".

"It's Cal", he said with authority, as he identified himself.

He heard a squeal from the other side, the safety chains dropped, and the doorknob turned.

He was home again – he wanted the time to stand still, he wanted to be back here and a part of things – but somehow he knew that he could never go back. Yes, he was still a part of them, but he was no longer a part of the life cycle of events that were evolving from day to day. He was different now, his experiences had made him different, and he could no longer relate to them or feel really a part of them. Cal felt the pull toward that which he knew and could most easily relate to. So again, he sought out those who had shared his experiences and he theirs. He would, in the years to come, come home less often and travel more to see beyond the hills that had trapped him for so many years.

The time had come for him to join the fleet. Another life was opening up for him, a life full of new adventures, new people, new challenges and places to see.

By the time his ride had arrived, he was packed and ready to leave. He flew out of Broome County Airport, making connections in Allentown, Pa and then onto Norfolk International airport. Somehow he found his way to the Naval Operations Base (NOB) and to his new home, the USS Fort Mandan, LSD 21.

The cabbie, upon entering the base, asked the gate guard at which pier the Fort Mandan was birthed, so as he traveled past each pier, he was amazed at the size of all the ships and the different types that were in port. They drove past Destroyers, Destroyer Escorts, supply ships, tankers, and tenders. On the far end were the aircraft carriers or "flat tops", as the sailors called them. They were dwarfed by the sheer size of the ships, their hulls seemed to loom far above them blocking out the scattered rays of sunlight that played between the ships.

Suddenly the cab stopped and, as it did, the cabbie pointed to his ship, "that be it over there tied to the Melifin, she's on a tender now", he said around a chew in his mouth. Cal hardly had any idea what he was talking about, but nodded as he pulled his sea bag from the cab and paid the man.

It was apparent that he'd have to board the Melifin to get to his ship, as she was tied on the outboard side to the Melifin. He watched for a moment as other sailors were coming off and boarding the Melifin as to how they were saluting the ensign (US Flag) and then the quarter master and Officer of the Deck (OD). He had scant training in such affairs, so he wanted to be sure he got it right.

Gritting his teeth, Cal swung his sea bag over his shoulder and started walking up the gangway. It was long and made of aluminum and pitched with every step. As narrow as it was, it was still able to handle two-way-traffic, that is, if you allowed a little leeway as someone passed you going the other way. Before he knew it, he was on deck.

He smartly saluted the ensign and then the OD, stated his wish to come aboard and that he was reporting for duty aboard the USS Fort Mandan LSD 21.

The OD smiled a knowing smile and returned his salute and then pointed to the other side of the ship, in the direction of the quarter deck of the Fort Mandan, saying, "She's over there".

Cal saluted again and continued his journey across the USS Melifin's deck and over to the Quarter Deck of the Fort Mandan, where again, he went through the same formalities. This time the OD signed him into his log and sent a seaman for the leading officer of the day from his division. A first class appeared, he could see that his name was Westmoreland. He was a short man, built like a tank with a quick smile. As he turned to lead the way, he pointed in the direction which they would be going. He led him through a hatch on the O1 deck, and as they made a left turn, they entered the "M" Division's sleeping quarters, where Westmoreland told him he'd be quartered.

He showed Cal to his locker and pointed out a rack on the third level. Cal was amazed at how many men were billeted in "this space" as he gazed at all the racks mounted between the pillars and lockers.

"The space" had the austere and crowded appearance of his first boot camp barracks.

Located a few steps away at the foot of his bunk was a table between two portholes. It was where guys off duty hung out, playing cards and writing letters to loved ones. Four men, smoking and playing cards, currently occupied the table. All of them eyed him with great interest and barely masked amusement.

Cal knew instinctively that he was the new kid on the block and that he'd have to pay his dues and part of those payments came sooner than he had expected.

He noticed as he glanced around, that everything was made of steel and painted an off white. Above his head were beams of steel and crammed in between them were all nature of pipes and cables. This would be his home for the better part of the next four years. It was an alien form of life that he would learn to tolerate, but never fully get used to.

For some, the structured life was a sort of security but, for him, he yearned to be free to come and go as he chose. He'd mark time and make the most of it, learn from it and move on. Any thoughts of making this a career were gone in this, his first glimpse of what life in the Amphibious (Gator) Navy was all about.

Chapter 8.0

His thoughts were suddenly interrupted by a voice asking what his discharge date was – it was a date that was burned into his mind like his service number and without hesitation, as he had been trained, he said, "12/17/1965". The man asking the question retorted in disgust, "If I had that long to go, I'd shoot myself," he cackled. "Ask me how long I've got left, boot", he sneered.

Playing to him, he asked, "How long you got?"

The other man playing up to the moment, shouted as loud as he could, "Two days and awake up and I'm off this F&*@% ship so fast that it will make your F&*@% head spin".

He would hear the "F-word" spoken more frequently than any other word in the English vocabulary throughout his stay in the Navy. (It was also known as the "F-bomb" or "the bomb".)

However, hearing this bit of information, the others hooted and sounded off the length of time they still had before they too would be discharged from the service, all their times were much shorter than his – it now seemed like forever at this tender point in his life.

Through the ensuing years, he would come to hear this theme repeated again and again and he too would have his turn at being a "short timer", although with the ability to use a much-improved form of grammar, one that he'd learned from his mother's knee and in a country school. That was not to say that there weren't times that he'd make a Freudian slip and utter a colloquialism and, should this happen at home, his mom was quick to make a clicking sound with her mouth, or remind him that was not the way we talk here.

After a few weeks, his newness wore off, and he was not looked at as a source of amusement – "he belonged" and was part of the routine that they had all fallen into.

His first bi-weekly payday came and, with it, he was $86.00 richer than the day before. There was not a whole lot one could spend their money on aboard ship, but in town, one could lose it all in a night, so his forays into town were very few at first.

In those days, to get paid, you had to fill out a "chit"[30]. As we proceeded, alphabetically, through the process, we would hand our chit to the Dispersing Officer, say our name and serial number and he'd check it against his list. It had to match the name on the list and service number perfectly, then he'd tell the man next to him the amount of money to be paid to each man as he proceeded through the line. We always got paid in cash. Once the man had counted it out, he handed it to a second man who also counted it, then he handed it to the one being paid.

He also noticed something else while going through the "pay line". After the pay had been handed out, there were other men further on down the corridor and at various times, a man would fall out of line and would stop and give one of the men some of his money. I found out that these men were like "bankers". They lent money to some people for various reasons. The money came from a "slush" fund that the man had created and the interest was high. For example, if you wanted to borrow five dollars, it would cost you seven dollars, ten dollars would cost fifteen, twenty would cost thirty and so on. Several guys on board, ran slush funds and they did very well with them. Should you not pay at the

---

[30] Receipt also known as Script

time it was due, the interest would double for the next pay and if you still didn't pay, you would be blacklisted and unable to borrow a dime from anyone running a slush fund - you might also get "roughed-up". Cal never lent any money or borrowed any, but many did - even officers.

There was also a lot of gambling – even though it was illegal, it still went on. There were arranged "card games" at different times at varies places aboard the ship – he knew of one, but again, he never played. Cal knew of one man who had lost over a thousand dollars, but over the proceeding months paid it back and went on to be "a winner". He was smart and became a student of the game. He also became an enforcer, collecting from those who owed money to the winners of a game.

During those early days, Cal learned his way around the ship, both physically and socially – where he had to go to work, where and when the meals were served and where the showers and heads[31] were located.

Cal also learned who the shakers and players were and who to be wary of. Like every community, they had rules, some written (Blue Jackets Manual), but most were only spoken and a few were unspoken. Like any rule, you break it and, one way or the other, you will eventually end up paying for it. But for the most part, it was a matter of routine, you did what you were told, kept your head down and you got along fine with everyone.

Although he had never done hard-time, he likened the duty on board this ship to serving time in a penal colony. They were every bit its captives, forced to labor day-in and day-out for a pittance. Cal's days in the service were a far cry from what the men and women enjoy in today's service, and the

---

[31] Bathrooms

duty he pulled was far better than that of his predecessors.

It was during the first couple of weeks that Cal was summoned by the Chief. He was a Master Chief (E9) who had served some 20-plus years, given the number of "hash marks"[32] on the left sleeve of his dress uniform. As he entered the chief's quarters, he noticed that they had a much larger common area and separate sleeping quarters – which were much better than his.

Chief Workman's first question startled Cal when he asked, "How do you like it aboard this ship?"

Cal thought for a moment before answering. "Well sir, it's not what I expected," he answered truthfully.

The old chief smiled through a deeply wrinkled, weather worn face, his steely gray eyes for a moment stared at the table, then up at Cal as he said, "I know how well you did in "A" school and by all rights, you should have been given a better duty station, but I pulled some strings to get you, as I needed someone who was smart enough to get along with this crew of derelicts and thieves, someone that I can count on to see that the work gets done and done right the first time."

He could think of nothing more to say, so he only nodded, wondering where this was all headed.

"Given your abilities, it will not be long before you'll become an E-5 and so on up the ladder as far as you want to go. The sky is the limit for you, and I'll do everything I can to see that you can take the tests as soon as you have the time in rate. As soon as you make E-5, I'll assign you to head up your own engineering space. In the meantime, I'll be asking you to work on equipment that I'd ask no other because your smart enough to figure it out and fix it. In return, if you have any problems with anyone

---

[32] Gold stripes placed on left sleeve of lower arm to denote years of service – one for every reenlistment term

aboard this ship, just let me know, and *I'll fix it.*
"Understood?"

"Yes, Sir."

"You're excused."

"Thank you sir," he said, as he saluted and left.

As it turned out, Cal would make E5 in a record 2-yrs from the date he'd entered the Navy.

After that, Cal only saw the Chief on rare occasions, as he sent his orders through one of his two 1st Class's; Westmoreland or Cook. Westmoreland was somewhat shorter than he and quite stout, but amiable and often wore a smile on his rounded face. Westmoreland never gave him any grief, nor were they ever buddies. Cook, in comparison, was tall, even taller than Cal's 6-foot and slender, never smiled and was distant. He rarely spoke to Cal. They operated on a purely business association. There would come a time later in his hitch, that the Chief would display a Solomon type of wisdom, amazing him, and cementing an even closer, unspoken friendship.

It was not long before they were off the Tender[33] and under their own power. Therefore, all the men had to stand more watches - four on and four off, plus his work day duties.

Once the ship was tied to a pier or on a Tender, they received power - elect, water, steam, phone and such. This was referred to as being on "Cold Iron". Even so, they had to maintain watches in the engineering spaces and above decks. Below decks, their duty was to check for leaks, fires and, or, any other abnormalities that might occur. None ever did, but it was part of the way things were done in the Navy and far be it for him to change it.

---

[33] A ship that repairs other ships

Somehow the diver training school knew he was in Little Creek and contacted him to come in for some refresher training and to attend classes for additional training. This would only require a couple of hours twice a week. The Chief and Master at Arms seemed to know all about it so all he had to do was to sign in and out and his duties were rearranged around this training. Again, it was all on the QT and not to be discussed with anyone. Soon he was requalified as a "hard hat" and scuba diver to 100-feet, or four atmospheres. After that came some additional specialized training, and the CO reemphasized that all their training was classified – that none of them was ever to mention any aspect of it or its existence, or suffer the penalty of going to prison. In effect, he was an embedded resource to be used at a future date and time should the need arise.

In a matter of weeks, the word was passed that they'd be going out for a couple of days for a shake-down cruise, to ensure that everything was in good working order, if not, the tender would have to fix it. If everything was okay, they were to get underway in a month for a Med Cruise. Everything must have been okay as they were cleared for sea duty.

As a Snipe[34], he was assigned to the Starboard Pump Room during working hours and standing underway watches. However during General Quarters, he was assigned to Starboard Main Control where he worked the Damage Control Board under the watchful eyes of the Engineering Officers.

During his four-hour watches, which he'd pull once every other day in port, and when at sea, 4-hours on and 4-hours off, his duties were to operate the varies machines in the "space". This consisted of taking readings and making adjustments as required for the "most efficient operation". During working hours he'd perform maintenance and repair work

---

[34] People who work in engineering below decks.

when and where required. During General Quarters[35] he was trained to man the General Quarter's headphones in Main Control and plot any damage to the ship on a large grease board and deploy fire and repair forces to those locations[36]. It was a big job, and he wondered at first if he was up to it. As time went on, he became very good at it and felt at ease standing along side of the Warrant officer and whichever Chief was on duty, as he did his plots and yelled out orders over the sound powered phones, to all the teams aboard ship as they went through one exercise after another.

They never stayed in port very long and before they knew it, they were again underway, back to the Caribbean.

It was April of 1965 and there was a revolution brewing between Haiti and the Dominican Republic. There was fear that if a war started, that it would endanger American lives. Our government wanted them to standby for possible evacuations. So, near the end of April, they were ordered to join the fleet already in the area. It took about three to four days to get there, where they cruised at 1/3 for the next several weeks, waiting to see if the revolution was on, or not, and if any Americans wanted to be evacuated.

To burn time, several guys decide it would be fun to fish for sharks. We had observed the sharks following the ship, waiting for the galley crews to dump soft garbage off the fantail. Some of the sharks were huge. So a few of the guys rigged copper wire to the homemade hooks and baited the hook with a chunk of meat from the garbage. Then they tied the other end of the wire to the ship. In no time, they were hooking sharks left and right. Some of them were very large and couldn't be hauled in and killed,

---

[35] Sound if there is a threat to the ship.

[36] Each frame and level number is unique to a given location on a board a ship.

so the Marines were enlisted to shoot them. Of course, this couldn't be just any old gun, it had to be a machine gun, and they had all kinds of them.

The water was turning blood red from the shark's frenzied feeding, on their own dead carcasses. The air was filled with gunfire and excited yelling. Suddenly the word was passed over the PA system, for all who were on the fantail, to secure themselves with a rope, as falling into the water would mean certain death.

The Marine CO felt that this was a good opportunity to get some field training for his men, in the use of their arsenal of weapons. It also allowed them time to blow off steam that was building up from the pressure cooker of the lower decks where the temperatures hovered at times well over 100-degrees.

At morning quarters, the shoe polish melted off their shoes and onto the haze gray 02-deck plates, where they stood inspection and heard the announcements of the day. By the end of the announcements, their feet were so hot inside their shoes that they felt as if they were on fire. Perhaps this was the reason for the meetings being shortened.

Their sleeping berths were so hot during the nights that it was difficult to sleep, even with the ports and hatches wide open. He could well appreciate what the Marines were going through in their sleeping quarters several decks below.

Finally, after weeks of cruising in circles at 1/3, they got word to report back to Little Creek. It was May 23, 1965 and apparently the revolution was over, settled more or less peacefully, without having to evacuate any civilians.

A feeling of exhilaration went through the ship like electricity. Immediately they went to "FLANK" speed[37] and headed for home. The morale on the ship climbed as the miles passed beneath our hull, with the guys making plans for liberty call.

They'd only have a week and a half before leaving again. It was an excited crew that manned the ship during their trip home. Even the Marines had had enough and the old man was livid about the duty that had been forced on his ship and its crew.

He felt strongly, that they had been the scapegoat, having to take on every tin cup job in the 6th Fleet. So, he had one of his men who was an artist, design and paint an Alligator with a wood screw through it, dripping blood, onto a piece of pennant sized material. As we approached Little Creek, he had the signalman run it up under the ship's flags, where it stood out boldly over those above it. To all nautical Navy men, the gator represents the Amphibious Forces and the screw through it, meant a "Screwed Gator". They all cheered as it went up to be seen far and wide ... and seen, it was.

When the old man found out that a pilot wouldn't be granted to bring the ship in until the "noncompliant pennant" was removed, he took matters into his own hands and brought it in himself. He earned major points from the crew and Marines but got himself a reprimand from the base commander. He was the only Captain we ever had who stuck up for their crew and, for that, he had our undying gratitude – we would have followed him through the gates of hell, if he'd asked.

After the shake-down cruise, they were immediately ordered back out to sea. The date was October 12th, 1962. It was all hush, hush as no one knew what was going on.

It was evident that it was something big as here and there they could see other war ships heading south. He could feel the Goosebumps rising up and

---

[37] Full speed

down his arms and legs, as the word was passed to maintain radio silence and the ship went black[38]. He could see the gunners mates hauling ammo up from down below decks, for the Quad 40s and stockpiling it around the armament.

The scuttlebutt was running like electricity through a wire; the word was, that they were going to war with Cuba and they were all speculating that it would be a 3-minute war.

The following day, they went to General Quarters. A state of war had been declared aboard the ship; "this is not a drill," came the word over the loudspeakers - the sound reverberated off the bulkheads and alleyways throughout the ship and the attitude on board became deadly serious.

Their mouths dropped open as they looked at one another – "*now what the hell was going on,*" they all wondered as they rushed headlong to their duty stations. The ship reduced its speed from FLANK to 1/3. They had apparently arrived.

Very soon it became apparent that they weren't alone, as across the open ocean, he spotted several other war ships in every direction, as far as the eye could see. Like us, they were slowly maneuvering in large circles. By then, they all knew that they were an integral part of a blockade to keep Russian ICBMs out of Cuba. No ships in – only out.

From this point forward, Cal partially lived in Main Control, ready at a moment's notice to start plotting damage.

"*What the hell was going on, everyone wanted to know?!*" They were in a news blackout – nothing in and nothing out.

As it turned out, a US Lockheed U-2, high-altitude, making a pass over Cuba on October 14, 1962,

---

[38] No lights

photographed a Soviet SS-4 medium-range ballistic missile being assembled for silo installation.

President Kennedy was briefed about the situation on October 16, and he immediately called together a group of advisors and officials known as the Executive Committee, or ExCom.[39]

We were at a point in history of being within a gnat's whisker of going to War with Russia and Cuba, and everyone was holding their breath, as they realized that they were on the verge of World War III. In retrospect, all it would have taken would have been for one of the young sailors to mistakenly pull the trigger on one of the quads, and all hell would've broken loose.

The days passed slowly as they held their breathes, expecting the worst, but praying for the best. Everyone in engineering, who worked and stood watches below the waterline, wondered if, at any moment, a torpedo might blast through the bulkhead[40] exploding and killing them all. There would be no escaping – if the concussion from the explosion didn't get you first, the flooding and subsequent drowning would. He preferred to think of other things; his plans for the future, their next liberty stop where ever that might be – they never knew ahead of time. It was a matter of security – they never knew. He also thought about what new things me might see when on liberty in a new port. For the most part, they were all silent only performing their necessary duties or when having to report in or in his case, respond to a report and pass it along to the OD.

---

[39] For additional information: http://www.history.com/topics/cold-war/cuban-missile-crisis
[40] Wall

*   *   *

For the next two weeks, President Kennedy and his team wrestled with a diplomatic crisis of epic proportions, as did their counterparts in the Soviet Union.

In a TV address on October 22, 1962, President John F. Kennedy notified Americans about the presence of the missiles, explained his decision to enact a naval blockade around Cuba and made it clear that the U.S. was prepared to use military force, if necessary, to neutralize this threat to our national security. Following this news, many people feared the world was on the brink of nuclear war and the world held it's collective breath. However, disaster was avoided when the U.S. agreed to Soviet leader Nikita Khrushchev's offer to remove the missiles in exchange for the U.S. promising not to invade Cuba.[41]

*   *   *

Finally, after nearly two weeks, they were ordered back to Little Creek, General Quarters was canceled and World War III had been averted. As soon as the Captain got the message from Fleet Command, he ordered the ship to go to FLANK speed and set their course for Little Creek.

Their hearts quickened, and their spirits soared, as they felt the ship come alive under their feet. It was an electric feeling as the mood of the ship's crew changed, and music from radios and guitars washed over and through the ship. To all of them, it was no

---

[41] For additional information: http://www.history.com/topics/cold-war/cuban-missile-crisis

small thing have the weight of going to war off their backs and minds. He would see it in all their faces – the relief ... it was palpably.

To the crew, seeing their home port was an emotional moment, but not near as great as seeing the hundreds, if not thousands, that were waiting to see them as they pulled in and finally disembarked. The moment was made even more poignant by the fact that had things not gone right, there might not have been a port or families to come back to and the families that waited for felt it too.

Without any fanfare, the pilot boarded and brought them into Little Creek and, the cheering could be heard even below decks. The pier was filled to capacity and beyond, with family's and friends stretching far out into the parking lots. It was an amazing thing to see ship after ship pull in and to hear the cheers of other family's on other piers and lots, and to be swept up in the spirit of the moment. Everyone has a grin on their faces – even though, like him, there was no one there for them.

The crew knew that in less than a month, they'd be leaving again to go to the Med. It seemed as if they had hardly settled into seeing loved ones when it was time to relieve the 6th fleet in Med.

By now, they all pretty much had had it and it was an ornery bunch of sailors that reported back aboard from leave and/or long weekends. They all knew they had precious few days to be with family and girlfriends, before leaving for the Med. This time, the day came all too soon. There were many, Cal included, who were not ready to leave so soon, especially after having been in a state of constant deployment. However, for many others, there was excitement in the air, as last minute preparations were being made. Large quantities of food supplies were brought aboard from the pier using our on board cranes. Then they made a quick stop at Roosey Roads[12] and, loaded canister after canister of ammo and explosives that were handed man to man until it was all stowed below decks in the armory. Because of his strength, Cal was often placed at the top of a hatch and given the job of physically lowering the canister to a waiting pair of hands below to move it on down the line, hand to hand until it reached the armory.

It was during one of these exercises that Cal hurt his lower back. At first it had only felt like a slight pain – a momentary stab and it was gone, but later it became increasingly painful and started limiting his ability to bend. He went to sick bay and then to the base medical center at Little Creek to see a doctor. The doctor ordered X-Rays and Cal was given medication. From that time on, occasionally, it would flare up and then go away. But, it was always there and Cal had to be mindful so as not to aggravate it.

It was early November of 1962; the morning of their departure had arrived, and the pier was filled with families of sailors hugging and kissing each other goodbye – something stirred inside Cal and then a cloud of loneliness settled over him. It was like nothing he'd ever experienced. It made him sick and dizzy, unable to concentrate. For the first time, he felt as if he might fall into an abyss and lose all control, never being able to stop his downward plunge. He wished he had someone in his life, someone to share his thoughts, someone who would care about him; someone he could love – truly, "ONE" is a very lonely number and he had been "alone" for a very long time.

In the past, when other guys had girlfriends, he had to work; they were too poor for him to be off in town somewhere dating as every cent had to go toward the family's survival. Subsequently, he was always on the outside looking in - always different. Cal watched the people on the pier, unable to tear

---

[42] Roosevelt Roads Naval Station located in Ceiba, Puerto Rico

himself from the port hole and wondered if someday he'd have a wife and kids, someone who would be seeing him off and waiting for him when he got back. He sincerely hoped he would.

The word was passed to prepare to get underway, and Cal ran for his assigned engineering space[43]. He had learned to descend the four levels without taking a step. By placing his hands on the copper-colored hand railings that led straight down, with his feet braced against their sides, he'd shoot downward at breakneck speed. Then, at the last minute, he'd tighten his grip and come to a sudden stop, just before his feet connected with the deck plates beneath the ladder.

Cal also learned how to move about the rocking ship and down four levels without spilling a drop of coffee. One of the secrets was, you never looked at your cup. The second, don't even think about the fact that you're carrying the cup in the first place.

Yes, Sir, Cal learned a lot on that cruise and became more self-assured than at any time in his life. He noticed that, in spite of the Navy's discipline and regimentation, he had developed a strong sense of self and, for the first time in his life, felt that he was as good as the next person - maybe even a little bit better. He'd earned the respect of his peers, for not only the quality of his work but for who he was. In the Navy, he became his own man.

It would be May of 1963 before they'd again, see "home port"[44]. The first few days at sea separated the men from the boys, as the old salts would say. There was a lot of seasickness, particularly among the Marines. They carried some four to five hundred men. While they were out to sea, they practiced man overboard, high-lining stores, high lining fuel and personnel exchanges. They also practiced going to

[43] Area aboard a ship identified with a deck and frame number
[44] Base of operations

war. This meant shooting at drones[45] and doing landings.

When their fuel ran low, they rigged for highlining. This time there was a heavy fog, so anything beyond the front or stern of the ship disappeared from sight. In no time, the USS Neosho loomed into view along their Starboard side. A shot from each side sent light lines to each ship. Once caught, they were used to pull in increasingly heavier lines across the expanse between the two ships until the highlining rigs could support the 5"-fuel lines. Then the heavy black oil fueling commenced. The fuel would be used to fire the boilers which turned the distilled water into high-pressure steam, that fueled the generator and propulsion turbines.

They were about midway into fueling when a contact was sighted by radar on a collision course with them. The ship was not one of their own, and it couldn't be raised before making contact, so an Emergency Breakaway was instituted. The rigging and multiple supply hoses were cut loose, and both ships safely parted, avoiding an open sea catastrophe. The praises from the other ships for their quick thinking and expert maneuvering were welcomed by one and all. (See "Ship to Ship message" at the end of this novel.)

However, it left both ships with large puddles of heavy fuel oil, on the decks and streaks up and down the sides of the ship. It took several days for the deck crews to clean up and repaint.

One night, word buzzed through the ship that they were going to make landfall the following day. They were currently just off the Azores.

One of the old salts stepped up to the air supply vent that brought fresh air into the engineering spaces from near the Quarter Deck and took a deep breath, then stated unequivocally, that he could

---

[45] Gliders pulled by a plane

smell European (expletive) and he was going to get him some before the fortnight. His rather crude reference to women, in general, moved him down several notches in Cal's estimation of this man's intelligence quotient and respect. However, in general, it was about the height of many of the men's aspirations.

The conversation ran the gamut that night: the best time they ever had, in what port, with whom and the sordid details of the adventure. It usually ended in being so drunk that it took several days before regaining full consciousness. Most of the events that took place were, of course, hearsay provided by an equally drunk buddy. If the truth be known, they probably went to a bar, saw a homely bar maid, and started drinking. As they drank, she started looking better and better, to the point where they were buying her drinks, and fighting over who would have her. While they fought, she stole their money and then called the Shore Patrol to pick them up.

After spending what seemed like an eternity at sea, doing drills and countless inspections, they finally saw land. Word was passed that at a given time that they would be passing through The Straits of Gibraltar. His only knowledge of this island was that it was inhabited with monkeys, served as a World War II storage place of munitions and served as Prudential's Logo. Beyond that, it appeared to him to be shrouded in fog most of the time and was no doubt one cold, windswept place to live.

*   *   *

In reality, having read up on it, today, the Rock of Gibraltar forms a peninsula jutting out into the Straits of Gibraltar from the southern coast of Spain.

The Rock's central peak, Signal Hill, and the top station of the Gibraltar Cable Car, stands at the windy elevation of 387 m (1,270 ft.). The near-cliffs along the eastern side of the Rock descend abruptly to a series of wind-blown sand slopes that date back to when sea levels were lower than today, and a sandy plain extended east from the base of the Rock. The western face, where the City of Gibraltar is located, is comparatively less steep and much more inhabitable.

The Rock of Gibraltar contains over 100 caves. St. Michael's Cave, located halfway up the western slope of the Rock, is the most prominent and is a popular tourist attraction, so I learned. It would have been fun to explore it and some of the others, I thought – maybe someday.

When World War II broke out in 1939, the authorities evacuated the civilian population to Morocco, the United Kingdom, Jamaica, and Madeira so that the military could fortify Gibraltar against a possible German attack. By 1942 there were over 30,000 British soldiers, sailors, and airmen on the Rock. They expanded the tunnel system and made the Rock a keystone in the defense of shipping routes to the Mediterranean.

In February 1997, it was revealed the British had a secret plan called "Operation Tracer" to conceal service men in tunnels beneath the Rock in case the Germans captured it. The team in the rock would have radio equipment with which to report enemy movements. A six-man team waited under cover at Gibraltar for two and half years. The Germans never got close to capturing the rock and so the men were never sealed inside. The team was disbanded to resume civilian life when the war ended.[46]

---

[46] https://en.wikipedia.org/wiki/Rock_of_Gibraltar

*   *   *

Their passage through the Straits was marked by rain and gale force winds, however, through the fog, he could just make out the mountainous formation that formed the Rock, as everyone referred to it. The Rock was shrouded in fog, and rain beat down on him incessantly as he tried to peer through the murky weather to make out more of its features, which then, was just the silhouette of a very large, green colored, mountainous-looking rock. Finally, he gave up and took cover from the biting winds that were whipping the seas into waves that were now breaking over the bow.

It was the beginning of winter for the Med and cold rain, and tortuous wind would be their constant companion throughout most of the cruise.

He had learned a lot, and he would continue to learn.

Chapter 9.0

T heir first port of call was Cannes, France. He'd never been in a foreign port, so he was all eyes and ears, not knowing what to expect, and he didn't want to miss a thing.

During this Med Cruise, their liberty ports would include, not necessarily in the order we visited them, Palos, Greece; Palermo, Sicilia; Genoa, Italy; Taranto, Messina; Cannes, France; Corfu, Greece; Athens, Greece; Barcelona, Spain; Rota, Spain; Valencia, Spain, Palma, Mallorca, Genova, Italy and Malta to name only a few.

He'd been below in Main Control when they anchored off Nice. He had recently been assigned to stand his watches in Main Control when they were underway. In that way, he'd be close to where he had to serve, should they go to General Quarters.

He had listened to the orders as they came down from the bridge, to go to "1/3" and then eventually to "STOP", then back "1/3" to set the "Hook"[47].

They had anchored out, which confused him as he thought they'd be tying up at a pier. But, as he soon learned, more often than not, they didn't tie up at most piers when making port. Either the water was too shallow or other ships had already reserved the dock space.

---

[47] Anchor

He came above decks in time to see the Old Man's boat, also referred to as the "Captain's Gig", being lowered over the side and then the word was passed, "Skipper's has gone ashore".

He was surprised and pleased to see that the sun was out for a change after so many days of wind and rain. He rushed to shower and shave and get into dress blues. He happened to be off duty and could go ashore. In no time, a handful of them had assembled on the starboard side, wing wall waiting for permission to go ashore. As soon as the word was passed, they saluted the ensign, and the OD and bounced down the gangway and then jumped into the Mike Boat.[48]

The Mike Boats were gray, front loaders designed to off load Marines on the beach during landings. These landings were a precursor to landing on hostile soil when at war. They would load Marines off the ship as they climbed down rope ladders hung from the side of the ship. They would then gather others from other ships and then rush head long toward the beach. Upon arriving they would beach the craft, the front of the boat would drop forward, and the men would run down it into the water and rush for the shore, hoping to get there without being shot. Thousands lost their lives in those first hours

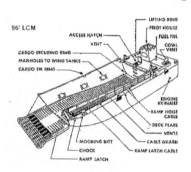

---

[48] LCM or LCU Landing Craft – front ramp, with pilot house. LCM's had 2-Detroit Diesel 6-71, Twin shafts for maneuverability, Engine Pwr: 300 to 400+ hp, 56-feet long, weighing ~ 64-tons, a crew of 5, cargo: 34-tons or 80-troops, speed: 9-knots, 130-miles @ 9-knots.

at Normandy while disembarking from boats just like these on D-Day.

Today's arrival would not be nearly so harrowing or would they run down the ramp into the water. The engine started, sounding very much like a hot rod at the tracks. It had a deep throaty sound muffled at intervals by the sea as it back washed into the boat's exhaust system.

There was a feeling of acceleration as they crashed into one wave after the other, some of which was whipped back over them by the wind. They cheered for it, as it had no bite on this perfect day full of sunshine. Being used to the feel of the sea beneath their feet, no one needed to hang on as they ran head long toward the pier approximately a mile away. It was a warm, almost too warm day for Dress Blues. He remembered the sea being a deep shade of blue and the water surprisingly warm as it drenched their faces.

He would learn that Cannes is located on the French Riviera, on the south east coast of France, bordering on the Mediterranean Sea, at the foot of the Alps. Its natural beauty and mild Mediterranean climate makes it a haven for world travelers wishing to spend their winters. For decades now, the picturesque Cannes surroundings have attracted, not only those in search of relaxation, but also those seeking inspiration.

As they neared port, he could see the town awash in pastels as it curled around the shoreline and up over the mountains in the background.

The harbor area was comprised of a long stone wall that served as a break wall and pier. At the seaward end of the break wall, was a large round stonework that held a harbor light. The harbor light, no doubt, served as a beacon for seamen returning home from the day's fishing. The break wall protected the marina on the far side, from the rambunctious moods of the sea. All that could be seen over the wall were the masts of sailboats large and small bobbing gently on the other side, safe from the ravages of the open sea.

Finally, they pulled along the stone and cement pier and some small boys from the village helped secure them to the bulwark.

They scrambled out of the Mike Boat and on to the pier, as if to take the town – however their mission was one of peace. It felt good to have something solid beneath his feet after weeks at sea.

Suddenly he felt small hands, deftly touching his ankles and lower legs – a couple of the other sailors yelled at the young beggars when they suddenly found themselves without their hidden cigarette packs.

He shooed them away, upset that they would even try such a stunt. Fortunately, he didn't smoke, so he had nothing to be stolen, nor was he a source for cigarettes from those aboard the ship who had turned bumming cigarettes into a growth industry.

Again, they were all dressed the same, no one better or worse than another, except for rank and pay grade. He felt a part of these guys who were all brothers aboard the ship. Many of them had forged friendships and confidences that would last a life time. This was the type of relationship that he had never enjoyed at school. The rules were different here; who you were and how people related to you was not only based on your rank, but more on your ability to take care of yourself and your brothers.

As he walked down the pier, a whistle-like sound pierced the air sending the gulls into swirling clouds of white and gray, calling out to each other in dismay. Then the church bells started chiming and, simultaneously, the stores all closed. Curtains with iron bars in them descended over all the windows and doors with a clinking din that echoed up and down the streets and alleyways.

In a matter of minutes the streets filled with girls from all over the village, all running toward the beach area. As they hit the beach, they were taking their shoes and ... yes, clothes off.

All the sailors, including Cal, came to a dead stop. He had never seen anything like this - mature women taking their clothes off, rendering them totally naked in public. Then, watching in amazement, as some of them put on a very brief bathing suit that he soon learned was a bikini. Some only put the bottoms on as they lay on large beach towels spread over the white crystalline sand.

The bikini consisted of a pair of triangular pieces of cloth, joined with a string to cover little more than the nipple on each breast and a single one with strings on it that looped up around the hips and struggled to cover the front and back. What a contrast from the one-piece bathing suit worn by the girls back in the States. Truly, this was a culture that required closer scrutiny.

After the initial shock had worn off, they all tried to walk along nonchalantly as if what they had just witnessed was an everyday event. The girls all seemed to be quite oblivious to them, though he was sure they were scoping them out for future dates.

After a couple of hours, the bell rang again, and the whistle blew, and the girls all took their bikinis off and put their dresses back on. This time, he stood in open awe at the sight of so many beautiful women in such a scenic place. God knew without a doubt what he was doing when he created them. There was something about every curve and valley that was intoxicating. He had to keep shaking his head to believe that what he was seeing was real - he marveled at the wonder of it all. Later, he would purchase one of those cute little bikinis as a souvenir, figuring that someday he'd give it to the girl he loved.

He would learn throughout his travels, that Europeans had much fewer hang-ups than their counter parts in the States when it came to sexuality. This was also evident with the use of public toilet facilities. It was nothing to see a man and a woman in a John side by side doing their business and unlike their covered systems at home; theirs freely drained into open gutters. *Though he suspected that due to the sanitation issues, this had all changed in the years since his trip aboard.* No one seemed to give it a second thought, as they rushed about their business.

Much to everyone's regret, they were in the picturesque village of Cannes for only a few days. Cal can still visualize the colorful houses against the brilliance of the waters of the Mediterranean and the blue sky as it bled into the turquoise sea. Sprinkled beside the sea, her fishing fleet bobbed at her feet, amid the sounds of laughter carried away on the backs of snow-white gulls.

After Nice, they went to Sardinia where they joined with the other NATO Forces and participated in "war games". This meant practicing working together to defeat a presumed enemy. Live fire, evasive maneuvers, planes and helicopters were all brought into play.

Sardinia is a large Italian island in the Mediterranean Sea. It has large expanses of coastline, sandy beaches and a mountainous interior crossed with hiking trails. The island has an ancient geo-formation and, unlike Sicily and mainland Italy, it is not earthquake-prone.

The weather was as nasty as it gets – sheets of wind-driven rain routinely soaked anyone foolish enough to go topside. When he wasn't working, or on duty, he stayed below decks, reading "shit kickers" as the cowboy western books were called. He had little-to-no interest in the numerous skin books, or books about deviant sex.

It still amazed him, the number of men aboard who talked incessantly about sex. In the back of his mind, he kept hearing his Mother's voice telling him about waiting until he was married, how it was a "great and wonderful gift to share between a husband and his wife".

In Cal's dreams, he'd often see a beautiful young woman. It wasn't a one-time thing, but it repeated itself in different variations, occurring from time to time over a period of years. In the dream, he knew beyond any doubt that she loved him and as such, he didn't desire any other. As he slept, they would be sight-seeing, laughing, and talking as they held hands or embraced - then the dream would end.

Cal knew that somewhere out there, God had someone special, just for him – he felt that she was his reward for his staying true to Him, never blaming Him for all the hardships and beatings, that he had endured. All he had to do was to remain patient and steadfast, and he would eventually meet her.

Each time they went ashore, his eyes would unconsciously search for that face, that special look, and perfect grace - the one that he knew so well and the voice tinged with that irresistible laugh. He knew that, once he saw her, he'd know her. After all, in actuality, he'd known her before they had been created. But he didn't see her anywhere or hear her laughter ... *not yet.* However, he had the feeling that it would be soon ... *very soon.*

He noted that the women of Italy were beautiful when they were young. Like their cities when they were new, they radiated strength and virility, but as they aged, cracks showed, and they fell into disrepair, with gravity taking its toll. The cities, so old, so proud, continue to hearken back to their age of greatness, now only a hollow cry above the din of poverty and indifference that languish at her feet.

Cal, Jack, Sean, Les, and Provost walked through the twisted streets, so old you could almost hear the wheels of chariots as they raced by. You couldn't see very far ahead in any direction, as the streets and alleys curved back and forth like a withering snake on a hot rock. Their streets, were paved with cobblestone and cement, separating homes that looked like they might fall at any moment.

They'd been walking and wandering for some time, hooting and hollering until they smelled food cooking somewhere up ahead.

They thought that by getting off the beaten path, they would find better prices, fresher food, and more receptive women.

Feeling hungry, they followed their noses and headed straight for the intoxicating aroma, like a hound after a coon.

After a couple of turns, they located a small restaurant like bar, built under one of the buildings. If they had not seen the activity coming and going from it, they would not have known it was there.

They piled down the old stone stairs and opened the heavy wooden door, ducking under the header, as they entered.

The floor of the establishment was yet another step-down, a fact that they didn't realize until they suddenly felt themselves falling forward into the bleakness of the room.

Some of the assorted tables were taken, and some men and women sat at the end of the bar clutching their glasses of wine as they peered at them through an alcohol haze.

A large woman came toward them speaking Italian as if they understood her. Cal thought she wanted to know what they were going to eat, so he sounded out the words "steak, " and she nodded approvingly. He happened to add, "is it fresh?" To which she added with great excitement, "bow-wow, this morning", as she animated a dog running around. They all looked at each other for a moment in stark disbelief. But their hunger for meat of any kind proved to be a stronger motivation than any hang ups they might have about the probability of it actually being a dog.

When it arrived at their table, the pieces of meat were small, dark and strong, like a pepper steak and a little tough as they chewed their way through the first few mouthfuls.

As they drank their lukewarm beer, they kidded each other about the side effects of having eaten a dog, as they were pretty sure that was what it was.

One of the guys joked that he had the strongest urge to lift his leg and scratch behind his ear, to which Cal commented, "if I see you lifting your leg, I'm afraid of what you're really going to do next". There was great merriment over that one and other more aberrant doggy behavior, that might befall them before the side effects of having eaten dog meat had worn off.

Somehow they all found their way out of the back street maze and back to the market area of Valencia, where he bought a fine lace shawl for his Mom and some jewelry for his sisters.

Along the journey from port to port, their ship pulled into Palermo, Sicily. To think that they were now tied up in the harbor, of a city where the Mafia got its start and was still thriving, gave life to the images of thugs hiding around every street corner and dead bodies bobbing just below the harbor's surface. Never had he seen a dirtier, poorer, more rat infested place. It was the first time, and only time, that the order was passed, to shut off the water purifiers and to pump as little water as possible through the ships condensers.

Once above decks, Cal could see why the restrictions had been ordered, they were literally sitting in a sea of raw sewage. It was also the only time they were forced to use huge metal rat guards on all the hawsers[49]. Armed Marine guards stood at the ready with submachine guns, with orders to shot any rat or man should they attempt to come aboard by way of the hawsers. The last thing they needed was for plague to break out aboard the ship.

Given what he'd seen and the port's reputation, Cal was not interested in going ashore to do any sightseeing. He still remembers feeling elated to see this port fading into the hazy distance from his vantage point, high above the churning sea, as he stood at the ship's stern[50].

The time that they spent at sea was always longer than their time ashore, and it was always Cinderella Liberty. With Cinderella Liberty, they had to be back before midnight, or risk being Away Without Leave, (AWOL). If you were AWOL, the OD or Master at Arms would write you up and then you'd appear before the "Old Man" (Captain). He would hear your side of it and then pronounce a sentence on you – usually, it would cost you a stripe, which meant lower pay and so on. Definitely not something Cal wanted to have happen, so he was always reminding the other guys who didn't seem to give a rip about being late or not making it back at all, what it would cost them. Irrespective, he got them back before the last boat shoved off for their ship. Every time they went out, he was fearful that, for whatever reason, he and the others would not make it back in time and they would all be in deep shit. So he was always vigilant as to where they were relevant to the ship and the time.

Things fell pretty much into a routine between ports of call and drills. It was about this time that he started noticing something that no one seemed to want to talk about. It was all very hush, hush, like

---

[49] Huge ropes that tied the ship to the pier.
[50] Rear of ship.

some kind of unspoken rule ... "what goes on overseas, stays overseas", so it was whispered.

Within minutes after docking or anchoring out, the first thing that would occur would be that some official looking person from the city would board the ship and be escorted to Officer's Country, which was one deck above theirs. Usually, it was a dignified looking man or two who seemed to be "someone of importance" and they were always accompanied by one or two young beautiful women. At first, he had thought nothing of it, probably their wives he reasoned. But when it occurred at nearly every port, he started to pay closer attention. They usually stayed an hour or two, then they'd leave with a couple of the higher ranking officers seeing them off the ship to their boat or on to the pier where much smiling and hand shaking went on. Within hours another boat, or car, would pull up and, as many as a half dozen to a dozen young and very attractive girls, stylishly dressed in somewhat skimpy dresses, would climb the gangway. Usually, their boarding was timed while the enlisted men were getting their showers and preparing to leave on liberty. Whoever was last out of the engineering spaces, was usually the one that got an eye full. You could tell that it was forbidden fruit, the way the OD would scowl at them for staring. Even so, they stole their looks and what they saw was profound. These ladies were hurriedly escorted up into Officer's Country and would not be seen until the next day, or they'd come out after dark and go ashore with some of the Officers. It didn't take much imagination to figure out what was going on.

Many of the guys wished that they were officers, but without a college education, they didn't stand a chance of ever becoming one. Besides, there were very few officers that were worth a damn - most were arrogant, self-righteous, spoiled brats that wouldn't give an enlisted man the sweat off their b&#@*, if he was dying of thirst. They seemed to delight in making their lives miserable, so he avoided them as much as possible. But somehow seeing this, and knowing that they also got better food than they, since they had their own cook, medical personnel, private, air-conditioned quarters, and a private mess hall, he had to seriously question the fairness of their "benefits". Especially since they were the ones that sweat all day and night, ate food that would make a dog barf and had to live out of a locker the size of some kid's toy box. If that wasn't bad enough, they labored all day, stood watches most of the night, got off the ship last – that was just for starters. So with the perfume of those fabulous girls floating around the ship, they'd pull out their cards or turn their books to a new chapter and try to concentrate on the things of their world, ignoring the laughter and other sounds from above decks.

Occasionally they'd get fresh supplies aboard from a supply ship, or dropped from a Fat Cow[51]. Usually, a few days out, the fresh eggs were gone and replaced by powdered eggs and every other type of food that could be turned into powder.

He remembered one time they were sitting down to eat macaroni with chicken instead of beef. As he dug around in it he noticed something that looked like rice, only they were pointed at each end and were not quite as white. He immediately recognized the intruders as being maggots. Feeling that this was something that the corpsman should know about, he immediately carried his tray from the galley to sickbay. Instead of indignation, the corpsman displayed a total indifference about the tainted food, saying, "don't worry, it's been cooked at over 212-degrees, there aren't any living bacteria in it that will

---

[51] Boeing CH-47 Chinook twin rotor helicopter - heavy-lift helicopter developed by American rotorcraft company Vertol and manufactured by Boeing Vertol

hurt you and there full of protein. He couldn't believe it, he was actually condoning the fact that they were eating what looked like maggots along with some kind of larva. He made a personal vow to himself that when he could get to a market, he'd buy some canned goods and bring them aboard, so when they served crap like this, he could get something else from his stash.

There was another time he recalled when the food was less than palatable. They'd been at General Quarters most of the night and part of the morning when the exercise was finally called off. It had been brutally cold and the warmth of the mess deck was more than just a little welcoming after standing in lines that wound around the upper decks of the ship. This was not usually the case, however, with several hundred Army and Marines on board, it made getting to eat right away much more difficult.

The ship had been rolling and tossing most of the night and all morning. The seas were high and running, so a large number of "their guests" were seasick. Finally, after waiting over an hour, he'd made it through the galley and headed for an open spot at one of the tables. They all looked like picnic tables, only these were made of steel and welded to the deck so they wouldn't move in heavy seas. They ran end to end in rows crosswise of the ship, separated by a steel bulkhead which had large ovals cut in it like windows only without glass, giving it the appearance of being one space. The area was full and seating sparse.

They'd been served a concoction that appeared to be stew. It was hot, and he started poking at the contents, trying to figure out what each item was before he ate it. It didn't help that the ship was taking huge rolls and they were all forced to hold on to their trays with one hand, even tilting it at times to keep the contents from running up and over the compartmentalized tray and onto the table or deck.

He could see that there was already ample evidence of other people's misfortunes here and there on the tables and deck.

The potatoes and carrots were easy, but the meat he had trouble identifying. He'd calculated that it was either beef or chicken or both. As he ate and poked, he found a curious item that he turned over, then rammed it with his fork. It was sort of grisly. Once he held it up, he recognized it for what it really was. It had a chunk of meat at one end, was long and hollow all the way through. The meaty end, had a puckered look to it with large pores. From his years of working on the farm and killing and dressing everything from hogs to chickens, he knew that it was the bunghole of a chicken, with a part of its gut still connected.

He called the attention of what he'd found to the guys who were sitting around him – a couple of sailors and six Marines. First, he asked them if they knew what kind of meat they were eating, most didn't, but concluded that it tasted okay. So he proceeded to tell them and from what part they were eating. He hadn't even gotten to the best part of his story when all the Marines within ear shot got up, most with the strangest color of green on their faces he'd ever seen. The two sailors hardly batted an eye, as one said, "I guess you separated the men from the boys," and they all started laughing. Just then the ship took another roll, and all the unmanned trays went crashing to the floor, causing a huge din and a mess beyond belief.

"Now", said another sailor, "this is why they call it a mess hall". Again, they all laughed as they continued to eat. The statement was further borne out by the sounds of dishes and utensils crashing around the galley. He was sure glad that it was not his duty to clean up the "mess" later.

Just before Christmas, they pulled into Athens, the capital of Greece. It was also, at the heart of

Ancient Greece, a powerful civilization, and empire. The city is still dominated by 5th-century BC landmarks, including the Acropolis, a hilltop citadel topped with ancient buildings like the colonnaded Parthenon temple. It is surrounded by mountains, Ymmytos, Pendeli, and Parnitha, northwards and eastwards, and the Saronic Gulf southwards and westwards. The sun shines over Athens all year round. The climate is one of the best in Europe, with mild winters and very hot summers.

A short walk around reveals old, well preserved mansions, others worn down by time, luxurious department stores and small intimate shops, fancy restaurants and traditional taverns in this historic city.

They were warned that there were Greeks who didn't like Americans. That they should be watchful not to be drawn into any confrontations and, in particular, not to walk under any second story windows, as they had the bad habit of throwing the contents of their pee pots and bedpans out the windows onto unsuspecting sailors. Cal thought that this was a disgusting way to treat foreign visitors. He couldn't imagine being so discourteous to visitors to the US.

The Master at Arms and the Warrant Officer also warned them about a drink called Ouzo. They said that it was lethal in its ability to render the user totally wasted faster than any other drink known to man. It also had another undesirable side effect that gave its consumer the false impression that he or she was invincible, as they could not feel pain. Of course, this warning fell on the deaf ears of some sailors who thought they were above the effects of such a drink – so it was like waving a red flag in front of a bull and they couldn't wait to try some.

On Shore Patrol duty, they were warned not to take any unnecessary chances with any men who were suspected of drinking Ouzo. They were told to call for help as it might take several men to subdue the drinker, and usually not before he had severely hurt himself and others.

Cal encountered this scene once while on Shore Patrol. He'd first heard glass breaking, followed by shouting, somewhere close by. They always traveled in pairs and were usually in sight of other pairs of Shore Patrol, particularly in "high-risk areas".

Night had fallen and the only light falling on the sidewalks was from bars and other night-club-type places. As they rounded the corner, they saw two sailors – both covered with blood. One appeared to be trying to contain the other – not fight him. He immediately blew his whistle to summon the help of all Shore Patrol within hearing range.

As they drew closer, Cal saw the broken store window; its glass lying on both the inside and outside the window. The fracture ran like a spider's web from corner to corner. He knew that, due to the glass's thickness, it had to have taken a lot of force to break it. If it had not been done with a brick or some tool, that part of the body which made contact had to have been injured. The two men were now out in the street with one man trying to get his buddy to calm down. The other was still swinging even though he had a broken arm that blood flew off of each time he attempted to hit his friend. He was also bleeding from cuts on his face and from his broken nose.

It sickened Cal to see what this man had done to himself and how it would affect his future. Upon waking up in the brig, he would stand court martial, be demoted to a seaman and given extra duty with no liberty for the foreseeable future and maybe even Dishonorably Discharged.

In the end, it had taken six of them to bring the guy down and cuff him, and not before having used their batons extensively on his legs – to no apparent effect. After the man was taken back to his ship, all of them had a whole new respect for Ouzo and what it could do to someone who was prone to drink and fight. That is not to say, that all people who drink Ouzo are prone to get into fights – many do drink it recreationally with no adverse effects. But, as with anything containing alcohol, which is consumed by someone who gets drunk and then inevitably wants to fight, they should never consume Ouzo. This had been the case with this young man, whose friend had said he was a heavy drinker who most always ended up in a fight. Being his buddy, he had always tried to save him from himself, even reminding him not to drink Ouzo. But he had been hell bent on giving it a go, saying that he could handle it.

There had been another time when Cal was in Palermo, Sicily. They had docked near the Banchina Crispi Harbor highway. The area was like most commercial harbor towns, filled with honking trucks, bikes zipping in and out, and people yelling directions as cargo was being unloaded, and brought to and from the freighters. He'd pulled Shore Patrol and was taken by the SP officer to their watch area. It was one of the streets leading off Via Francesco Crispi. During the day, their beat area was quiet, until the evening when the people were rushing home from a day's work.

For the most part, the streets were void of any architectural facades, only barren pale yellow walls with the occasional window – all on the second story and above. There was only one bar on their whole patrol, and it seemed to be very quiet – no fights. He reasoned that it was a home town bar and most likely only frequented by the locals – too far back from the harbor to interest any sailors or soldiers. As they made the next turn on the block, they spotted a man lying on his back, half on the sidewalk and half in the gutter. There was a knife sticking out of his chest. It must have happened recently as they had passed by this location over an hour ago. They stopped only long enough to see that he was dead and that there was no one in sight – only silence met their inquiring stares and hearing. They had been instructed not to get involved with any civilian matters, so moved on. He could only imagine what had happened. Given the situation, they both agreed that it probably was a "hit". Whatever had happened, the body and any traces of blood were gone by their next turn around the block, no doubt relegated to the deep, as it was not uncommon to see a body occasionally floating out to sea.

Life, Cal learned in various old world countries was not as valued as it was in the states. He was glad that he had been born in the US.

Not all ports of call were indifferent and devoid of visual stimulation and they were again in another port. The day, like most, was gray and cold. Cal chose to take advantage of a tour to see a greater part of the city, and hear about its history, instead of aimlessly walking around on his own.

There was the famous Acropolis, the Amphitheater, and the Seven Muses. The architecture was stunning and, of course, as he viewed the huge stones and fine carvings, he had to wonder how many people had died to accomplish this. As with most things of this stature, thousands of people were pressed into near slavery if not outright slavery by some all-powerful king or ruling despot to build these great wonders of the world.

Cal sat for a time on the stone seating in the amphitheater and, for an instance, he could hear the sound of clapping and the cheers of those who had witnessed a stoic moment on stage. As he looked, he noted a few people milled about the stage. He could hear every word, even the sound of their footsteps, from his vantage point approximately fifty yards away. It's said that the acoustics are perfect and, because of this, it had become the model for all great theaters around the world.

He walked below the Seven Muses; one was gone, leaving only six. The seventh had been taken somewhere for repair, so it was said, or perhaps, she was just destroyed by some conquering army. He could not recall the details from that long ago. They stood there, their slender arms and heads bearing the weight of the structure's roof. Their bodies perfect in every way as depicted in the artist's rendering in marble, wearing only a wind-blown gown of sheerest material.

The Greeks of old were very much involved with their Gods. They had one for just about anything that happened. Diana was their Goddess of love, Neptune their god of the deep, Hercules the God which supports the earth and more that captured their imaginations. All of whom, it was said, lived on Mount Olympus. It was located a short distance away and, at this time of the year, obscured by dense cloud cover and torrential rain. They stayed in Greece for only a few days before leaving, never to return.

Next, they pulled into Florence, Italy. They docked at the Imbarco Sardinia Ferries per Golfo Aranci deep water piers and Cal signed up for a day Tour that would take in every interesting place there was to see.

He was glad he took the tour as he got to see the best of Florence; the priceless art, the splendid buildings, the iconic Leaning Tower of Pisa and so much more. Truly, it is one of his best memories of his time in the Navy.

First, they'd visited the Piazza Della Signoria, the home of Michelangelo's David. Cal's breath was taken away, as he admiringly gazed at the closest thing to a human being in the form of a statue – so life like that it seemed to defy its own reality. Michelangelo was not even 30, when he finished this master piece after 3-years. He was so successful in his renderings, that the Pope immediately called him to Rome where he eventually painted the Sistine Chapel. He and Leonardo da Vinci stood shoulders above all of the other famous artists of their day.

The next stop was the Fine Arts Academy in the city. A place within it was put aside for learning about art. It was designed to show students examples of the masterworks from the past so that they could practice and study art. And what a place it was. It contained statues depicting examples of design perfection. In particular, the choices were limited to the Renaissance, the period in which Florence held the undisputed record for fine art. Over the years, the collection has grown enormously, and today, the Gallery is a vast museum that exhibits many fine masterpieces.

Next, they were on to see the Leaning Tower of Pisa. Although only a third as high as the Washington Monument, it was a miracle of medieval engineering, probably the tallest bell tower in Europe. The construction of the Tower of Pisa took 200-years to build due to the onset of a series of wars. Till today, the name of the architect is a mystery. It was designed as a circular tower that would stand 185-feet high. It is constructed of white marble. The tower has eight stories, including the chamber for the bells. There is a 297-step spiral staircase inside the tower leading to the top, and Cal counted everyone. They told them that the top of the leaning tower of Pisa is about 17-feet off vertical and Cal believed it. They also told them that it was slightly curved from the various attempts by architects and engineers to keep it from falling over.

During that day, they visited the Appian Way, an accent highway that endures to this day. The main part of the Appian Way was started and finished in 312-BC. The road began as a leveled dirt road carved out of the ground. To this surface were applied small stones and mortar. Gravel was leveled over this, which was finally topped with tight fitting, interlocking stones which provided a flat surface. It was written that the historian Procopius observed that the stones fit together in such a manner that they appeared to have grown together. The road was cambered in the middle for water runoff and had ditches on either side which were protected by retaining walls. During this day, Cal saw so much of Florence that he wished he could stay. Truly there would be no end to its magic to crunch his thirst for more.

Another port of call was Barcelona Spain. The first thing he saw as he walked down the pier was the statue of Christopher Columbus in the Plaza Portal de la Pau.

This old city, like the others, spoke of time, and one could hear the echoes of history whispering among the cobblestone streets, which were lined with buildings that had been dragged into the 19-century kicking and screaming. From deeply carved ornamental stone edifices, hung neon lights that fizzed and hummed, whose illumination stood out in stark contrast to the history all around it.

He had, upon leaving the ship, signed up for a tour to Mt Tibidabo. This mountain overlooks Barcelona, Catalonia, Spain. At 1,680 ft., it is the tallest mountain in the Serra de Collserola. Rising sharply to the north-west, it affords spectacular views over the city and the surrounding coastline. At the top is the Temple del Sagrat Cor visi des de la Talaia del Tibidabo. It is a marvel to behold, both out and inside. Truly, a work of art, beyond belief. Standing on the summit of Mt Tibidabo, Cal looked out across the expanse and was reminded instantly of his small place in this world. As his eyes scanned the sea, and then closer, looking down to the pier, he could make out the needle size ship from which he'd come. It was truly a moment like none other he had ever experienced as the clouds rolled in, passed over and around his feet as it encircled the top of the mountain, and then disappeared. For him this was a spiritual experience – one is which he felt that God had just touched him, as He passed by.

Later, when Cal caught up with his friends, they followed the sound of music, like a snake follows the haunting sounds produced by a snake charmer's flute; they zigged and zagged until they came upon the source – a night club.

They entered the club and found a round table at one side of the room near the stage. There appeared to be some 30 to 40 round tables with fine linen table clothes and a heavily ornate bar near the entrance.

Suddenly, the curtain opened, and the stillness was broken by the sound of music and tap dancing. They all stopped talking and drinking to watch. Four of the most beautiful women they had ever seen, along with four handsome, slim men dressed in black Spanish costumes that harkened back to the days of the conquistadores, were moving their feet with the speed of light over the floor.

They had been admiring the young ladies for some time, talking and drinking as they watched, mesmerized by the sight. From time to time, there were sometimes two, three and even four couples dancing at a time. The dances ranged from the very fast hat dances with castanets and fans waving wildly in the air, to the slower more exotic dances. In all of them, the movements were pure grace and elegance, and the couples were extremely talented. Each of the male dancers was incredibly slim, their skin the color of freshly poured copper. The women, as pretty as any you would see on the cover of Cosmos. Cal noticed that they were small, none above five one or two and probably weighing no more than 100-pounds, if that. As he watched them, he felt attracted to the one which he saw as the most beautiful of all. She'd caught his eye during several of their numbers, though he thought nothing of it –

only stage presence, he remembered thinking. Shortly after their numbers ended, a waitress approached their table and, addressing him, asked if the dancers might accompany them at their table. They were all surprised and pleased, and Cal told her, "by all means, that they would be honored to visit with them".

In a moment there was a rustling sound behind the stage curtain, and suddenly they were all around the table talking with each of them. He immediately stood up, and the rest of the men followed suit. The waitresses brought over more chairs, and they all made room for them. As he turned to address the girl next to him, he saw immediately that it was the girl he had singled out on stage and the one who had been catching his eye. He moved behind her and guided the chair toward the table, seating her.

She tossed her head, sending her shimmering, jet black hair trailing about her slender shoulders. She smiled a smile that was as dazzling as she was beautiful. Her dark eyes were luminous in the low light and said volumes about things that were and could be.

After the waitress finished bringing chairs the rest of them sat down, and he asked the young woman beside him if she cared for a drink. She did and ordered it in Spanish. After each of them completed their order and the waitress had hurried off to fill them, she asked him his name.

Cal said it slowly. As she struggled to pronounce it in English, he was surprised at how it sounded with a heavy Spanish accent - very sexy, and he told her as much. They all laughed as each of his friends heard their names being said in Spanish.

Then Cal asked her for her name, and she rattled off about thirteen names. He had never heard such a long name before.

He asked her about its length and she laughingly explained that it was a combination of family names, going back several generations and, of course, he tried to say them all. It came out rather terribly.

She then put her slender finger against his chest and, placing her full lips near his ear; she whispered, "you ... can call me Francesca".

He could feel the heat from her breath against his neck as she spoke the words.

As they talked, he noticed that the other girls would stop and listen and look their way from time to time. It was as if the girl with him was someone of importance – but it would be later in the evening before he'd come to that conclusion.

Call it youth, call it inexperience or being somewhat self-absorbed at the time, but, Cal failed to pick up on the clues. To this day, he's not sure who she really was. As the evening wore on, it was obvious that she really liked him ... a lot. She asked him quietly under her breath if he would wait until after the last number and go home with her to meet her family.

Of course, Cal's head was already in the nodding mode, and before it registered what she had just asked, he'd nodded, "yes" as his voice had suddenly failed him.

*   *   *

They had been briefed on the cultural differences of various countries before going on liberty. In some of the countries, if the young woman asks you to her home, it means that she is presenting you as her betrothed and that, in time, you will become her husband. It was well known that, very often foreign girls would compromise a serviceman and the next thing he knew there would an incident involving not only the women's honor, but the country. They were told at all cost, to avoid any "political incidences".

*   *   *

After nodding his head "yes", she squeezed his hand, and gave him a gentle kiss near his ear and whispered something that sounded very sexy. She slowly rose, allowing him to take in the full view of her low cut dress and, as she left, she allowed one finger to trail through his hair and down around his neck leaving behind a trail of fire.

He swung his head around to watch her departing figure and with every step and sway of her hips, the promise of greater things to come echoed within his senses.

As he turned back toward the table, he grabbed for his drink, hoping to find a quick answer to the questions chasing each other through his head and that he knew were soon to come from the guys around him. He heard them, almost in unison, say, "Man, she's hot for you, what did she say"?

Clearing his throat, as his nerves were still shaking, "Well she said a lot, most of it, he admitted, he didn't understand".

"Shit", one of the guys spit out, "I F#&@^* well know what she said, he all but shouted. "She wants your sorry F&$#*@ ass so bad that it's about to kill me."

To that, the whole table cracked up, and he felt embarrassed at the man's brazen language in a place that looked to be one of the town's most prestigious nightclubs.

He nodded to the other guys to get him under control. But they were all looking at him for an answer to his question, their mouths open and panting like dogs after chasing a rabbit.

"Well, she wants me to go home with her ..." before Cal could finish, he heard one of them say, "Jesus, you aren't already out there warming the car up?"

Of course, they had no car to warm up, but he caught the gist of what he was saying. They felt he should be making every effort to go with her but, he intoned, you are all forgetting one little, but very important thing. "One", it's now after 2200 hours and we are all here on Cinderella Liberty. *There is no way in God's creation, he was going to let some girl take him back into the middle of ya, ya land to meet her parents and go beddy bye and expect to be back before 1200 hours.* "Two", like the old man says, you go meet the parents and you better be ready to marry that girl. Who knows, maybe she's looking for citizenship; a lot of them marry a serviceman for just that reason.

All of them tried to shred his reasoning but, in the end, they all knew he was right. Even so, a couple of them, without cooler heads to prevail, would have gone AWOL.

The sound of music crashed through his senses, and he abruptly turned to see them all out on stage dancing. This time, the girls were doing a number that sent their dresses far over their heads, showing long slender legs and left no mystery as to where they were attached, and the brevity of their underwear left no illusion that they were all female. Francesca, without a doubt, was the leader and what she did, the others did. As they twirled and tapped their feet, she spun ever closer and closer to him, until her hands touched his hair in one of her spins.

Cal didn't know how many numbers they would be doing, but he knew he'd better get out of there before she finished her dancing or he'd be dead meat. He had a feeling she was not one to trifle with and who knows how many male friends she had who were fully capable of hauling his sorry butt up some mountain to never be seen again.

As they finished the number and darted behind the curtain to change for the next, he told the guys that he was leaving with or without them – now! And with that, he left enough money on the table to satisfy his bill.

Grudgingly they all rose, muttering under their breaths as he headed for the door as if a five alarm fire had just sounded.

Once outside, Cal took a deep breath and started jogging toward the piers as fast as his two legs could carry him. There was no way that he wanted some kind of scene in the middle of the street back in the hinter lands of this city. He could just image who they would believe, some teary eyed native girl or a sailor - one of their own or a foreigner. His step quickened even further as several scenarios played out - none of them good. He didn't let up until he was safe aboard the ship and, even then, he wondered how far the fingers of their government could reach. Hopefully, there was no way she could get him.

The next day came and passed. The following morning the guys who had been with him on liberty the night before said, "God, damn, that girl of yours is pissed off at you. She was looking for you after you left and she had a knife. She has rallied all the other girls and her male friends, and they are going to cut you up into little pieces if they ever see you".

As their story unraveled, it seemed that he had dishonored her, caused her great shame in front of her friends and so on and so forth. He breathed a great sigh of relief that he was safe aboard the ship. There was no way, that he was going to get off until they hit another port, and he didn't.

Chapter 10.0

The days came and went and finally after six months had passed, their time in the Med was coming to a close, their last port of call would be Rota, Spain.

*　　　　*　　　　*

The Naval Station Rota, Spain, the "Gateway to the Mediterranean", is strategically located near the Straits of Gibraltar near the Southern Spanish city of Cadiz. NavSta Rota is the largest American military community in Spain and houses more than 3,000 U.S. Navy Sailors, Marines, and their families. There are also a small US Army and US Air Force contingents on the base.

The base provides support for U.S. and NATO ships; supports the safe and efficient movement of U.S. Navy and U.S. Air Force flights and passengers; and provides cargo, fuel, and ammunition to units in the region. The Naval Station is the only base in the Mediterranean capable of supporting Amphibious Readiness Groups with secure, pier side maintenance and back load facilities. Rota supports Amphibious Readiness Group (ARG) turnovers and hosts Sailors and Marines from visiting afloat units.[52]

---

[52] https://www.thebalance.com/installation-overview-naval-station-rota-spain-3354741

*　　　　*　　　　*

Spring had arrived, with its warm, sunny days and he could feel the excitement on board; everyone was anxious to be on their way. Married men with families, single men who had sweethearts waiting for them back home, were beside themselves with the need for them. Many of them had read their letters over and over until they were nothing but limp pieces of ink stained paper.

We would pull into port one last time to load stores and mail. Once there, the word was passed that they would be forming teams of boxers and wrestlers to compete from the Navy, Army, Air Force, and Marines, pulling men from all ships and the base.

He had no desire to box or to play any other games, so opted to stay aboard and watch a ship's flick. They were free and usually fairly recently released - they took his mind off home. Since Cal had no wife or girlfriend, he couldn't feel what the other guys were feeling or fully understand why they read their letters over and over and looked for hours at their loved one's pictures.

Over the course of his hitch, Cal would see men pitch their wedding rings overboard, and see grown men, as tough as any he'd ever known, completely breakdown. For one man, it was more than he could bear and he had hung himself because of a "Dear John" letter.

When they left Rota, the trip back was not filled with endless drills as it had been on the way out. The old man wanted to get the ship back as soon as he could. The pilot had brought them out of the harbor and had taken his leave, now the helm was in the Old Man's hands, and he wanted to get home. They heard his voice come over the Com as he said, "This is the Captain, and we are going home, men". Then they heard him say to the Helmsman, "Go to flank". Cal was on watch in Main Control and knew that they usually cruised at 1/2 to 2/3s, never at flank speed, which was only for emergency navigational situations. It certainly wasn't used in the "Pond", as they called the Mediterranean.

The remote speed control on the control board swung to FLANK, accompanied by the sound of a bell announcing that a change in the controls had been ordered from the Bridge. Instantly, they spun the twin control wheels to the wide open position, allowing the high-pressure steam to pour unabated into the turbines. Immediately, they could hear them speeding up. Slowly the deep down humming sound in the Reduction Gears started up the pitch scale to successively higher pitches. Soon the deck under their feet was vibrating from the tens of thousands of pounds of torque.

They doubled their watches on the shaft bearings and in the Shaft Alleys until they were sure that the bearings could take the higher RPMs. Also the turbine and main thrust bearings were being closely monitored for an increase in temperature and a close watch on the Delaval Oil Purifiers for any signs of metal chips on the magnets. If any were found, it would mean that a main bearing was going or was about to go causing a misalignment of the turbine shaft and the main shaft would have to be immediately stopped and locked until a new bearing could be put in. If it weren't, it would ruin the reduction gears.

This situation did happen later on another cruise, causing around the clock hard work to replace the bearing, while they continued with only one "live shaft" or on one *"screw"* as they called a propeller in the Navy.

He could hear cheering throughout the ship, when the word had been passed that they had just cleared the Straits. It would be a week and a half before they'd see land again. He knew that they could do this standing on their heads. It had been over 6-months since they'd been home with their families. Some had babies born, others had lost loved ones, and still, others had lost their entire families through divorce. Only an immediate death in the family, with Red Cross notification, would allow you get off the ship during a cruise; otherwise, you were stuck as sure as if you had been in jail.

To Cal, this had all been an adventure, but now he was tired of seeing just open seas day after day and week after week. He'd hoped to see more of the world than he had. He longed to set foot on land and be free to explore the highways, free to go where he wanted when he wanted and most of all, he wanted to have a hamburger, not just any hamburger, but a special one. There was this place just outside of the base within walking distance of the ship, which served up the biggest, juiciest burgers he'd ever had, and he could taste it already.

Guys with super sensitive radios would sit out on the wing-walls in the evening and dial through the stations trying to find anything that sounded like it came from the US. For a time they could only get Radio Free America and some British stations. They carried some music and a lot of news. He spent most of his time reading. He liked Westerns like Louis L'Amour and, more recently, had discovered Ian Fleming's; James Bond - Double-O-Seven books. Occasionally, he wrote his mother a letter but, at the moment, they were in a sort of blackout zone – no radio stations and no mail.

Suddenly, one morning they started hearing stations from all up and down the east coast, and they knew they must be only a couple of days out. It was great hearing what was going on in the states; the newest songs, who was on top in sports – essentially, the heartbeat of home. Cal could feel the mood on board immediately soar.

Another clue that they were not far out, were the number of dolphins that toured alongside the ship. He loved to watch their acrobatics as they leaped and dove in unison on both sides of the ship. He spent hours watching their antics from his favorite vantage point on the far end of Starboard Wing Wall. He often sought this location out when writing letters or thinking things out.

They stopped off at Roosy Roads (Roosevelt Roads), Puerto Rico and off loaded ammo at the base, then headed for Little Creek. They arrived the next day and soon, the pilot was on board, to bring them in.

As soon as they tied up and secured from being underway, Cal was released from his underway duty station and was at liberty to assume his watch duties or go ashore if he was off duty.

As was his custom and, weather permitting, he'd usually come up from Engineering and out onto the deck, where he'd look around – his eyes adjusting to the light. As he did, the first thing that struck him was the smell of perfume. He had forgotten that it had been months since he'd smelled female cosmetics and the odor abruptly caught his attention.

The second thing that he noticed was the shouting. He looked down over the side to see what was causing all the noise and saw that the pier was full from one end to the other with throngs of people. Various people were shouting to a loved one on board, trying to get their attention and find out if they had liberty or not.

Cal had never before witnessed a home coming welcome, so was surprised when he saw how many people had turned out. The word had gone out long before they'd "made land" that the fleet was coming in. Some had children with them, and others were alone. All of them were waiting for a glimpse of their loved one. He noticed that here and there were some very attractive young women and wondered who the lucky guys were.

Then something completely unexpected happened. From deep down, a sadness suddenly welled up out of nowhere. It was so profound, that tears started running down Cal's face - he wished more than anything, that there was someone there for him. He felt enormously lonely. It was the way it had been his whole life – this feeling of being alone – bone marrow loneliness that extended through the core of his very being.

Even though Cal liked people and got along with everyone, he never had what he'd call a really close friend - even now. He considered a close friend, one with whom he could share his deepest secrets without fear of retribution. It was like the men he knew spoke different languages. Everyone talked woman, sports and cars. The first and second, he knew nothing about, the third - quite a bit. He also knew a lot about hunting, trapping, fishing and survival stuff. But no one he'd met yet had even an inkling about any of these things.

Chapter 11.0

As he went into his quarters to change, the word was passed that civilians were coming aboard. That meant that they couldn't run around naked from the shower to their quarters. Those who brought family aboard had to keep them out of the men's bunking area. Often some would end up in the mess hall, which for M-Division, lay between their quarters and showers, making it pretty dicey if they happened to be caught in the showers without anything but their towels. Also, if they were in the mess hall, they could see right into their quarters, which meant that they often got an eyeful when the they were dressing. Some of the guys didn't care and were of the mind that the civilians were on their turf; it was up to them to beware.

The local town was Norfolk. It is a sailor's town. However, not everyone enjoyed having the sailors as neighbors and often one could see signs along the urban areas that read, "Dogs and Sailors Keep off the Grass".

Active duty servicemen and retirees had been settling in Norfolk and the surrounding areas for years - one serviceman knows another and how they think, so they aren't going to let a serviceman, especially a sailor get within a mile of their wife or daughter(s). If you want to date a Norfolk girl, you had better be anything but a serviceman. All military men were painted with a wide brush, so the bad actions of a few had poisoned the water for the rest. Even so, he held his head high and kept his eyes open for any opportunity to meet and date a good looking young woman, that he might come across in his travels.

After trips to the park and roaming the streets and an occasional look around at the various bars, it was obvious that he was not going to find any acceptable female companionship anywhere in town. He gave his situation considerable thought and turning the situation around, he asked himself, "Who would socialize with a military man?"

The answer was, "Out of town college girls, tourists, people who lived over 50 or more miles from the base – in fact, the further the better". Of that group, the tourists sounded as if they would be the most likely to date a military man, in fact even being a military man would be a plus. Never underestimate the pull of the uniform and the mystique that it embodies.

"Now, where do the tourists hang out?" he asked himself.

He had it – the beach and or amusement parks. It was always the first place that women liked to go. So after telling Larry and Jack his plan, they thought that it was pure genesis and they all headed for the Ocean View Amusement Park, just down the road from the base.

Ocean View had a large wooden roller coaster, a small zoo and lots of kid's rides, plenty of places to eat and miles of beach.

They picked their lookout spot well up the beach where they could scan for likely candidates. Of course, a lot of speculation ensued, but not much action. All the girls that walked by seemed to be looking the other way or would be in large groups. The girls knew the sailors were dying to meet them, but didn't want to make it obvious, and there was no way that they would approach any of them if they hung out like a pack of dogs ready to attack. So he suggested they split up, he would work the concession stands and they should work the shoreline and rides.

He'd watched the concession stands and in particular, those selling drinks and food that had long lines. Perfect he reasoned, as that would give him time to strike up a conversation and talk at some length.

Even though he was still somewhat shy, his urge to meet a good-looking girl was stronger. He watched from the cover of one of the parrot cages until a lone, good-looking girl got into line, and then he walked up behind her. He waited for a few minutes, acting disinterested, until she knew he was there, and then, working up his courage, he said, "the water looks great today, doesn't it"? Or, he'd say, "long line, been here long"? Either way, depending on the tone of her voice and how she answered, he'd know whether to pursue her or to just drift off to another line and try his luck there.

His first time out, he scored, and in no time she was carrying on a dialog with him as if he was some long lost friend. He fed into it, gently probing and holding back while she filled in all the missing information. In no time he learned that she was down here from Vermont with a friend on vacation. She was single, no boyfriend and bored. He knew instantly that she was looking for a good time. He told her about himself; that he was active duty Navy and was based here. Not being from there, she thought that was pretty cool as he could come here any time he wanted and enjoy the scenery and rides.

For some reason, women who did not live at ground zero near a military base liked being with a serviceman, maybe it's the idea of being with a man who is in top physical shape, a warrior type person, maybe it was the carefree life style they seemed to project or maybe it was just the pull of the uniform – some woman just can't resist it. Whatever it was, Cal wasn't going to tell them any different.

They agreed he'd pick her up at 8 pm and they'd go bowling and then out to eat. She gave him her phone number, a big smile and waved as she disappeared into one of the houses along the shore. He was elated – he'd scored.

Cal quickly found his shipmates, one of them had scored, and the other hadn't. Larry wanted to double up with him, but he wouldn't hear of it. He operated better alone. Besides, he didn't want him messing up his opportunity with his bad language and leering looks. He'd seen it before. He was like "OFF" Deepwoods mosquito repellent ... devastating.

Cal went back to the ship and freshened up with a clean pair of dress whites and called a cab. There was no way he was going to be taking her on a date on a bus from here to there and back again. Even so, he wished he had his own car.

The cab stopped at the address Cal had given, and asked him to wait. The driver displayed a frustrated face, as he nodded. He hurried up the brick steps and knocked on the weathered door. It opened almost immediately by another girl who invited him in and motioned for him to sit down on the couch. He only had to wait a few minutes before she came into the room. She had replaced her swimsuit with a pair of white slacks and a brief yellow blouse. Her toenails gleamed with red polish as they peeked out the front of her white sandals. Her hair was up and curly. She looked quite cute and somewhat preppy. He knew from the way she talked that she was a college girl without her ever having to say so. He also knew she came from money and it made him nervous, as he had neither. He began to wonder what he was doing taking such a woman out – he was doomed to failure he thought. Even so, he was polite and opened the door for her. As they exited the house, she saw the cab sitting there and seemed to hesitate for a moment, then went on. He explained that he didn't have a car yet and that they'd have to depend on a cab to get around. She nodded noncommittally and got in as he held the door. Then he came around on the other side and also got in. The cabby, somewhat perturbed, asked, "Where to buddy"?

"Ocean View Bowling Alley," he replied with as much authority as he could muster. He didn't know why he always picked bowling alleys to take a date, it must have been because he felt at home there and could bowl reasonably well. He strained to make conversation with Judy, feeling that she had cooled down quite a bit since they first met. Of course, that was before she found out that he didn't own a car. He knew without a doubt that not having a car was queering the whole date and he felt like a back-woods jerk. He was relieved when they finally pulled up to the bowling alley and he'd paid the driver, plus a tip.

Before he could ask if he would swing by in a couple of hours and pick them up, he was gone in a cloud of exhaust fumes.

He turned and caught her hand, and they walked into the bowling alley. For an early evening, it was relatively busy. Even though this was a Navy town, he was the only one wearing whites. He made another mental note to buy some civvies[53], wearing a uniform was not going to make it in a military town. He led the way to the counter where they got shoes, and he paid for a couple of games. He found an alley ball right away that he felt comfortable with and she made mention that she had one at home that was custom made. Something told him right then that she knew her way around a bowling alley and that he'd better be on his game.

He motioned for her to go first and admired her backsides and legs as she took two steps and laid the ball down soundlessly. It hissed down the alley and

[53] Civilian clothes

tore the first eight pins off the floor like a cannon ball being launched from a battlewagon. She mumbled something about being rusty since playing in the leagues. Something in his stomach moved south and he grabbed another swig of his Coke, putting it down just in time to see the 9 and ten-pins fly into the air. She had made her spare, and now it was his turn to show her how it was done – he hoped.

He picked the ball up and approached the line, stopped and concentrated, forcing himself to relax. He was not sure which spot to use, the second from the center or the third. He was a spot bowler, and when he found his spot, he could usually deliver a pretty consistent ball. He decided on the 2nd to the right from dead center. He felt the ball fall the length of his arm, feeling it's weight trailing backward as he moved forward, one step, two steps and then he extended. The ball thankfully connected with the floor nearly as quietly as hers. He watched as it tore down the alley, veering to the right then slowly coming back toward the strike zone and connecting. The pins all headed for the sky, and his heart jumped with joy. He had done it, pulled off a strike in the first frame. For one brief second, he was hot - he was the man.

He turned to catch her eye, she was putting their scores down, and as she finished, she smiled slightly and said, "nice job".

He had the feeling that he wouldn't hear that complement again the rest of the night. Again he watched as she picked the ball up, allowing the blower to dry her perfectly formed fingers tipped with perfectly manicured nails. "Yeah, she was definitely high maintenance," Cal thought as her perfume washed over him. He slid over slightly in his seat, so he was sitting just behind her. He knew that this was all he was going to get this or any other night with her. He watched as she moved up to the line, and lined her feet up perfectly. As if in slow motion, she started to move, the ball started its downward arc as she moved forward. The lights over the pin-setting machine illumined her white pants in a psychedelic way as they stretched to contain her muscular thighs and firmly outlined her long legs where they joined her body. There was no doubt that she was one sexy, thoroughbred through and through. He knew that no poor farm boy with a cab was going to get to first base with her – not in a million years. His thoughts evaporated as he saw all the pins explode, flying every which way.

He knew he had his work cut out for him, as he told her that was one of the cleanest strikes, he'd ever seen. She smiled ever so slightly, and he knew what she was thinking, *"guess I showed you how it was done – now let's see what you've got"*.

He approached the line again and prayed for another strike. Again he picked the same spot and this time telegraphed his will over the ball all the way to the strike zone. He could feel it before it even started and the explosion of pins in his ears confirmed it.

Again he turned, savoring the moment, and mentally thanked God for another strike. So it went, five strikes in a row before he spared, then she spared followed by another, he threw three more strikes to her two, and when the game was over they'd come within two pins of each other. He had thrown the best game of his life, a 238 and she'd gotten 236. He'd never forget it.

They both decided they had had enough and after returning the shoes, he called a cab from a nearby phone booth as she headed for the little girl's room. Even so, they had to wait over 15-minutes before it finally arrived. He apologized for the wait, and she graciously said, "not to worry". There was only just so much conversation one can have over a game of bowling. She told him about some of the tournaments that she had been in and he told her about how he had learned to bowl in a country bowling alley in Marathon, NY. Of course, she had never heard of it or, for that matter, of Binghamton either. Though she had heard of Syracuse, so he was able to make a connection, but somehow it had lost its moment if there had ever been one.

The cab finally came and again he fought to come up with things to talk about. After exhausting his entire knowledge of anything that might remotely interest her, they lapsed into long moments of silence. It never occurred to him to talk about having just returned from a Med cruise and the things he'd seen there. Probably because it was just so routine to him that it never occurred to him that it might be of interest to someone else, not to mention some of his diving experiences.

They arrived at the restaurant he'd heard about and went in. Upon entering, he learned that they had to have reservations and he didn't have one. It was embarrassing to have to shake his head, "No". It had never occurred to him to have to call ahead of time. He turned in time to see Judy's face. It had the look of pure disgust on it. It was obvious that she was used to being with men who knew their way around, who were not total klutzes. "If only he were more experienced in these sort of things," he silently lamented. He could have kicked himself all the way out of the place. He had never eaten at a place where he needed reservations, but he was not about to tell Judy that.

Again, he sought out a phone booth and called a cab, this time Judy took a very long little girl's room break. He had a feeling she was making a few calls of her own at the booth in the hallway and could only imagine what she was telling her roommate. Frankly he would have been just as glad to take her home, an idea that she soon suggested.

Just before the cab arrived, she made her appearance and simply said, "perhaps they had better call it a night, besides she had to pack and get ready to leave early tomorrow".

He was relieved to have her off his hands and to be free to just roam around without having to worry about entertaining some fancy pants, high society broad.

Again she was quiet all the way back to her place. He got out to open her door, but she was already out and shutting it.

Even so, he saw her to her hotel door and, as he turned to leave, she politely said, "thanks". She quickly told him that she'd had a good time bowling and hoped things would go well for him.

Before he could reply, she had opened the door and was gone.

He went back to the cab, got in and told the driver to take him back to the base. He had had enough of dating to last him for a few weeks. All told, he had spent a small fortune and what did he have to show for it? A nearly empty wallet, a bad memory and the knowledge that he was far from being "smooth".

He knew one thing; his friends would be full of questions as they always were when one of them had a "big date". Knowing them, he could only believe 10-percent of what he heard, the rest would be pure fiction. Even so, they were always entertaining to listen to. He was more content to be truthful, so he told them what had really happened, to which they offered all kinds of future advice. The most popular consensus was that he should have dumped her before he'd even gotten to the bowling alley.

Waters, a slow talking sailor from Florida leaned over and told him in a deep rumbling voice, "You can borrow my car anytime you want". He was deeply moved by his offer. It would be an offer that he would take him up on several times in the future. But for now, he knew that he was more determined than ever to have his own wheels. Mentally, he made a note to start saving for it starting with his very next paycheck. He'd never again allow himself to be caught without wheels and embarrassed in that way again.

From his most recent experience, he'd learned several things about dating in a military town. A hip sailor, never is without a car, even if it's rented or borrowed. Not having wheels is a date killer. The second – buy some classy civvies – there are times when being in uniform doesn't cut it, particularly when meeting and dating a girl from a military family, where the uniform have zero WOW power. Third, never, ever, travel in packs. There is nothing more scary to a young girl than having a half dozen or so guys descend on them like a pack of dogs. It's always better hunting by yourself or with a "wingman". Fourth, know all the venues (things to do). For example, know what restaurants require reservations, when and what movies are playing, and having all these places with phone numbers written down in your wallet. And just in case you get lucky, add a couple of motels to that list. Fifth, late mornings are the best time to pick up girls – not too early as they are still waking up from the night before. Late afternoons are not the preferred time to find a girl, as you will have less time to plan your evening, particularly if you've met a classy girl and are planning on showing her a special time. You will need time to get reservations, particularly if there's entertainment and dancing involved. If you plan on going to a movie, be sure you know what's playing where and when – being knowledgeable earns points – remember, a klutz ends up holding an empty wallet and not the girl.

Chapter 12.0

One of his buddies also had a brother on board who lived only a short distance from the base. His name was Larry, and his brother's name was Leroy, neither of them looked as if they were brothers. Larry was small of stature, bold and adventuresome. Leroy was much large, masculine, handsome and reserve, but every bit as capable of finding adventure. He was also married and had two sons. His wife's name was Sherri. She was a petite redhead, with freckles and very pretty.

Larry wanted to come right over to Leroy 's house as soon as they got off the ship, but Leroy warned him off – "hey, let a man get a "little" before you guys come barging in ... OK?!" He said as he twisted his mustache and winked.

Larry smiled and nodded saying, "that shouldn't take more than 3-minutes - knowing you". To which Leroy took a swipe at him, but Larry saw it coming and ducked in the nick of time. They often kidded with each other as both had a quick wit.

During his off duty times over the following weeks, Cal met Larry's brother, Leroy at his home. He gravitated toward his family; Sherri and he would have long conversations about girls and what they liked and didn't like, with Leroy butting in with his two cents, which usually led to Sherri calling him a caveman.

She told Cal how she and Leroy had met and they laughed about some of his antics. Leroy didn't seem to mind him being around and he came to be like another brother to Sherri. He'd pick up groceries for them and, in turn, Sherri would wash and iron his shirts and pants, even though she hated ironing in the worst way. He tried not to wear his welcome out and so hung with Larry most of the time.

Larry had a knack for picking up women. For a guy that was half Cal's size and homely as a hoe, he could sure attract the women and usually always had one waiting in the wings. Perhaps it was his personality - He did have a way about him, which showed through when he flashed his killer smile. If you weren't careful, he'd talk you out of your freshly shined shoes in a wink. So it was, that one day he met Carol and Brenda. Larry was seeing Carol, Brenda's younger sister. The family were poor as dirt; their father was a drunk. He never saw him sober and the mother looked as if she'd been pulled through a knot hole. He had no idea how they even got along.

Every time Larry stopped over, he'd slip the old man a bottle of hooch[54] and off he'd go with Carol. She was cute as a new born calf and fun to be around – she was a girl you could talk to about anything and who was content to just sit in the park and watch the squirrels run up and down the numerous Oak trees.

Larry would try to cop a feel now and then, and she'd playfully fight him off. Cal discreetly turned his head pretending not to notice. She often conned Larry into buying cigarettes for her, and he'd do it hoping to earn some redeemable points, which would later get him a kiss now and then. That was as far as she'd ever let him go.

Cal would often catch her looking at him and then she'd smile mischievously, when his eyes met hers. He knew she liked him, but he never acted on it – she was Larry's girlfriend and that was it.

---

[54] Liquor

Cal had finally got his nerve back, and was again approaching attractive women. His favorite place was the amusement park; it was more relaxing and informal. He found that by just being friendly, things worked out a lot better than being pushy. He'd meet them in line, talk small talk and, if they seemed interested, they'd ask him if he was alone. That was his cue that they were about to ask him to join them. It never failed. Of course, he was always alone, even if he wasn't. The guys knew the score. After all, they were all on the prowl and were happy to see one of them score.

Long before Bo Bridges came along, they had worked out a scoring system for women on the basis of one to ten, with ten being perfect.

One day he was at the beach alone; the other guys had wanted to go bar hopping, something that bored him. He just wasn't into drinking.

Cal had been hanging out on the boardwalk at Ocean View taking in the sights when a couple of girls caught his eye, but one in particular interested him. There was something about her that and he was compelled by a force he had never felt before to keep an eye on her.

He noticed that she was wearing a very loose-fitting, sleeveless blouse and a pair of form fitting shorts. She was very attractive, "perhaps a ten". He could tell that she was athletic; she moved with the fluidity of a deer. He guessed that she was maybe 18. With some girls, you can't tell if they're over 18 or slightly younger and she was no exception. However, as he studied the two of them, how they interacted, he knew that they were related. They were also with an older women, that he guessed was their mother.

As the afternoon waned and Cal moved about the park, ever watchful for a special lady, he noticed them again and so had some other sailors. For whatever reason, the two girls had separated from the older women and were feeding the fish in the fishpond not far from the coaster. He watched as several sailors descended on them and he could tell that they were frustrated by so much attention. He didn't know why, but it bothered him, so he decided to do something about it and approached the group, saying, "There you are, the others were starting to wonder where you guys had gone" as if they were all together.

He was dressed in civilian clothes, so the guys in uniform presumed that he was an older brother.

The girls looked startled until he winked and instantly they caught on and played along with it.

The other guys got the message and left.

The two girls laughed about his intervention – how clever and heroic he was. "Sir Galahad", they'd called him, all in good fun.

They hung out for awhile near the gold fish pond and talked. They introduced themselves as Kinsey Connors, from Cumberland and her cousin, Renee, from Virginia Beach and that she was staying with her Aunt. Kinsey was the one that had caught his attention. As they visited, he learned that she was an identical twin. Her sister's name was Delia. Being "an identical" surprised him because he'd never met an identical twin and that meant there was another person in this world as pretty and charming as she.

He told them that he had never met an identical twin and wanted to know what that meant to her. They talked for some time about that and then when he asked her where she was from, she told him, "Cumberland, a little town in the Maryland mountains - you probably have never heard of it," she stated. She was right, but he had heard of the Cumberland Trail and Cumberland Gap, which she said were also familiar to her but not the same place. He went on to tell her where he was from and a little about it.

It was obvious from how she spoke of her town that she was very proud of where she was from and of her family.

He noticed that as they talked, she tilting her head, as she listened to him, which showed that he had her full attention and he also found it to be just a little sexy. As they visited, she had a way of making him feel like he was the most important person in the world to her. Before he knew it, they were talking about his family, their likes, and dislikes. He had to keep telling himself that she's a bit young for him and she lives a zillion miles away – so forget it!

It was about then that her Aunt showed up and both girls told her how several sailors had been hitting on them and how he'd come to their rescue. She nodded her thanks and told the girls that it was time to get going.

Before Kinsey left, she'd surprised him by passing her address and phone number to him in a handshake, and with a smile, she quietly asked if he would write her from time to time. He'd agreed, more out of desiring to send her off with a happy memory of her day, than anything else. He also doubted that he'd ever follow up.

Over the next few months, he had forgotten about her until coming across a wadded up piece of paper in his locker's "personal draw". Not knowing at first what it was, he unrolled the crumpled lump, and there was her address and phone number, with some Xs and Os on it. He had never gotten a note like that before with "X"s and "O"s, but figured out that the "X"s and "O"s most probably meant - hugs and kisses. At the time he looked at it as the frivolous fancies of a young girl of little consequence.

He remembered his promise to send her a letter, and since he was not all that busy at the moment, he dashed off a short note, on his Navy stationary depicting "the Fort", telling her about his daily routine. He also included a few stories about living aboard a ship, since it was all in the vein of keeping a long overdue promise and promises were an important part of who he was. He also imagined that his letter would be a real trip for her, particularly since it was written on the "ships stationary".

He'd been trained since childhood about the sanctity of making and keeping promises. It was right up there with "not lying and keeping your word. It was all about one's "honor". It seemed that no sooner had he sent the letter than she answered.

Several weeks went by before Cal sent her another, and it was very brief, as he'd been extremely busy recently keeping up with his duties aboard the ship and going on liberty in various ports of call.

As before, he'd gotten another from her at the next mail call. The days passed, and then it was a couple of more weeks, and Cal still hadn't gotten around to answering her last letter. Finally, he forced himself to sit down and answer it. It was more out of some sort of duty now than anything else. He had half a mind not to bother further with writing her again, after this letter. In her next letter, she'd enclosed a picture of herself and her three other sisters in their PJs, on top of a bed playing board games. Again, he felt a ping of recognition, like he should know her from somewhere, but he couldn't put his finger on it, which was odd since he never forgot a face.

Life, while in port or on liberty, had pretty much settled into the routine of pulling their "eight" with the occasional cold iron watch, playing cards during their time off or writing to their girlfriends or wives and, if they didn't have the duty, going off ship on liberty. Once on shore, most of them would go drinking. He preferred to go off base to his favorite hamburger place right outside of Gate 1 on Shore Drive, for a huge, juicy, all beef hamburger, garnished with sliced dill pickles, fresh sliced tomatoes, sweet onions and mayo, along with a plate full of fries, and one great big icy cold Coke. As he bit into it, the juice would stream down his forearms – but no matter, it was beyond heaven after living on sea-rats (sea rations) for months. Then he was off to Ocean View or Virginia Beach to see the sights. Which is military talk for "scanning for pretty girls".

When visiting foreign ports, he enjoyed absorbing each country's culture and taking pictures. Occasionally, he'd visit some of the shops and buy gifts for his family.

During Cal's time in the Caribbean, one of the many islands he visited, was St John, the smallest of the three US Virgin Islands, where 60-percent of the land area, is a pristine national park. He took advantage of the self-guided Annenberg Historic Trail, which took him through the restored ruins on the plantation grounds and the Annaberg Sugar Plantation. As always, he never missed an opportunity to go swimming in the translucent waters that bathed in the crystalline white sands surrounding the island.

St Thomas, St Croix, Trinidad, Barbados, Antigua, Dominican Republic, Grenada, Jamaica, St Kitts, St Lucia, St Vincent, Haiti, Porto Rico, Curacao, and Guantanamo were all like jewels from afar, set in the never ending blue Caribbean waters.

Of them all, the poorness of Haiti will forever haunt him. The poverty Cal had endured as a child, didn't come close to what the everyday citizen of Haiti endures. When all you have are the clothes on your back and a piece of tin in your hands that forms the roof over your head during the frequent tropical storms, he realized how lucky he was.

Of all the islands, Guantanamo, Cuba is a US base, on the island of Cuba. Liberty was restricted to the base which was fully militarized, so the scenery was severely limited. As for areas around the base, it would appear that it was a microcosm of any small village, right down to a new school teaching K-12 with slightly over 100-children.

If you liked to drink, there was a bar and places to eat. There was also a place to shop for everything from food to electronics and furniture for your home if you lived there.

Most often, he stayed on the ship writing letters, and catching up on his sleep and lifting weights. They were usually there only a couple of days before going elsewhere.

The following day, started out like all the rest but would change all of them forever.

He had been lounging in M-Div.; it must have been a weekend, as he was still in his boxers, sitting on the edge of his bunk watching the guys playing cards. The radio had been on. It was playing Cuban music when all of a sudden, the music stopped, and an announcer broke in yelling something in Spanish. We could only pick out bits and pieces – something about our President and the word "Kennedy". (el Presidente Kennedy ha sido asesinado.) It was enough to know that something terrible, involving our President, had happened. A few of the guys who understood a little Spanish told them that Kennedy had just been assassinated in Texas.

Then our PA system came on, and the Captain said in brief, "President Kennedy has been shot. The flag will be immediately lowered to half-mast. And he ordered the ship to go to General Quarters until more information was available. Immediately, GQ was sounded and the crew ran to their stations. In the meantime, all liberty was canceled until further notice, and the men on shore were recalled".

You could have heard a pin drop, as, for a moment, everything stood still – grown, battle trained sailors wiped away tears, caught their breath, and scrambled to their GQ stations. Slowly, through the scuttlebutt news line, we learned what had happened, and GQ was later canceled. The following morning we left port, believing that either Khrushchev or Castro were somehow involved in this heinous crime. Later we'd learn that Lee Harvey Oswald had shot Kennedy and a man by the name of Jack Ruby, in turn, shot and killed Oswald.

To this day, over 53-percent of Americans believe that someone else killed Kennedy, and the government was complicit in the cover up.

Chapter 13.0

One of the many stops the ship made during our numerous Caribbean cruises was St. Thomas. Cal loved exploring it, both on land and under the water.

The Pilot, who had been ferried out to the ship, boarded and piloted them in. When we were safely tied to the pier his job was done, and liberty was piped over the ship's intercom.

Previously, Cal had made a trade with a sailor in his division for a Heathway single tank, scuba outfit for his brand new 30-30 Winchester lever action rifle, which he purchased through the ship's armory by way of a civilian gun dealership. He had thought about using it to hunt deer in his civilian life. However, this deal seemed too good to pass up, so the trade was made.

As Cal was already a trained diver, he was anxious to use the equipment. The standing rule, of course, is never to dive alone but after asking around on both the ship and at the UDT diving pier, no one felt like going with him - they would rather go drinking and play cards.

So off he went on his own, feeling, what the heck, he's not really diving because he's not using a scuba tank or weights. He caught a ride over to West Port in an old jeep and headed for the beach, with his snorkel, mask, and fins in hand. It was a beautiful day, with a slight breeze - not too hot or humid.

Reaching the beach, Cal noted that there was no one else there and its remoteness fed into his need for privacy and quiet. He kicked off his flip-flops, leaving them at the high tide mark, slipped his fins on and pulled the mask down to his forehead. With his snorkel in hand, he headed for the water. He saw that there were no waves, which made it all the better for snorkeling. After dipping his mask into the water to keep it from fogging, he put it on and continued to back into the water – the easiest way to enter the water with fins on.

Soon he was bobbing up and down, in his quest to find a coral reef. After approximately 30-minutes, he found one complete with several grottos – it was like a 3-D kaleidoscope of color with animated fish swimming in and out of an array of holes. He circled it a couple of times, then swam out deeper to see if he could find some more. After several minutes of coming to the surface, he'd dive again and again, until he finally found another one in over 30-feet of water. Just below was the granddaddy of all coral reefs. Its color was brilliant, beyond comparison, with tall white coral trees, red ribbon coral, green, blue and even black. The grottos were so large that he could swim through them with ease, following all colors of fish. It was like a Disney Wonderland. In the course of following these schools of fish and the lure of grotto after grotto, he noticed that his snorkel had started to foul when surfacing for air. At first, he disregarded it but, as it got increasingly worse, he stayed on the surface long enough to see that it was not the fault of the snorkel, but the waves that were being picked up by the wind.

With horror, Cal realized as he turned around looking in all directions, that any signs of land had disappeared. He had been pushed by the tides out to sea but, in which direction land lie, was anyone's guess.

His heart started to race, and he had visions of eventually, drowning. He knew he had to calm down, to think – that was what they were taught in their diver training – "think or die" was the saying. So as the swells came and went, he rode atop them, looking in all directions. Finally, in the far distance, Cal spotted a slight variation on the horizon along the ocean's surface. It had to be land, as it appeared to be slightly darker than the ocean's surface against the sky. With each swell, he became more certain of it and started swimming in that direction. Since the sun was over his left shoulder, he knew he was swimming north. Given the rule of "line of sight", he knew he was approximately nine miles from land. Calhad trained to swim or run 5-miles before breakfast, so a couple of more shouldn't be that big a deal. As he swam, he noted that the tide was still running against him and he was not gaining any discernible distance.

What time was it, he wondered – it was not his habit to wear a watch unless he was using tanks. He'd left the ship at around 9 am, and the tide had still been coming in. So during his dive, it had started going out and would continue until around noon at which time it would shift and start going back in. Given that he could see no shadow in the water from his head, it must be around noon. The best thing he could do was to start swimming back toward shore, or risk being pushed even further out to sea. So he dug in and kept swimming, hour after hour.

When Cal stopped and looked at the angle of the sun to his location, he estimated that it must be around 14:00 hours (2 pm) and by his reckoning, the tide had switched and was pushing him toward land and would continue to do so until approximately 19:00 hours (7 pm). If he didn't make it back by then, he was totally screwed.

He could kick himself for not waiting until one of the guys could go with him – but then there was no guarantee that he too wouldn't have been caught in the same situation. He was feeling the fatigue in his muscles, and the salt was biting his lips and burning the inside of his nose.

Whatever he did, he mustn't cut himself in any way, which might lead to bleeding. If that were to happen, the sharks would scent it and finish him off in seconds.

Cal started swimming in earnest – thanking God for his fins and mask, they might just end up saving his life. As he swam, the hours were ticking off, but he could see that the land mass, he was headed for, was drawing closer. He was nearing exhaustion, and he could feel the beginnings of cramps setting up in his calves and thighs. If that happened, he could drown. So he reached forward and grabbed the top of first one fin and then the other, pulling it toward his chest while keeping his leg straight. After doing several of those, he knew he'd have to modify the use of his legs to take the pressure off his leg and calf muscles.

Landfall was still a good ways off, perhaps 200-yards. It was now closing in on 1900 hours, and Cal was running out of time. He'd been in the water nearly 10-hours. Again, he dug in, gritting his teeth as he pulled, mentally reaching deeper into his body than he had ever gone before. Cal was also praying. This was something he had not done in years; he struggled to remember the last time. Then he remembered that it had been on the farm when he saw the bear rear up and head for him – he'd thought that he was dead meat and he had prayed to God to spare him and his family. Since then he couldn't remember a single time that he felt that he needed God. Yes, he'd gone to church during boot camp, but that had been so he could get away from the RCPO and to get some rest. Then on the ship, every Sunday, they had church just outside M-Division, and he'd ignored it.

So once again, Cal prayed that his life would be spared. He knew that God had no reason to listen, after all, he hadn't listened to God. He'd ignored Him. He did know that faith played a huge part in prayer, so he also prayed for faith. He was beyond exhausted, so tired that he was feeling woozy; his body was giving out, but he kept swimming – only just a little ways more he kept telling himself. It was then that he saw the bottom. He forced his face down into the water and it looked like the bottom was only a couple of feet away, so he allowed his feet to drop downward, only to have the water close in over his head. The clear Caribbean water was so clear that the depth was deceptive. Again he dug deep down and kept swimming. Twice more, he tried it and twice more his head went under. He could see the water breaking against the shoreline – so close, but yet so far. He could hear a faraway buzzing in his head and knew he was fast running out of time. Once more his feet dropped, and this time, he felt his fins catching on the rocky bottom – but there was one problem ... Sea Urchins. They were everywhere, like clods of grass growing on the rocks. They were so thick that there was no way of avoiding them – he had to make land or drown in the surf and be dragged back to sea when the tide went out.

With each step, Cal could feel the spines penetrating the thick rubber fins, but he kept going until he was on the beach, it was all he could do to remain upright.

Once he felt the sand under his feet, he said, "Thank you, God," then collapsed. How long he laid there, Cal didn't know, but when he woke, the waters had surrounded him, and he was starting to be dragged down the beach and back out to sea. The tide had turned and was going back out. Arm over arm, gouging his elbows into the sand, he dragged himself up to higher ground.

Cal's feet were burning as if he'd walked through a fire pit. Rolling over, he pulled his fins off and, as he tipped them up to examine the bottoms, blood ran out of them and dripped onto the sand. He noticed that the bottoms of the white fins were sprinkled with black dots like pepper on mashed potatoes. Even though his feet burned, he put it out of his mind, as he grabbed his gear, stood up and walked toward a bluff that ran along the beach. He located a path of sorts that led up through the brush and onto a large yard.

To his left, was a white table and four chairs occupied by four women drinking tea.

They noted his arrival and one said to the other, "Lord, mercy, it's "a Yank" – you'd think they owned the island the way they just trod all over one's property." Cal ignored them as he headed for the road that he knew lay just beyond the houses.

As luck would have it, he had only walked a few yards when a jeep came wheeling along over the clay packed road. Driving it was Plank, one of his ships corpsmen. He had always liked Plank; he was easy to get along with, and they often talked. Plank had dark brown hair, nearly black, depending on how the light hit it. He was also extraordinarily handsome. It was obvious, judging by his build and smooth hands, that his job did not require hard labor.

Quickly, Cal stuck his thumb out as if he was hitchhiking, which he was, but he knew that Plank would stop anyhow as soon as he recognized him ... which he did.

He quickly threw his gear into the back and shoved himself into the seat. Plank hit the gas pedal and let the clutch out – "what's up?" he asked, as they went speeding down the crooked road.

Taking a deep breath, he looked over at Plank and said, "got a bunch of sea urchins in my feet, how about getting them out?"

Plank took a long look at him and asked, "how'd that happen?"

"Did a little morning swimming off the point, and got caught in them."

"Where's your partner?"

"He went home by another way."

As they came into a small village, Plank stopped at a bar that apparently was frequented more by the natives, than any tourists.

They walked inside and sat down at a table by the window. Plank had a medical bag with him and, after he sat down, he signaled for Cal to raise his foot, grabbed it, put it on his knee to examine it.

A waitress stopped by and Plank ordered a bottle of gin and two beers. He also asked for a couple of towels. At first, she started to ask why he needed the towels and he pointed at my foot. After one look, she nodded her head and disappeared. Upon returning, she brought the towels, the beers and a bottle of gin. She also had another bottle that looked like some kind of home brew medicine.

She noticed their inquiring looks, and said, "we get a lot of that around here, the herbs in the bottle will help make the burn go away and make it heal faster."

Plank nodded his thanks, and put the towel under my foot, then poured some gin over one end of the other towel. Without further ado, he started washing the bottom of Cal's foot off with the gin soaked towel. It only took a second before Cal felt as if his foot had caught fire. Clenching his jaw, he didn't make a sound, as Plank took a hypodermic needle and injected his foot in several places. Then, with another needle, he started to dig each spine out of Cal's foot. It took a couple of hours to get all he could, and the towel was soaked with blood.

The barmaid had been watching from a distance and, seeing that Plank was finished, retrieved the towels and brought over a pair of used flip-flops, no doubt left behind by some drunk. Plank applied the herbal medicine to his feet, saying, "You never know – it might just actually work. If not, you may only lose your foot" he added with a grin.

Upon finishing his work, Plank put his gear away, zipped his bag up, and got up, saying, "if they should discover that, for any reason, you can't perform your duties, you'll be written up and should turn himself in".

"Thanks, Plank for helping and, don't worry, we're cool."

A few days later, he no longer felt a thing – his feet had healed perfectly, even Plank had retorted that he should have bought a bottle of that home remedy.

The Caribbean Cruise came to an end, and it was time to go into dry dock in Savannah. For him, it would be a whole new adventure to tack on to the many he'd already had.

Chapter 14.0

In preparing for dry dock in Savanna, he was told to create a list of all the mechanical things that needed repairing or updating. The ship, in essence, was going to get an overhaul of all its systems. Within his engineering space, the evaporator needed to be pulled down and the tubes cleaned and any leaky ones replaced. All of the five DC pumps needed to be pulled, the armatures rewound, bearings replaced and new wearing rings put in. Also, the two steam driven ballast pumps needed to be pulled and new bearings put on each end of the turbine. In addition, the turbo generator needed it's hot well pump pulled and the bearings, brushes and wearing rings replaced. There was a lot of work in this space alone to be done by the yard. It was also up to him to oversee, not only the yard work, but his own men and their work while working with the yard people.

They were also told that, on this trip they would be allowed to bring their cars – which meant signing release forms to relieve the Navy of any responsibly for any damage to, or by, their car. It was explained that each car would be chained to the built-in steel cleats just as they would have a tank, boat or any other piece of equipment to ensure that it wouldn't start careening back and forth in a storm and damage either its self or the ship.

Once the fifty or so cars were all loaded and secured, they untied and were soon underway. The trip was short, taking only a couple of days. Even before they had tied up, a strange putrid smell started permeating the ship. The smell was akin to hamburger rotting in the sun. Later, they learned that it was actually the pulp mills that were causing the horrible stench. After a few days, they got used to it and for the most part, ignored it.

They quickly learned that the weather here was hot and very humid, making working in the engineering spaces nearly intolerable. Thank God for the huge, below deck ventilation blowers, salt pills and their prized cold water cooler, or they would never have survived.

By the end of the day, he was beat and ready for a shower with the full intention of hitting the rack. Instead, he usually got talked into going out for "just one drink, a burger and some fries" at the end of the pier. By then, he was ready to go into town.

Savannah is a town that takes you back in time to the days of the "Old South". Its stately, moss covered trees line every road, street, and driveway beneath a pale blue sky. It's a place where the work is done in the morning and the rest of the day is spent looking for more leisurely pursuits.

Often the women from the "better homes" are seen lounging on front porches, drinking sweet tea or mint juleps and discussing the affairs of those who appear to have more of a life than their own.

The men are usually found gathered at the local watering hole or at one of the fashionable men's clubs around town, smoking cigars or having a good chew while they played cards. The topics of conversation being sports of any kind, the new hottie working the counter at the golf club, politics, commerce and not necessarily in that order.

Savannah is a contradiction in commerce. A throw-back to the days of cotton and tobacco exporting. Vintages of this can still be seen in the harbor with its derelict piers and old, falling down warehouses. To think, that these old piers bore the weight of carts that hauled tons of cotton from the warehouses, to waiting ships, and now languish, rusting away to rubble, with the farms round about hardly able to grow a weed. The soil poor fields lay abandoned under the torturous heat and, here and there, a scraggly pine was trying to grow. Now paper is king, dock work is second, and graft can be seen everywhere, if not felt in the day-to-day living.

To the less observant, life is idyllic and laid back. The young women around and about are bored with the slow pace of the local boys and are looking for excitement ... something new. This was the Savannah that they found when they, the sailors of the USS Fort Mandan came to town.

Along the way, they had to stake out their turf. Word quickly got out, that when a few of their brothers had ventured into the bar at the end of the pier, they were roughed up and thrown out.

Once the word was out and, after the day's work, about fifty sailors stopped in on the way out of the yard and evicted the local muscle in a matter of minutes. From that day on, any sailer could go in there and expect no more than the best service in town.

Larry and Cal used to stop in for lunch and throw down a Colt 45, while they waited for their half-pound hamburgers to arrive. At first, they had all they could do to hold on to their bar stools so as not to fall off while waiting for their meal. After the food arrived, it helped to stabilize their stomachs and therefore their equilibrium. After refueling, they were ready to take on the town.

The first order of business was to find out where the women hung out. Cal's vote was always for the beach and that was where they headed. Women love to sunbathe; a good tan was a rite of passage, and no matter what they tell you, they love to show off their bodies, especially if they have one that is worthy of being shown off. And besides, what better way to see what you're getting than to go to the beach where it's all put on display, like goods in a store window.

Again, Cal would locate the concession places – when you are sun bathing, you tend to get thirsty and hungry. However, Savannah's beach didn't have a concession stand or any restaurants nearby. In fact, it was a rather long drive out to the beach. So Cal hit on another idea. If you can't get a cool one at the beach, - bring it to the beach and they will come. So, carrying this premise one more step, why not make a drink that is both satisfying and that eases the tensions? After doing some research, Cal hit upon a lethal mixture of Hawaiian Punch, Ginger Ale, and Vodka. The Punch was sweet, the Ginger Ale gave it a bit of a kick, and the vodka took the starch out of the most puritanical girl. The punch was a real crowd pleaser. Cal called his drink, the Sneaky Pete.

It was not long before the girls with the stiffest upper lips were singing their praises – never had they had such a good time, and soon the word was out that they were the coolest bunch of guys around. All they had to do was see their car coming, and they were there to help unload. At that time, their car was a flat black, flathead six, 51 Ford, 2-door coupe, that burned almost as much oil and it did gas.

Money was always a problem, they needed it for gas, and thankfully the used oil was free and easily obtained from most gas stations. They needed cash for more than just gasoline, they also needed it for a burger and some suds every now and then. They took to taking short cuts with the car. Cal can't remember if they ever changed the oil or filter, bought new plugs or had a tune up. In fact, the lack of funds to maintain the car would later get him in a heap of trouble. It was more a case of guilt by association than actually having committed the deed. However, one more, in a long string of lessons, would ensue. These were lessons life doled out to him, its eager student.

They all soon discovered that they had immunity from the cops in Savannah. Several of the guys, in the course of having a little too much fun, got pulled over and were let go when their military ID's were shown. Anywhere else, they would have had to pay a fine, but here, the police would just say, "Guys, take it easy". Later, they learned that the old man and the mayor were tight. They hung out together and went golfing every day and finished the day off with a few drinks and a game of cards.

Much to the chagrin of all of them, the day came when they learned that they were going to be leaving Savannah. Many of the men had become romantically involved with the girls from the area and were now caught with the problem of how to continue their long distance relationships or how to get out of the relationship without any repercussions. For one man, in particular, it was like a rope that was tightening around his neck. His name was Jerome Thomas, JT for short, and he was a married man who had become involved with the daughter of an old southern family, one with position, money, and power. Because he had a southern accent and the manners of a gentleman, they'd accepted him as one of their own. He'd liked to brag to his fellow shipmates about his good fortune, how he had worked his way into this rich family's good graces and how he was bedding their daughter, whenever he pleased.

Cal suspected that JT was telling them this bit of information as a way to get back at them for not including him in their day-to-day banter. He was, for the most part, an outcast. No one trusted or respected him. He also acted like he had a chip on his shoulder like he was too good for the rest of them. So life went on pretty much as if he didn't exist. They hadn't respected him before, and now they respected him even less, because they knew he was married and not to just any girl, but to a drop dead good looking girl who thought the sun rose and set on him. As transparent as he was to them, he had a way with the women who all seemed to fall for his line. So it came as no surprise that, at the end of each day, a limousine pulled up at the end of the dock and, as he approached, the driver would get out and open the door for him. For anyone standing close by, they could see a very attractive girl, reaching for him as he entered. They'd embrace and, as they did, he'd start getting intimate with her, so there would be no doubt about what they were about to do on the way to her home.

It made them all boiling mad, that he was not only disrespectful to her, but he was also cheating on his wife. And moreover, he was rubbing their noses in what he was doing and it sickened them that he was using her for not only his own pleasure but to get back at them for ostracizing him.

There was nothing they could do, at least, not without hurting someone else. After a time, they didn't hear any more bragging from him, even though the limo would show up daily and off he'd go, coming back just before duty call, the next morning.

He always seemed to have money, and his clothes were always newly washed and pressed before reporting for duty. The lack of his bravado was not lost on them, but even so, he slipped back into obscurity for all practical purposes and didn't reappear until the day they pulled into Little Creek.

Life had been good to Cal in Savannah; he was meeting lots of young women and having a great time. Over the course of the next few months, he first met a girl who was a telephone operator, then a nurse trainee and finally an x-ray technician. The telephone operator he met one day while strolling along a street that bordered a park. He saw her outside eating her lunch and sat down nearby, appearing to rest. They struck up a conversation, and soon she was telling him where she worked and lived. Over the course of the next few days, she told him that whenever he needed to make a long distance call, to ask for her and she'd put it through for free. This would be a big help on his budget when calling home and he was grateful and told her so.

Next, Cal met a nurse trainee; there were a lot of them around Savannah due to a huge nursing school nearby. Once you met one of them you got to meet a lot of them and, in no time, they were all up to their armpits in nurses. A tall, slender Polish nurse took a liking to him and quickly put together a plan to hustle him up to her place and break him in. He had found her to be modestly attractive.

In her campaign to win him over, she had arranged for a car for them and cooked a big special meal. She'd even invited several of her relatives and friends over for the function, to show him off. The only problem was that he completely forgot about the date and was off somewhere else with another girl.

He later heard that she was so mad at him that she'd threatened him with bodily harm if she ever saw him again. So he stayed clear of that part of town for a while.

In the meantime, his group took to hanging out at the USO, as it was cheap, if not slightly square. They could get a room, food, and be entertained for practically nothing. Every weekend they had a dance and would haul out a bunch of old records that must have been recorded back during the Civil War, and enlisted some of the colleges to send over some girls to dance with "our boys in uniform". This is where Cal met Shelley Channing. She and her cousin Wanda stopped by because their Aunt was involved with the USO and, given the culture of the day, they were always on the prowl for "husband material". Perish the thought that should their daughters ever become an old maid, they'd be accused of failing them and their families for generations to come. No self-respecting girl would dare show her face in public if she wasn't wearing at least an engagement ring by the time she was 20.

Given the looks on both Shelley's and Wanda's faces, one would have thought that they were being escorted to their own lynching. As soon as they appeared in the door, Jack and he went over and met them. He had his eye on the petite red head and Jack the tall, slender brunette.

She was the first blue-eyed redhead Cal had ever met; he estimated that she was about five feet tall and a dead ringer for Shirley McLean, the movie star. When she said, "Hi," he heard a voice that had a killer southern accent. No matter what she said, it sounded sexy, and then those eyes said volumes about the possibilities that lay ahead. They hit it off right away and became inseparable. For him, all the other girls he'd been dating fell into the background; he only had time for her. After a few dates, he learned that she and her cousin were heading back home to Greenville, SC in a few days. To him, her home town might as well have been located on another planet as he knew of no way to get to see her again anytime soon.

The last weekend they were going to be there, he bought some records featuring music he could dance to. They were the newest Chubby Checker releases. He was an artist who was doing great things with music and he knew how to do some wicked twisting to it. There was also a new sound out that had been sweeping the VA area, from which he learned to dance the Thunderbird.

After dancing to several slow songs, he edged over to the record player and asked if they'd mind if he played a couple of records from back home – and gave them a home sick look that would have made a nun cry. They quickly relented and put them on.

From that moment on, the place was never the same. The music went from the slow swooning sounds of a very young Frank Sinatra, to rock and roll. At that moment, there were probably over fifty guys and their dancing partners on the floor. When old Chubby wound up and started singing, "Let's Dance Again", the place became galvanized. He was feeling pretty good and proceeded to show them all how it was done. By the time the first song ended, the floor had refilled, and they were all twisting to the hottest thing in town.

After that record finished, he put the second one on. The speed of the music about doubled, and he started doing the equivalent of the "Dirty Dog". He thought he saw a couple of the chaperones faint. Another one of them came over and tried to tell him to tone it down, but all the guys and girls booed her off the floor.

They'd tasted something new and were not going to be shut down. Shelley was having the time of her life; she was a born rebel and rallied to the moment. Her red hair flashed in the light like fire racing over a bone dry, grain field as her graceful body curved to the heavy beat of the staccato music, her feet moved in sync to his as the records were played over and over by popular demand.

After the dance was over, Jack and Cal saw the girls back to their Aunt's, and they regretfully said "goodbye". Before they left, he got Shelley's phone number and address. She made him promise to call her before they drove away. After they left, he went back inside the USO. The dancing had ended and the chairs were all back where they originally were assigned and only a few lights next to the overstuffed chairs were left on. Gratefully, he sunk into one as he felt as if his world had just collapsed. After an hour or so, a glass of Kool-Aid showed up on the table next to him along with some homemade cookies. He thanked the kindly looking lady as she departed.

Cal was big on promises, and he made it a point to call Shelley nearly every day; it was during one of these long distance calls, that he happened to get his telephone operator girlfriend. She made it a point to deliberately mispronounce Shelley's name and made sure that he knew, that she knew, what was going on. He knew, without being told, that his "free calls" had come to an end. From that point forward, he didn't care what she, or any other girl he'd been dating, thought. He had found someone he cared about and he stopped going ashore every night.

It was about killing him, not seeing Shelley. A few weeks passed, and he got an idea how he might get to see her again. He knew that Jack was interested in Wendy and Sean already had a girlfriend in Savannah that he was seeing. So, he proposed that they pool their resources and take the weekend to run up to Greenville and see the girls. Everyone thought it was a good idea. So, after they'd stopped for a fill-up and a five-gallon can of used oil, they headed out. Since they all knew how much he liked to drive, they were soon off on another great adventure with Cal in the driver's seat.

They had started at daybreak and, after driving all day, they'd arrived just after sundown and checked into a motel, booking two rooms. One for Sean and his girlfriend, and one for Jack and himself.

After settling in, he gave Shelley a call to let her know they'd arrived. She was so surprised that she started screaming and talking all at the same time. After she'd asked, and he told her where they were staying, she said, "no man of mine is going to be staying at such a place, I'll be making other arrangements for you all".

The following morning, Shelley and her cousin Wendy arrived at the motel and guided them over to her Aunt's and Grandparents. Sean and his girl ended up staying at Shelley's Uncle's place and Cal and Jack at the Grandparents.

It was readily apparent that friends and family did not stay in motels – "these places were for the "seedy side of town's use" and no self-respecting person would go near one," Shelley told him with a look of pure disgust written over her face. As we were preparing to leave, she looked over her shoulder several times, no doubt hoping that no one she knew saw her as it would mean the end of her reputation, as she had later informed him.

After they'd settled in their respective places, Shelley's Uncle Louie, lent them the use of his power boat and car, as it had a hitch on it.

In no time, they changed into their bathing suits and went boating and then swimming in a nearby lake. Once there, it was quickly discovered that he was the only one who knew how to back the boat into the water and drive one, so he was nominated for the job and to be their captain for the day. It was a real plus that an old talent from his farming days would now come in handy.

He noticed that Shelley looked particularly good in a bathing suit and he saw her openly sizing him up while they'd been swimming and again on the boat, as they ducked the spray, as he powered in and out of tight turns.

Suddenly, looking over at him she said, "do you know, you have the perfect symmetry of an all American male". I've been studying bone structures and flesh formations in my X-Ray classes, and have to admit that the combination of both bone and flesh make you particularly handsome.

He'd never gotten such a compliment, but then, he had never been out with anyone like Shelley, nor had he had that many girlfriends. He could quite honestly say that the subject had never come up before. However, her observation was somewhat startling as he'd never regarded himself as being handsome or a stud, as young men of virility were often referred to. His mother had often told him that he was a good looking young man, but then she was his mother, and they were somewhat biased when it came to their sons and daughters. So he'd always dismissed such observations as being just something that mom's say, because you're their kid.

They all swam in the warm, clear waters and sunbathed. It was relaxing, and he enjoyed his time with Shelley – having her close, where he could put his arms around her and kiss her whenever he wanted.

The following day, Sean took off, citing that he was on leave and was going home and we were to take his girlfriend back to Savannah, which we agreed to do amid our surprise at this turn of events. Later that evening, we drove him to the Greensville airport, where he flew out as we all exchanged waves and well wishes.

His girlfriend didn't seem to mind his departure nor did she show any signs of missing him. This surprised Cal since she and Sean had been very romantically involved with one another in the back seat of the car during the trip to Greenville.

All too soon, it was time to leave. Cal knew he'd miss Brenda, Lewis, Bill and Bess and Shelley's Uncle Bowie. They'd all been good to him, but more than anything, he'd miss Shelley.

They'd taken some time to be alone – walk and talk some more. She'd put her arm around his waist as they walked and it felt good. Then, at long last, Cal bent over and kissed her, holding her pear-shaped face in his hands and then he felt her starting to sob. The tears ran down and coated her lips, reminding him of the sea – restless and beckoning. It was time to go.

They promised to write and he to call. He felt something stir inside of him – was this "the one".

They loaded all their stuff into the car. Jack got into the front seat, and Sean's girlfriend was in the back, with Cal behind the wheel. They were only a few miles down the road before Jack moved from the front seat to the back. He thought this was strange, but kept his eyes on the road as the miles rolled under their wheels.

After a while, he knew they were doing more than just sitting back there talking and wondered what Sean would think when he found out. Sean was a whole lot bigger than Jack, and no match for his temper, so he didn't have to use his imagination as to how that was going to turn out. Even though he felt uncomfortable with what was going on, he managed to put his thoughts back on Shelley and think about when he might be seeing her again.

They were about halfway into their trip when Cal saw a car coming up on them. He could tell by the car's contour, even though it was only a speck, that it was a cop car. The car was coming on fast, as he watched the distance narrowing by the minute. He started to wonder what in the world would warrant him being pulled over. He alerted Jack that there was a cop closing in fast on their 6.

The cop's lights came on, then the sirens squawked, and Cal pulled over immediately, not wanting to upset the local law-enforcement. He knew that some of these small town cops were not too bright and would take offense rather quickly if they had any excuse to. He'd let him do the talking first and then tune into his dialect.

He could hear his tires crunching on the gravel as he pulled over and slowed to a stop, shutting off the engine. The oppressive mid-day heat came rolling into the car, causing his forehead to break into a sweat.

Cal watched his rearview mirror and saw the cop get out of his car, and come up beside theirs. He was dressed in a wrinkled blue uniform, dirty black shoes and wore a policeman's brim type hat. As he approached their car, he had his right hand resting on the butt of his gun and the other on his hip. He immediately asked for the car's registration and his driver's license.

As he reached for his wallet, he asked Jack if the registration was in the glove box.

Jack's voice was low, barely audible, as he said, "should be unless Sean has it on him".

So he reached over to the glove box, pushed the button, causing it to drop open with a thud. Inside was a bunch of wadded up papers, a couple of packs of rubbers, a half pack of Winston's amid a lot of dust.

"Guess Jack Billingsley, has it and he's in Steubenville, Ill." He told the officer. He then produced his Navy ID, as did Jack.

The officer looked both of their IDs over and then looked at them. Cal could see the disappointment etched on his face, he'd obviously thought he'd caught a couple of rubes and was going to give them a hard time. The last thing he wanted was to have the government messing with his business, so he gave them back their Navy IDs and told them that they had a tail light out, waved and went back to his police car. In two minutes, he was out of sight on down the road.

"F&^#@*," stupid cop Jack shouted. "I'll say one thing, these Navy ID's put the fear of God in those F%$@&* cops. He could hear the girl, shushing him, as he started the car and pulled back on the road, continuing on their way.

It was late Sunday night when they pulled into the ship's parking lot in Savannah, after dropping Sean's girlfriend off at her house. He could hardly walk, as he stumbled toward the pier, his legs still waking up.

He could hear Jack lamenting about crossing the line with Sean's girlfriend – that he'd have to tell him as soon as he got back since he was planning on marrying her and that he shouldn't, as she's nothing but a tramp. Seems that she had been messing with

Jack until he'd finally relented and got into the back seat.

Irrespective, the whole thing was very distasteful to him. It wasn't the way he'd been taught, nor was it the way he was going to live his life. He made a mental note to start disassociating himself from them as soon as possible.

The days passed quickly, and before they knew it, Sean was back from leave.

Jack had ask Cal to back him up when he told Sean what'd happened on the way back from Greenville. Jack quickly explained to Sean how his girlfriend had baited him, that they'd had sex in the back seat, and that, he didn't think it was a good idea for Sean to marry her.

All the time Jack was talking to Sean, Cal had been nodding to add validity to what Jack was saying, while watching Sean's reaction to this bit of, what he was sure was, unwelcome news.

After Jack had finished, Sean stood there for a long moment, his jaw and fists clenching and unclenching, as he looked at first Cal, then Jack. Finally, he nodded and said, "that he was not surprised – come to think of it, he'd thought that she was too easy, and now he knew what kind of a girl she was – she was just using me, and I'm better off knowing now before they'd gotten married.

That was all he ever said about it, and the incident passed from our rearview mirror of life like so much dust in the wind, as he continued traveling from one adventure to the next.

Chapter 15.0

He was about to learn a new and very important lesson about life, one that had to do with associations. His two friends, Jack and Sean, were a couple of hard cases who apparently had dubious reputations and, most likely, were well known by the police where they came from. Having such friends can lead to trouble, not necessarily of your own making. It is known as "guilt by association". The old saying, "birds of a feather flock together," can spell real trouble for disassociated people, as well as for the birds.

It was during this time that Sean announced to Jack and Cal that the car's tires were so bald they were running the risk of having a flat at any time. Cal had noticed that whenever the car needed something, it became "their car" and, when Sean was flush, they found they had to remind him that they were all sharing in the car since they had all paid into its up keep.

At this time of the month, none of them had the money to buy new tires, so Sean came up with an idea which seemed brazen to him and, of course, dishonest. However, Cal didn't want to lose out on being able to use the car, so offered no objections to Sean's underhanded plan. He told them that their tires and those of another sailor's car, whom they all had little use for, were the same size as their car's. He went on to say that old Chuck was too dumb to figure it out and would more than likely figure that his tires had worn out prematurely and simply go out and buy a new set.

The only problem was, that old Chuck wasn't as dumb as he looked. Apparently, Sean had waited for Chuck to have the duty and then switched the tires and rims. Later, Sean informed them that he had made the switch, and again they had not raised an issue with what he'd done.

A few days went by, and suddenly Chuck accosted them about his tires being switched, and he knew from where. Of course, Sean shouted him down and told him to go suck an egg. His size alone was very intimidating, so Chuck went stomping off.

A weekend passed, and then the Master of Arms accosted each of them with the charges that had been brought against them, and they were told to prepare a statement of fact, involving this incident.

It seemed that old Chuck had gotten a hold of the tire dealership where he'd bought the tires, and they had recorded the serial numbers of each tire sold to Chuck and they matched the ones on Sean's car and the color of the rims also matched Chuck's car's color. It was cut and dried as far as he could see and he knew he was in "deep shit" as they say in the Navy when something goes drastically wrong. Cal knew that the car was not legally his and he had not participated directly in the crime. But he had prior knowledge of what Sean was about to do.

If it had been up to him to have made the switch, he would never have done it – he couldn't, but he was associated with those who did and by saying nothing about not doing it, he had, in effect, sanctioned it.

Sean came to Jack and Cal several times during the day and told them that they couldn't prove a thing and that if neither of them cracked, they'd be okay - they could beat this thing. For the life of him, he couldn't see how and told Jack as much.

Since they had not actually done the tire switching, they wouldn't be as culpable and hopefully, the "old man" would take this into account. For his part, he was deeply disturbed that he had been seduced into somehow believing that what he had sanctioned by his silence was okay. How far had he allowed his scruples to be compromised? What was he becoming – a petty thief?

He couldn't remember another time when he had been more disturbed or troubled than at this moment in his life.

He wrote a long statement, outlining the details of the incident and framed it with information about where he had come from and what the Navy had become to him and how he was willing to take his medicine for his involvement in this dishonorable act.

The day of their Captain's Mass came, and they all lined up before the Captain. He announced that he had read their statements and the Master of Arms spoke up in each of their defenses. When he came to Cal's defense, he was, he felt somewhat more passionate and articulate. The captain then asked each of them for a final statement. When his turn came, he simply said that he was very sorry for his lack of good judgment and stepped back.

He gritted his teeth as his name was read and listened as he was pronounced guilty and would have to serve 49-hours of extra duty and after one year of probation, the incident would be sponged from his record - if no further incidences occurred. A great load suddenly came off his shoulders, and he thanked God for answering his prayers.

Jack and Sean were reduced in rank and also had to perform extra duty. From that day forward, he had little to do with them. He had learned his lesson. Compared to the sentence that the Captain had handed down, the sentence, that the crew doled out, was even worse. He had been a part of stealing from a shipmate, and that was deemed unforgivable, at least for some time.

He did not try to defend his actions; he only listened to them as they braided him for his actions. He went about his business, serving out his extra duty, completing it just before arriving back in Little Creek. He again started hanging out with his old friends and redoubled his efforts at saving for the day he'd be able to buy a car.

This time when they pulled into Little Creek, he wished that Shelley was on the pier, he longed to be with her, to see her again. So it was that he made plans to see her once more. He knew that he had some leave coming and would put in for two weeks. He would spend a few days down there and fly up to see his family and then fly back, returning to the ship.

Along with the throngs of people waiting for them on the pier was JT's wife and family. And parked at the end of the pier was a long black limousine with JT's very pregnant girlfriend and dad, standing beside the car, watching for JT to come down the gangway and onto the pier.

JT was white as a sheet and visibly scared to death. He was wearing "dress whites", the uniform of the day, so we all knew he had liberty. Quickly the word was passed not to cover for him – let him take his medicine. However, he eventually found someone to take a message to his wife, stating that he had the duty and wouldn't be getting off until tomorrow night, and he would call letting them know the time and place that they could pick him up, off base. Word had it that he'd paid a handsome sum to get that message to her.

After the pier had cleared, the young girl's father approached the OD and asked about JT. He was told that he was not free to divulge any information on any of the crew.

Somehow JT managed to give them the slip and the following day he met up with his wife, off base. They never again, saw the limo.

On the way back from Savanna to their home base in Little Creek, the ship was fraught with so many engineering problems that it had to go on a tender for several weeks to make it sea worthy.

There was quite a flap over that, and so duty was limited again to cold-iron while a tremendous number of problems were resolved. This time it was the crew who had to make the repairs. Even so, in a matter of weeks, they had the ship back in tip-top shape. But before he could go on leave, the ship was sent to the Caribbean for a short tour of duty. In all, he'd see over 13-Caribbean tours and two Meds. Of all his time aboard the Fort, they'd be in the US a total of slightly over eight months out of the nearly five years of duty. Their saying was, "You Call, We Haul".

Finally, upon returning, he was granted leave and, in no time, he'd flown down to Greenville and was staying with Shelley's grandparents. Before he'd left Norfolk, he had a little side trip to make and a purchase. Shelley and he had been communicating by mail and phone for months. He loved to hear her voice, and she had a way of saying his name that nearly drove him nuts.

Shelley's grandparents were wonderful to him, and he had the run of the house. He kept them up to date about their plans (their comings and goings). His feelings for Shelley continued to grow. He couldn't wait to see her every day, after her X-ray classes.

The mornings were spent with her grandparents, Bo and Bess or with her Uncle Lewis and his wife Brenda. Afternoons, Shelley and he would take the car, which her dad (Arden) had loaned them, and they'd drive around seeing the sights.

He later learned from Shelley's grandparents that Shelley's dad never lent anyone anything, especially his car. It was sort of like seeing a miracle that Arden had loaned Cal his car, and a lot was made out of it around the family.

One day they were out driving and he took a right turn on this hardly used dirt road. He loved to take the road less traveled. The road twisted around and headed across a field and went toward the woods.

Suddenly, Shelley hollered, "Stop ... back up as fast as you can". He didn't question her as the tone in her voice said everything. As they backed up, she said one word, "Moonshiners".

After they were back on the main road, she said, "we'll likely get ourselves shot if we don't skedaddle out of these parts fast". He didn't need any further encouragement, and soon they were far down the road from that place. It was a long time before he took his eye off the rearview mirror.

Another time they were traveling along, and in the distance, he saw some men along the highway. He couldn't make out what was going on as they were still a long way off. Again, Shelley said in a voice that was all business, "chain gang - don't stop, don't look left or right and drive as if you have somewhere you got to get to yesterday". He did as she said, with the exception that he did look ... a little.

He had pretty good peripheral vision and saw, as they passed the men, that there were several men in black and white, stripped jail outfits with several more men with shot guns who were sitting on top of the trucks watching over them. They paid them scant attention, as they flew by.

Shelley proceeded to tell Cal some stories that she'd heard about how some people had gotten shot for stopping to ask directions from one of the guards.

They had thought they were stopping to help some prisoners to escape. After that story, he hoped that he never saw another chain gang.

The days seemed to fly by and, up to this point, he'd been happy just being with Shelley. He could sense that she was getting restless, but couldn't put his finger on a reason. The last couple days of his stay, Cal was overcome with the need for her; he felt that she was the one that he wanted to spend the rest of his life with and it was now or never – he had to tell her how he felt.

They were sitting on the swing in her uncle Bowie's yard, talking idly about this and that when he gently told her that he didn't have a lot of time to go out with her like normal guys might, taking her here and there, to court her properly. What he was trying to say was that they'd been calling and writing for some months now and he couldn't tell her how much it meant to him and how he really felt about her."

By now his tongue was getting so thick that he had all he could do to swallow. His heart was pounding, and he must have been breathing like a wind broke horse. She'd been holding his hand and looking into his eyes with those big blue trusting eyes of hers; her red hair framed the freckled face of a cherub as he stumbled over his words like a two-year-old. Finally, he just blurted it out and asked her to marry him. Before the sound of the question had died in his ears, she nodded her head, as she answered, "Yes".

He quickly told her that he'd ordered her a diamond ring, but he couldn't get it in time to bring it with him.

She said that it didn't matter, the important thing was that their feelings for one another were pure and unshakable, that she would be happy even if it were just a simple band of gold.

He was dizzy with the emotions that were washing over him. He bent toward her as they threw their arms around each other and kissed.

It felt so right, so special – he couldn't remember another time in his life that he'd been happier. There were the whirlwind meetings with her parents and them getting to know him better. Before he had been an oddity, a passing person in their daughter's life, but now he was someone to be reckoned with and a Yankee to boot. For most of the Old Timer's, the Civil War was still being fought - in the bars, barbershops and their homes, and a Yankee in their midst was fair game for pot shots. Her grandfather, no matter how many times he was "shushed", was bound to try and provoke him. Finally, on Thanksgiving Day, Cal looked him in the eye as he said, "Sir, if it were up to me, I'd have let you win the Civil war, cause you're such a poor loser".

You could have heard a pin drop, and the old man didn't say another word to him after that.

In spite of those who wished to fight the Civil War all over again, the rest of the family gave him a feeling of belonging, and it felt good. At long last, he would be part of a "whole" family, that was as good and caring as the one back home.

The following morning, Cal was talking with Shelley's grandparents, trying to draw them out – he yearned to know more about Shelley - what she was like as a little girl, some precious moments that he could cling to. They seemed strangely reluctant to say anything, though he didn't pick up on it at that time. Only in retrospect did he remember the mood of that moment. Her grandmother had hesitated and then reluctantly said, "*Shelley can be ... well, difficult at times, fiery, and well ... she'd paused before adding - be careful, she doesn't mean much about what she says when she gets upset*".

At the time, the sketchy words said with such care, didn't register ... not fully; all he could see was that beautiful face and those blue eyes and lips that drew him in. But he was soon to find out the other side of Shelley.

His nature, when he was happy, was to kid around and when he picked Shelley up, he felt particularly happy. After giving her a big hug and kiss, he said with a grin, "You won't believe all the good stuff I heard about you from your grandparents". He was totally unprepared for her retort as she, with the language of a seasoned sailor, launched into a string of profanities about how her grandparents had better learn to keep their big mouths shut. If there was anything she wanted him to know, she'd tell him". He couldn't have been more surprised if she'd picked up a shovel and hit him upside the head.

Quickly, he retrenched and told her that he'd only been kidding, that they hadn't told him anything. He was totally surprised at her reaction to his attempt to make a little humor and her strong feelings about no one telling him anything about her, puzzled him. He couldn't image what was so terrible, that she'd sworn everyone to secrecy.

She also had another quirk that surprised him. He had been raised in a loving environment, where the kids were referred to by all kinds of colorful eponyms. One of those had been, "cotton picker", as in "why you little cotton picker". Apparently, this was insulting to her, as she insisted that neither she nor any of her kin had ever picked cotton. To say that they had was just plain insulting. So he'd dropped it from his repertory of endearing sayings.

Not knowing what would or would not sit well with her, he adopted the philosophy of not kidding or using nicknames for her other than her own. This seriously cut into the spontaneous type of person he was, causing a slight personality shift. In spite of this, he was in love and so, he just swept this and other things under his romantic carpet.

The next morning, he'd packed and was ready to go to the airport. It was time to fly out and go north to see his Mother, brother, and sisters. It was time to tell them the good news.

He wanted to stay, he wanted to see Shelley again and to hold her close. He needed to feel her nearness more than anything, particularly at this moment.

The phone rang and Shelley's grandmother answered and then handed it to Cal. It was Shelley, full of tears, hardly able to talk, wishing him well and missing him already. He mentioned something about coming down to see her, but she said, "No, it was better for them not to, that he should just leave now – besides, he'd miss his plane if he weren't on his way." So they said their goodbyes.

He had never had a girl cry for him, at least not one that he loved. Yes, there'd been Penny, whom he'd met at the Great Lakes Training Center, but in his mind, she had only been a friend. This was different; he loved Shelley and wanted to be with her forever, and it tore him up to think that she loved him so much that she was crying at his leaving. He desperately wanted to hold her.

His body may have traveled home, but his heart remained with Shelley. He went through the motions of greeting family members over the next few days. The only high point was when he told them that he was engaged and all about Shelley and her family. In telling them about her, it hurt not having her near, to share in this important announcement. Now he only had the memories of all the great times they'd had together.

Upon returning to the ship, he learned that they were scheduled for another Med trip. It was like being sentenced to eight months of solitary confinement. He dreaded that trip, dreaded not being able to phone Shelley or to see her. He only had her letters, that were full of love and news about home and her training.

At each port, he bought her gifts and had them shipped to her. Then one day, he got a letter telling about how she'd gone out with a group of people and how much fun she had had and that their was another guy there - "how funny he had been and how much fun she had".

A terrible feeling gripped his heart, and he felt like his lungs were in a vice. He had to fight to breathe, to even stay upright. The pump room spun, around and around, and he was feeling sicker by the minute. He knew what was happening as surely as if he'd pulled the puppet's strings. The horrible thing about the whole thing was that he was powerless to do anything about it. He could only write back, telling her how distressed he was that she was going out – after all, they were engaged, that her seeing another man meant that she couldn't be thinking much of him.

The next letter from her was full of vehemence and simply stated that their engagement was over and that he would be getting a package from her with all the things he'd given her. The thing that surprised him all most as much as her breaking their engagement, was that she pleaded with him not to come back there again and not to make trouble for her. The letter also led him to believe that she had been seeing this fellow long before it was mentioned in her last letter.

He was stunned, the memories of her and all that they'd been to each other, her parents, uncles and aunts and all that had been said and done spun around in his head like so much dust in a whirlwind. His first thought was that he wanted to get back there – if he could only see her, he could work this thing out. Even though he knew that he couldn't get emergency leave, he tried. He went to the OD and pleaded his case. The OD sympathized with him but said that it would have to be a life or a life-threatening problem and that they would have to be notified by the Red Cross before he would be granted leave. He was trapped like a dog in a tub in the middle of the ocean; he could now understand how guys could, and did, throw valuable wedding rings over the side of the ship and how they could hang themselves in a Paint Locker. Women have no idea what it's like to be on board a war ship thousands of miles away from family and friends and to get a "Dear John" letter. What it does to a man is akin to killing him emotionally. Some cannot handle it and they never recover.

For days, he went through his private hell. To be so in love and feel so much a part of another person and then to be told, "that you're not good enough to wait on, that you were not as much fun to be with as their new guy. How can you fight that, how can you show them that they're dead wrong?" A part of him shouted, "you never gave me a chance". But all he heard was the echoes of memories, laughter, and tears and after a while, these faded away in the distance of time, but not forgotten.

A week later a package arrived from Shelley. He knew what was in it and took it unopened, down to the Main Control Engine Room and stored it away in the Gyro space, back in an obscure corner. He couldn't bear to open it, to look at the things he'd bought her, to remember the smiles, the warm embraces, all the special times – then the Dear John letter. He was not strong enough yet. So it would sit for months, hidden away until one day one of the guys told him that it would have to be moved as they were going to have a Zone Inspection. He knew he had no room for it as it was and would have to open it and store the items in the personal drawer in his locker until he could send the things on home.

He'd written home telling his mother about their break up and, of course, she tried to console him, but strangely enough this time her words of kindness only served to further exasperate the rawness of his nerves. He guessed, of the "five stages of grief", he was going through the "hate stage" of getting over her.

He suddenly felt as if he was the victim, used and abused – tricked and now he was being laughed at. Even so, he still wanted to see her - one more time – he longed for closure. But it was not to be, and like most things, time and a new relationship does wonders to heal a wounded heart.

In the many times that he mentally reviewed their time together, he came to the conclusion that he was better off – that he had missed the bullet. Given her temper and his love of joking around, their marriage wouldn't have lasted. *Surely, God in His infinite wisdom had other plans for him.*

Chapter 16.0

Letters had started coming more frequently from Kinsey. He had told her about meeting Shelley and about their engagement. She'd been full of encouragement and then later, supportive after the breakup.

After several months, he'd finally come to terms about Shelley and had put that part of his life behind him, a fact that he'd shared with Kinsey.

He had moved on to other things, one of which was obtaining a car. He had told Kinsey about his plans to buy a car and, after saving for it, having the money stolen. Again she was supportive. He was devastated, remembering how hard it had been saving for it. After figuring out how many more "pays" he'd get before the end of the cruise and deducting his expenses, he went on a crash savings program to again try and save up the six to eight hundred dollars he'd need to buy the car, as he had no past financing experience in borrowing money.

It was tough not treating himself to the occasional ice cream or Coke and having to pass up all the super buys that were offered from time to time in the Ship's Store. But slowly, pay by pay, Cal restored his savings. By the time they arrived back in Little Creek, he'd saved enough to buy a plane ticket to Allentown, Pa., some traveling cash and enough to buy the car and insurance.

Step by step, he shared his plans, hopes, and fears with Kinsey. In one of her letters, she'd asked him to come by and see her after he bought his car and he promised he would.

Later, he could have kicked himself for making such a promise, all he really wanted was to buy the car, drive home, and see his family. It had been months since he'd seen his Mom and siblings. Having a car, would help Cal feel like a man of substance. The car would represent a freedom Cal had never known. He could draw a mental line that denoted a change in self-esteem between before the car and after the car. Before the car, although he felt that he had worth among his shipmates, he still lacked that extra something that gave him true independence, that special feeling of autonomy.

Cal had heard the guys on the ship talking about a great place to buy cars. Some were actually making money on the side buying cars up there, driving them back to the base and selling them. He had to know more about this place. He found out that it was called Reedman's, located in Langhorne, Pa. Cal looked on the map of Pa. and found it near Allentown. He called the airline and bought a one-way ticket. It was very reasonable as long as he flew "Military Standby" – which meant traveling in uniform. His leave had been approved without hesitation, and he had made E5 while at sea and with it, not only came a nice raise but, also more clout. He was now a man of means and could easily afford a car.

For the first time, in a long time, he felt empowered; he had money in his pocket, a plane ticket in his hand, 15-days leave, and he was headed for good times and adventure. He couldn't believe that in a matter of a couple of days, he'd own his own car - his very first car! He felt like he'd "arrived". No more excuses for not having a car, not having enough money, not having enough to eat, and not being on par with the best of his old school classmates. He had arrived, "Look out world, here I come!" Cal felt like shouting.

The plane touched down in Allentown on Sunday afternoon. He knew that Reedman's wouldn't be open on a Sunday, so opted to go to a motel - the closer, the better. Since he didn't want to stay at an expensive one in town, needing to save every dime he could, he was looking for an inexpensive place nearby.

Cal spotted a sign that read, *"This way to the Airport Motel bus,"* so he picked up his luggage and off he went. He noticed as he got in the car the motel had sent, that it was full of airline hostesses. In fact, it was so full he was sure there was no room for him and was prepared to wait for another car. However, the girl next to the door got out and pointed to him to sit where she'd been sitting and asked if he minded if she sat on his lap. Cal was so surprised at her request that he didn't have a chance to speak, as she pushed him down into the seat, then sat on his lap and closed the door.

Even so, there still wasn't much room, as he was practically sitting on top of the girl next to him. It didn't take but a moment before Cal started to feel very warm. It didn't help any that she'd shifted her behind slightly, presumably to get more comfortable, but it was having a curious effect on him.

He could feel how soft she felt and she smelled good too. One of the other girls jokingly said, "Gee, Mary gets all the luck, " and another girl said, "Hey, if you get tired of sitting on his lap, I'd be happy to trade places," to which they all laughed.

Having so many young and extremely attractive looking women in such close proximity unnerved him. One on one he could probably have held his own, but this many, he couldn't concentrate on all the vibes he was getting, so switched his concentration to the car he'd soon be driving.

A voice suddenly broke into his thoughts as the girl next to him asked where he was going. He told them that he was going to Reedman's to buy a car and expected to be driving it to upstate NY. They seemed intrigued by the idea, and several of them told him that they wished they were not flying out tomorrow, so they could go too. Cal was just as glad, that they couldn't, as their presence would have been too distracting – he had to concentrate on what he was doing to negotiate the best possible deal, so he just nodded and smiled.

After getting to the motel and checking in, he noticed a small swimming pool just outside his window. There was only one girl reading in one of the lounges as she sunbathed, so he felt this would be a good time to take a quick dip and also get some sunshine.

He remembered ruefully that there was no sunshine five decks down in the engineering spaces on board the ship and he was sure if he didn't get some sun, he'd soon look so pale, that everyone would think he'd been in jail.

It didn't take long to slip his uniform off and put his swimming suit on. It was one that he'd purchased while in the Virgin Islands. He was still darkly tanned and muscular from working out on the ship and diving. Weight lifting and body building had become a passion of his, and he'd been working out with Nick for the past two years – they spent hours pushing each other to do more and more weight.

Nick had been working as a body builder, most of his life and was ripped – the closest living thing Cal had ever seen to a picture of Sampson, with his black wavy hair framing a chiseled, square copper toned face. He was Italian and could easily have passed as an enforcer for the mob.

Cal grabbed a magazine off the rack on the way out of his room and walked silently over to the pool, opened the gate and went in. The girl he'd seen seemed deeply involved in her magazine. He bent over and laid his magazine down on a reclining chair only a few feet from hers, and went over to the diving board, took a couple of measured steps and dove into the pool. As an experienced diver he liked to enter the water clean; without so much as causing a ripple. The water felt refreshing, not too warm or too cold. He could hear the buzz of the filtration pump through the water as it gurgled around him. At the end of the arc, he felt the bottom brush his under arm as he propelled himself through its depths with long powerful strokes.

To him, this was child's play compared to some of the training he'd had before being embedded on the ship, where the Naval Department had told him if he was ever needed, he'd be activated. He knew that he would always be subject to recall until his enlistment time had been completed and that meant his Reserve time at the end of his active duty hitch.

Suddenly he felt the bottom pitch upward, and he broke the surface on the other side of the pool. He rolled effortlessly over on his back and, out of the corner of his eye, looked toward the side from which he'd come and caught the girl watching him. When she saw his gaze meet her's, she abruptly raised her magazine and continued to read. He could tell she was self-absorbed or shy and didn't want to visit and that was okay because his mind was on other things.

He'd no sooner made himself comfortable and started thumbing through the magazine when he heard voices and laughter behind him. Usually, he didn't sit with his back undefended and even now, it felt uncomfortable. Turning, he noted several good-looking girls in bathing suits coming toward the pool. Again, he went back to cruising through the pages, looking for articles about cars, specifically, 59 Chevys.

After a while, he was startled by one of the girls addressing him. She asked if he was the guy whose lap she'd sat on during their ride to the motel, to which Cal answered, "Well, it depends on how many guys laps you've been sitting on". To whit, they all broke out laughing at her.

He was happy to have scored one – usually, he was lost in his own thoughts, so wouldn't have responded so glibly, to her query. Nodding, Cal smiled, enjoying his moment in the sunshine. Then he, as a mock gesture, apologized for any discomfort he might have caused her, smiling mischievously as he nodded in her direction. Again, they laughed approvingly, glad to see that someone was her match and they laughingly told her so. Once the laughter had subsided, she again, asked him about the kind of car he was going to buy and about his trip and plans. When they found out that he was single and alone and that he had no plans for supper, they all wanted him to join them for some "good times".

The prospect of being out with so many girls horrified him – he couldn't begin to tune into all of them and answer all their questions. He knew he would go into a total melt down, and besides, he didn't have enough money to pay for everyone's meals and "good times" and still be able to buy his car. So, he declined their offer of supper and some "good times" afterward, whatever they may have meant by that, and got up to escape to the peace and quiet of his room. Cal said, "got to get my beauty rest, leaving early tomorrow for Langhorne". As he left, he heard some moaning and a couple of cat calls and just waved over his back as he proceeded through the door and into the motel.

It was cool and quiet in there, just what he needed to wind down from being at sea. His nerves were still jingling from the flight and planning the logistics of getting to Reedman's to buy the car, fix anything that might be wrong with it and still have enough money to cover traveling expenses and, most importantly, having enough to be able to get back to the ship. That was all-important, as he remembered the military trainers drilling it into their heads, that being AWOL was about as bad as it gets. They had also said, that if you're ever under orders and come back after the ship has left, go immediately to the Shore Patrol Head Quarters, check in, and you'll be okay.

As for a place to keep the car, he'd already figured that out. He had a place to park it on base, and when he was out to sea, he'd made arrangements to park it at Leroy and Sherri's place.

Cal knew that there was always the unexpected, so he had to watch himself closely to not spend himself into a hole. He must have counted his money a hundred times just to be sure that he wouldn't short himself. He knew he was limited to only 600-dollars on the car's purchase price, anything over that and he wouldn't be able to stop off and see Kinsey, go home or afford to support himself for two weeks without cutting back somewhere.

He put his money back in the envelope he'd been carrying since leaving the ship and put the rubber band back around it. He debated whether to put it in with his undershorts in the duffle bag or in the pillowcase under the pillow where he slept. The last thing he wanted was to be robbed again. The under-the-pillow option won out. He knew that he was a light sleeper and if anyone tried to dislodge the pillow, he'd immediately wakeup.

Cal heard laughter outside his window, and got up to peek around the curtains and see what was going on. A group of airline hostesses, still in bathing suits, were gathered between the pool and his room talking very animatedly. Then suddenly, one of them looked in his direction and pointed as she spoke to the girl who'd sat next to him in the airport motel car. Then another girl pushed her toward his patio door.

Cal's heart stuck in his throat as he recoiled from the window and held his breath, as a timid knock resounded through the silence of his room.

What should he do? If he answered the door, they'd be at him again about going out. Better to have them believe he was sleeping or just out somewhere. After a couple of more knocks, they went away, and all was quiet.

He laid on top of his bed watching the shadows creep across the walls as the sun went down. The silence was only punctuated by the sound of airplanes taking off and landing scarcely a mile away and, the occasional sound of someone coming and going from the adjacent rooms. The only thing he could think of was getting his car; nothing was going to get in the way of his goal.

Cal had lived for years for this very moment, ever since being stuck on the farm, landlocked, without transportation - short of using his bike or the generosity of a relative, neighbor or friend. He had few opportunities to go anywhere. There was no independence, no freedom - not in its truest form. When Cal did need to go to a social function, he'd been forced to borrow or rent a car, but now that was all about to change.

It was 1963; he'd studied all the cars on the market and liked the 59-Chevy the best. It looked good, rode good and was big enough to live in. He'd read the Motor Trend Reports that claimed it fish-tailed when making sudden stops and was sloppy on corners, but Cal knew that was largely due to the light duty shocks that came stock. They were far too light for the car's weight. The first thing he intended to do was to change the shocks to heavy-duty road handlers like the stock cars used. He also intended to have it tuned up, and a set of Uni-Royal Rain Tires put on it. They were guaranteed not to hydroplane.

Cal must have dozed off, as suddenly he was awakened by a thumping sound. At first, he didn't know where or what was making the sound. He was on his feet like a cat, ready for anything. It was all a part of his training.

It was dark as coal in his room, so if someone was trying to break in, Cal knew he'd have the advantage. Slowly he moved across the floor, feeling his way until he was standing behind the door, should it open. Holding his breath, he listened for even the slightest sound. All they had to do was to jimmy the lock, and he'd know what he was going to do next. With his knees slightly bent, his right shoulder lowered and his hand down near his knee, he was ready. Then he heard it again - another thump, followed by nervous laughter.

Cal slowly let his breath out in a long even release as he'd been trained to do. It was the girls again, no doubt back from having a few drinks and wanting to party some more – probably at his expense. The knocking came once more, and then they moved on. He could hear doors opening and closing and more laughter on each side of his room and across the hall. Cal realized he was in the middle of a bunch of party hungry airline hostesses looking for a good time and, he couldn't care less. He knew that, had it been the guys back on the ship, they'd have been all over those girls like bees on honey.

Leaving the lights out so as not to attract their attention, he took his dress whites off and folded them neatly along with his jumper. These he placed under his mattress, so in the morning they'd be freshly pressed. This was a short cut he learned back in his boot camp days. His underwear, he dumped unceremoniously into his ditty bag[55] and threw it back into the corner of his duffle bag, for future laundering. Then, thinking about whether he'd have time to do them later, he decided to do his laundry as he showered. He could hang the stuff on a line he carried by stringing it across the bathroom, and it'd be dry by morning.

---

[55] Laundry bag

Once in the bathroom with the door closed, he turned the light on knowing no one could see it. The last thing he wanted was to have the girls knocking on his door again. He slowly ran the water, filling the sink and lathered up the hand soap, then briskly moved his hands back and forth over his shorts and shirt until they were all lathered up, then he took them off and left them to soak in the sink as he finished showering.

Remembering the bathroom exhaust and heat timer, he twisted it, then stepped back into the shower and pulled the curtains closed. Just as he'd finished soaping up, he heard the shower come on next to his and felt a temperature shift. He was used to that on the ship, so didn't give it much thought, other than to think that barely a few inches away, was a naked girl, showering alongside him. Then he heard a tap, tap sound – he stopped for a moment and listened, wondering what it meant. Was it something to do with the water system or was it something she was doing on the other side of the wall between them, like adjusting the water pattern? After a moment it came again, like some kind of a signal, waiting to be answered. Part of him wanted to tap back, and another part said, "No," leery of what would come next. He was inexperienced in such matters, and he also knew that because he was a sailor, every girl thought that he was somehow endowed with all the knowledge known to man about how to satisfy a women and leave them begging for more – or so the guys told him. There was no way that he could live up to that kind of expectation. Sure he had read a couple of skin books and had some ideas about it, but nothing that came close to practical experience.

So he let the knocking go unanswered and quickly finishing his shower, turned off the temperature controller and silently dried himself with the oversized motel towel. He absently wondered how many other airline hostesses had used the same towel as he drew it back and forth over his shoulders and then lower. Momentarily he stopped drying himself, to smell the towel; he didn't want to be using it if it had the slightest "used smell". But it smelled fresh, not musty or moldy, so he figured that it must have been well laundered before it had been put in his room.

Silently as possible, he washed, rinsed and wrung his clothes out and then strung them up across the bathroom to dry. Next, he laid out his civilian clothes for the next day. Since he wasn't traveling the airlines, he wouldn't need to wear his uniform.

The rest of the evening was uneventful. He watched a little TV, but kept it as low as possible to still hear it. He didn't want to disturb anyone or cause more knocking on his door. After an hour or so, he tired of the TV and turned it off and went to sleep.

By 5 am he was up, showered, shaved and dressed. He checked out and ate something from one of the machines in the front as he waited for his ride back to the airport. From there he'd grab a bus to Langhorne.

It was Monday morning, and there was bustling everywhere with people checking out and rushing ahead to make their flights. Everywhere he looked, there were airline people. He never knew there could be so many good-looking girls in one place. After waiting for what seemed like forever, a car came and the same guy who had brought him out grabbed his bag and put it in the trunk, just as several girls walked up. He recognized them as the girls that had ridden out to the motel the day before and, along with them, was the one who sat on his lap. He could feel the color rising in his face.

The driver graciously opened the door and stepped back to allow them to enter the car. The one who had sat on his lap, grabbed his hand and pulled him in beside her. As she slid in next to the driver, she said, "you're sitting with me".

He was surprised by the move and the laughter it evoked from the others, but went along with it good-naturedly. She asked him where he was off to today and when he told her, she wished him well in finding a good buy.

All of them seemed oddly interested in where he was going and if he'd gotten enough sleep last night. They mentioned that they had come by and knocked, but he must have been tooooo exhausted to hear them.

He caught their smirks and knowing smiles, but decided to play dumb. He nodded in agreement and apologized for not being awake to hear them. Then one of them turned toward him and whispered, "how was your shower last night"?

So she was the one that had been showering next to him. He replied, "oh, it was great; even had time to do laundry - though the pipes in the place must be really old, as they kept making noises".

They all laughed at this. His ploy had worked, and the monkey was off his back. Now they all knew that one of them had been trying to gain his attention by "pipe talking". *"No telling where that might have led had he answered it,"* he thought. Each of them picked that tidbit up and ran with it, kidding each other about past experiences using the pipe knocking ploy.

In a matter of minutes, they were back at the airport. However, before he had a chance to get out, the girl next to him gave his hand a squeeze and whispered, "good luck with the car and if you're ever this way, ask for Suzie McKenzie, someone will know where I am or where I can be reached", and his hand came away with a piece of paper in it.

He got out of the car and held the door for Suzie, watching as she slid across the seat. He didn't know if it was because of the dissimilar fabrics (the seat and her dress) or if she was trying to give him a covert message, but a lot of leg and more was showing by the time she made it out the door. Like the gentleman his mother had raised, he turned his head and made like he hadn't noticed, even though a flush was spreading through his body like a fire through dry hay.

As soon as she stood up and cleared the door, he shut it. The driver got their bags from the trunk and handed them out like lunch to school children, calling out their names from each tag.

Suzie waited next to him until her name was called and then walked over and took it. She turned around one last time and winked at him. He was amazed and totally unsure of what to do or say. He'd never had a girl hit on him like she had. So he nodded, waved and then smiled at her as he put his hand in his pocket, releasing the piece of paper that she'd given him as he started walking toward the shuttle bus service.

After asking for directions, he was soon on the bus that would take him to Langhorne and Reedman's car dealership. He was so excited that he could hardly stand it. He looked anxiously out the window watching every sign, hopeful that he wouldn't, somehow miss it. Before long the bus stopped, and the driver looked over at him and winked as he pointed across the street.

Earlier, he'd shared with him where he was headed, and he had nodded – so he was reassured that he was indeed on the right bus. Apparently, he'd remembered his asking and now was letting him know they were there. On the way off the bus, he reached over and shook the driver's hand and wished him a blessed day. The driver smiled and wished him the same.

The road was wide, over six lanes and divided by an island median. He jumped off and the dust from the bus, as it accelerated, blew his hair down over his eyes and laid a layer of dirt over his clean, short sleeved shirt and blue jeans, turning them momentarily a light shade of gray.

With the smell of diesel fumes still burning in his nose, he picked his way across the street, dodging a few cars that were no doubt carrying their passengers to work. Panting, he stopped to catch his breath, finally arriving in front of a huge sign, which read "Reedman's". The sign in front of the automobile dealership, although as large as a transit bus, didn't betray the true size of the business, which he was about to enter.

As the front door closed behind him, he was struck by the speed in which he was waited on. Immediately, a man in a dress suit asked if he could help him, "Yes," Cal replied, "I want to buy a used car". The man then asked him what price range, and he replied, "Five to six-hundred.

The man motioned for him to go to the door to his right and that a cab would be by momentarily to pick him up. "Tell him what make and price range you want, and he'll take you right to them."

He did as he was directed and before he got to the door, a cab pulled up outside with Reedman's painted on the side. "Talk about service," he thought, and to think that they have their own cab fleet too.

He got in and told the driver the price range and model, and before he'd finished, they were off in a cloud of dust. In a few minutes, they'd pulled up in front of one of many car lots, each having the make and cost range printed on a large sign. There were Impalas, Biscayne's, and Chevy's of all makes filling the lot. Some cars were in rough condition, others like new. He pretty much knew what he was looking for, so he got out and walked over to the first car that caught his eye. It was a four-door, white Chevy Biscayne. Nothing fancy, he didn't have the bucks for an Impala; they were sportier and therefore more costly.

A thin layer of dust had settled over all of them from the dirt roads that ran around the lots. He looked at several more but kept coming back to the first one he'd seen. It seemed to have the lowest miles and looked the best for the money. He did notice that the tires were nearly bald and it needed cleaning. The sign said that all the cars were "as is" on the lot, but that any discrepancies noted, would be fixed after the sale.

He looked up toward the small shed and raised his hand. One of the men got up and came down with a big yellow tag. He asked Cal his name and address, home phone number and working address, and then directed him to a building a short distance away. He told him to go in there, and he'd be directed through the process of buying the car and that it would be waiting for him in the "Sold Lot" when he was done.

"*Sure he thought,*" he'd heard about these long waits at other car dealerships.

The day was uncommonly hot, but once he'd walked through the door, he noted gratefully that it was as cool as a fall day and all his tensions drained away.

A young girl with long black hair, shouldering a wraparound smiled, asked him as soon as he entered if he was financing or paying cash.

He said, "Cash", and smiled back at her.

She pointed to the yellow line and said, "Follow it". Her smile seemed to follow him down the hall as he followed the yellow line, much the same way that the little girl followed the Yellow Brick Road with Toto in the Wizard of Oz.

Somehow, as soon as he'd told them his name, they knew what he was buying and gave him a receipt for his money. When asked if he had his own insurance or not. He said, "Not" and they directed him to another line. After buying the temporary insurance to cover him for a couple of weeks, which he felt was enough time to see Aden in the Point, where he'd buy his own car policy. He remembered that he was Grandfather's best friend and everyone bought their insurance from Aden. There just wasn't any other way of thinking.

The place was bustling with activity, there were people in lines all over the place – but it was efficient, and things were getting done. He must have been in there a total of 30-minutes, and he was done. He had his temporary registration, temporary car insurance, papers of ownership, receipt, and a conditional warranty.

Just as he signed the last forms, a man came up to him and quickly went over all that they'd done: washed and cleaned the car inside and out, put new tires on it, tuned the engine and changed the oil and filter. The only thing they hadn't done was to change out the shocks – sighting that they were not worn out to the point of having to be changed. Otherwise, it was fit to go and so was he.

He couldn't believe the difference when he saw the car. It looked brand new, as it sat there gleaming in the late morning sun. He couldn't have been prouder if he'd just had a baby. His chariot to the stars was waiting for him, and a new adventure lay just around the next bend in the road. Never again would he be tied to looking at the same piece of real estate with no way out. He tossed his bag into the trunk and watched as it almost disappeared into its voluminous depths. The trunk was big enough to hold a queen size mattress.

As soon as the temporary plates were installed, the man shook his hand, gave him the keys and told him it was a pleasure doing business with him. A feeling like none he had ever had settled over him – free at last – thank God, I'm free at last. It was a dream come true.

Chapter 17.0

He looked the car over from stem to stern and popped the hood and took another look. It looked clean, radiator hoses weren't cracked, and he couldn't feel any soft spots, likewise with the plug wires, there weren't any signs of dry rot. He pulled the dip stick, and the oil was clear, and all the engine's gaskets appeared to be dry - not showing any oil stains which would be a clue that the gaskets were failing. The doors all opened and closed easily, and the seats felt comfortable, no matter where he sat.

He walked around the car looking for any sign that it had been in an accident, and saw none. He checked the exhaust pipe – black meant it was burning oil, the rings might be bad, but it was gray, which meant good combustion, showing an efficient use of fuel. He also gave the tail pipe a kick to be sure there were no broken pipe connectors – it was stiff.

He got behind the wheel, the inside of the car smelled okay, no smell of mildew. Then he started the engine. It sounded smooth and didn't smoke. Not bad he thought for a four-year-old car with just over 60-thousand miles.

Next, he unfolded the road map and looked at his route out of town. He'd promised Kinsey that he'd swing by her house before going home, a promise he now regretted having made. He could have kicked himself for ever making it, as every cell in his body wanted to point the car north and get on with his trip. But he'd promised, and promises to him were sacred. He'd learned at a young age, that a man was only as good as his word – grandfather had taught him that and he was a respected man, and that was what Cal wanted – respect.

So, after plotting his route west through Pennsylvania to Cumberland, he was off. The car drove well and felt good. It had lots of pick up and cruised easily along Pennsylvania's flat roads and gentle hills. After a few hours, the hills started to become big hills and then mountains, and he started noticing how the car was becoming increasingly lethargic. After a while, it took almost all his gas pedal to get up the hills and, added to that, the engine temperature gauge was rising. As luck would have it, after descending into the next valley, a large service center came into view on his right. It was a large, white concrete block building with four stalls and a waiting room. Over each stall, painted in large red letters were the words: Lube, Tires, Muffler and Tune-up.

Without hesitation, he swung into it determined to find out what was wrong with his car. He knew that it probably needed a thorough tune up – plugs changed, new points and the timing adjusted. After telling the service rep how the car was performing; its lack of power and overheating, he nodded and said that they'd fix it and have it back to being as good as new.

He was sick over the fact that his new car was not running as he'd hoped. He also told them to put a new set of extra heavy-duty shocks (Road Masters) on it. He remembered what the article in the Motor Trend Magazine had said about the car pitching on corners, and he knew that he needed to be making better time, and not having to hold back on the treacherous mountain curves.

While they were working on it, he roamed around the place. They had a sales department displaying all kinds of gadgets for cars and trucks. He saw a small compass and bought it. It was the kind that mounted to the windshield or dash, and it didn't cost that much. He knew it would come in handy, especially when he hit a road junction that had a route number but no compass indicators posted, so inevitably it was always a 50/50 chance whether he'd be going in the right direction – north, south, east or west. The device even had a light in it for night driving. By the time he'd finished looking around and bought a snack and Coke, the car was ready.

They'd installed the new shocks and rebalanced the tires, tuned the engine (new plugs, points, flushed the radiator, changed the thermostat, put new coolant in and replaced all the old radiator hoses). The car had had a thorough going over, and they told him that it should do him for a long time.

Since he was a serviceman, they went easy on the bill, so it came to only 96-dollars – a lot of money in those days, but it was worth it for all the work they'd done.

He was grateful for the break, as his money was going faster than he'd anticipated. He paid the man and was anxious to get back on the road. Mentally, he was timing his trip, figuring he'd arrive in Cumberland sometime in the late PM, check out where she lived, get a room, get up early, drop by and say, "hi" and be on his way in a couple of hours. That way, he'd have fulfilled his promise. He had much better things to do than to waste his time on this young girl.

He was mentally scolding himself for having anything to do with her – after all, he was spending money that he didn't need to, coming all the way out here, just to keep a promise. But a promises was a promise and he was duty bound to keep it.

He hit the gas pedal, as he'd been accustomed to and a loud screeching sound immediately erupted in his ears as the car leaped forward like it had been shot out of a cannon.

He was almost giddy with its new found power. Now he was able to fly up the mountain roads as if they weren't even there. It gave him a whole new feeling of power. Power to go anywhere and do anything. Taking corners was no longer a problem as the car hung tight to every curve like a cat on rails. Now driving was nothing but sheer joy and he bent into it like a man on a mission. The radio was on, playing Thunder Road, and he was the man straightening out all the curves as he blew through one valley after the next.

He never dreamed it was so easy to go so fast in his life and the feeling of the air blowing through his hair was beyond words. "*God, this was living, and he loved every minute of it*".

As he drove west through Pennsylvania and later dropped down into Cumberland, he noticed how low the sun was, in fact, it would be setting in a couple of hours. He reluctantly stopped for gas and to check his oil and radiator level. They were good, and there were no signs of leaks from any of the new hoses. He was relieved that the engine had been running cool since the flushing, and the new thermostat certainly was helping to maintain an even engine temperature.

He grabbed another bite to eat, being careful not to get his dress whites dirty. He'd decided to put them back on at the garage where he'd had the car fixed. He wanted to save his civvies for later, figuring that he could get his "whites" washed anytime.

It was after 2100 hrs. when he pulled into Cumberland also known as the Hub City, according to the City Limit sign. It was an old manufacturing town by all accounts, clawing its way into the late 19th Century. He was hard pressed to see a new house, or an updated one for that matter anywhere. It looked like a town that was hanging on for dear life to whatever meager existence that could be wrung out of whatever resources that were available.

Given the number of railroad tracks running through it and the size of its rail yards, he guessed that it was a major transfer point between the rail-lines to the east – west, north, and south.

As he bumped along over pot holes and man hole covers that stuck up inches higher than the surrounding pavement and over part brick and part macadam streets, he strained to see the names on street signs, of which most were non-existent. Some were even bent backward around the post, no doubt the work of a bored juvenile or a drunk snowplow driver.

He had no idea where he was in relationship to New Town Road, so stuck his head out the window and asked a guy, that he'd noticed standing on the corner.

He told him, "to keep going down the street, along the railroad tracks, turn left at the end of the block then right and keep going and he couldn't miss it".

Sounded simple enough, Cal reasoned, now to find out. Just as he told him - he made each turn and then went straight and as he strained to see the names on the street signs in the darkness, he suddenly noticed that they all read "New Town Road". Now to figure out which house was hers.

He poked along as slow as he dared without incurring the wrath of the natives, as he looked at the two story homes that lined both sides of the street. It was difficult to see the numbers in the dark - some didn't even have numbers. Finally, after making two passes, he saw it next to a small filling station and across the street from a film processing business. Well at least he knew now, where to go tomorrow and that would save some time, time that he could use on the road going home. He felt that since it was after 2100 hrs. (9 pm), fast closing in on 2200 (10 pm) that it was not a proper time to be dropping in on a young girl and her family.

Cal went back up the street the way he'd come, but instead of swinging back down the hill again, he elected to turn up the hill. This brought him around to the left surprisingly enough, and after traveling a short distance, he pulled into another filling station. He had the man top his tank off, as he got out to stretch and visit for a moment which was his nature. The attendant asked him where he was from and he told him the ship he was stationed on and the base and added that he'd been invited to stop by to see an old friend.

After a moment, he started to laugh, and since Cal was the curious type, he asked him what was so funny. As he finished topping the tank off, Cal handed him a five, and he said, "Well, that's the third time those girls have gone around this block, you're quite the attention getter". Surprised, Cal asked, "why's that"? "Well, we don't get many sailors up here - long ways from the sea", he said with a cocked eyebrow.

This time the service attendant waved at them as they passed and they all laughingly waved back. Cal had no desire to encourage them, so he turned and asked him about a place to stay. The attendant pointed across the street at a non-assuming building with an old, faded sign that read, "RR Boarding House" as he said, "not much for looks, but it's cheap and clean".

"You're singing my song", Cal said, as he thanked him and got into the car. He liked the way it gleamed under the station's lights, and it looked like it was going 90-miles an hour, just standing still.

He drove down the street and around the next building and parked behind it. Grabbing his duffle bag, he locked the car and bolted up the creaky old steps and opened the heavy oak door. The hinges squawked as it opened, announcing his presence as well as any doorbell.

An old, unshaven, partially bald man with kinky wire hair, sitting behind the aged oak counter said in a gruff voice, "Yes".

"Can I have a room for the night", he asked. The hotel keeper, nodded as he swung the register around for Cal to sign and then he wanted to know the make, model and license plate number of Cal's car.

Cal hadn't memorized it yet, and started to turn to go get it, but was interrupted with, "don't bother, I'll just put a number in there". In a moment, he handed him the keys to his room and said, "First on the right, top of the stairs".

Cal thanked him, grabbed his stuff and swiftly ascended the faded, badly worn carpeted stairs. With each step they squeaked, making a different sound. Absently, he wondered how many hundreds of feet had trod those steps over the years.

Cal inserted the key into the door lock; it could have been opened with a skeleton key, he noticed. It, like its predecessor, squeaked as it opened and again as he closed it.

The room smelled old, like the upstairs in their old farm house – it brought back memories of home and how much he missed his Mom and the rest of the family.

He was restless and again wanted to be on his way. For a moment he hedged on whether to stay or not. He knew that if he left now, he could be home by morning. He could make up some kind of excuse why he couldn't make it, and she'd be none the wiser. But something inside him said, "No ... you promised, now keep your word". He could have sworn that it was Grandfather's voice and it wasn't the first time that he'd heard it. Often when he was looking for the right answer to a problem, he heard his grandfather's voice advising him.

He quickly took the room in at a glance. It had twin windows with dark velvet curtains and black shades to block the sun or to give more privacy. The bed was visibly lumpy, the carpet old and faded from what appeared to have been hundreds of years of usage. The wallpaper's design had long ago lost its definition, and in places, it was even threatening to come lose from the old plaster walls.

The bathroom was also showing its age. The walls were tiled like a greyhound bus station. The sink, a single post with 18-century fixtures and a tub that looked like it'd served as a part time cattle dip.

He walked over to the dusty window and looked out. He could see part of the cobblestone street he'd traveled, but most of the view was obscured by the roof on the aged building next door.

Again, he washed the clothes he'd worn that day, hung them up, and piled into bed. The springs in the old bed made an unearthly noise with each movement he made – he could only imagine what it must sound like if someone was having sex.

Soon he was asleep; the events of the day washing over him like the sea over a beach at high tide.

Outside the hotel, a black limousine sat. It had followed him from the airport to Reedman's. The man inside had observed his purchase, followed him to the garage and then to Cumberland, always keeping a discrete distance.

"It appears that our young man is coming up in the world – becoming his own man, as it were," he said in a British accent to no one in particular, though the driver heard him and nodded in agreement. He made his customary notes and then returned the file to its alligator clad brief case, momentarily patting the side. He then said to the driver, "I believe it's time for us to find lodging, as we'll need to rise early to keep up with our young man".

The service had conditioned Cal to rising early. Long before sunrise he was up and dressed, packed and ready to check out, later that morning.

He drove by her house a couple of times, very slowly, weighing the pros and cons of whether to park or just keep going. Finally, he parked in the lot next to her house and waited until 07:00 hours (7 am). It was Tuesday morning, the sky was clear and not a breath of air was stirring or a single person. Occasionally a car drove by barely making a sound.

The time seemed to drag unrelentingly. Cal listened to the radio but, found nothing on it that didn't bore him. He tapped his fingers on the steering wheel; even it seemed to beg to be on its way. Surely by this time, they'd all be up.

Finally, Cal moved the car and parked right out front of her home. He'd practiced his little speech a hundred times and, if everything went as planned, he'd be well up Rte. 220 by noon.

The steps up to her front door were extraordinarily high, and from the vantage point from the porch, it seemed like a long way down to his car. He looked up and down the street; not a creature was stirring, not even an old alley cat. The town was still asleep, at 0800 hrs. (8 am) on a Tuesday morning.

He turned and walked up to the door. It was huge and had an ornate design. Each opening in the design had cut glass panes in it that allowed some vision into the interior. As far as he could see, there was no one stirring in the front of the house.

Timidly, he knocked and then waited. He was half tempted not to try again; after all, he'd tried. After pausing a moment, he half-heartedly knocked again, this time a little harder. After not seeing or hearing anything, he knocked yet again, even harder. This time the curtain moved ever so slightly, so he knew that somewhere in the house someone had opened and closed a door, causing a slight convection of air pressure. He turned away from the door, so as not to appear to be looking inside like a peeping Tom. That would have been considered impolite.

He heard footsteps and then the door was unlocked and opened. He turned to see a young girl with her hair still in curlers, wearing a bathrobe over her PJs. He smiled and nodded as she stepped back from the door and gestured for him to come into the living room. As he passed by her, she gestured for him to go to the right and into a secondary living room or parlor, as some people call them.

He noted a brick fireplace on the far wall, framed by two windows - one to each side. The couch was located to the left of the entry way from which he'd just come, on the near wall, directly across from the fireplace. To the right of the fireplace was a large, leather, over-stuffed chair. To the left of the room was an opening that led to the dining room. Midway between the dining room and the left window near the fireplace was an opening that he knew must lead upstairs. Again, she motioned for him to sit on the coach, and she sat down beside him at a respectful distance.

His mind was running 90-miles an hour – something wasn't adding up. First, this young women had let him in as if she'd been expecting him, but yet, he didn't recognize her.

She asked him how his trip went and if he'd had a hard time finding the house. He politely answered, as he thought, "*she's asking all the right questions, but I still don't know who she is*".

One of his little voices was saying, "*boy – you better start shucking corn or get out of the bin*". Just as he was about to clear his throat to make his getaway speech, he heard a sound across the room from the stairway.

Looking up, a vision of loveliness such as Cal had never seen before, came into view. He had the distinct feeling that his legs were turning into jelly and his stomach was doing forward rolls at one a second. He was glad that he was still setting or he'd of fainted.

Suddenly Cal recognized her – he knew who she was; his mind remembered her face – it was the same face that he'd seen again and again. She was the one in his dreams – he felt as if he was having a revelation or something and that at any moment, the heavens would open and God would speak.

Cal also recognized her from the picture; only she looked much older and even more beautiful. He hardly noticed or heard her sister getting up and saying that it was nice to meet him. He could only nod mutely as he stared incredulously at Kinsey, and watched her come over and sit down next to him.

She had a way about her that took his breath away. Cal couldn't believe the transformation that had come over her in the past couple of years, since last seeing her at the Ocean View Amusement Park.

She asked him how the trip had gone from the ship and if he'd gotten the car that he'd wanted. He remembered writing her about his plans and about how he'd had all his money stolen – she'd been his sounding post, his cheerleader of sorts when he faced some of his darkest moments. It was during these times that he'd written to her like she was a close friend and confidant, a sister perhaps – but suddenly, something was happening, and he was powerless against its pull. His mind was trying to bridge the gap between his communications with a sister-type person and now to this apparition of a person he'd known within his soul since the beginning of time.

Things became a blur, through which he moved with no awareness of anything around him. Before Cal knew it, her mother was insisting that he move out of the hotel and stay with them. It was as if he was suddenly a member of their family, and had just come home after a long absence. He also had a little

brother and three sisters and another mother and a
father, though he hadn't, as yet, met Kinsey's dad
whom she'd told him was a military man - Air Force.
Seems he was a crew member on a B17 during World
War II.

Time stood still for the next few days. No thought
of going home entered his mind – he was in a trance.
All he could think of was that God had rewarded him
for being steadfast and not blaming HIM for the
abuse he'd suffered during the first years of his life.

As he looked at her, a feeling of wanting to protect
her came over him. He also wanted all the wonderful
things that life could hold for her, and because of
her, he knew he could be and do anything. He felt
drawn to her like a metal filing to a two-ton magnet.
The way she held her head, her warm smile, the deep
Kelly green eyes, that drew his gaze like nothing else
could – she was poetry in motion, and he felt himself
falling, falling, falling in love.

Somewhere during the next few days, they started
holding hands, then there was that first kiss - it
seemed so natural. When he told her, without
reservation, that he loved her, she quickly assured
him, that she felt the same.

Finally, and with great regret, he had to go home
– but he'd call and write. He knew that he had to
keep his distance, even though she was within a
month of 18 and he was 21, it was still an age thing.
There was not only the age thing, but his duty to the
Navy that he had to fulfill.

Cal had very little experience with "girl friends"
other than Shelley, whom he had known for a very
short time. They had never really "courted". Little did
he know that he was about to learn some personal
things about her that he'd never heard, nor had ever
entered his mind to know - and she was very open
about this, feeling that given their new relationship
that these were personal things that he should know
as her man.

He was terribly naive, inexperienced and as his grandfather had said, years ago, "that he was still wet behind the ears" when it came to things of the world.

There was a very special feeling he got knowing that they were a couple. Finally, the time had come to leave, at least for now. He said his goodbyes to Kinsey's Mom and thanked her for her hospitality, and to her sisters and brother for having met them. They had all turned out to see him off. He had breakfast and had earlier packed his stuff in his car.

After the goodbyes to the family, he took Kinsey into his arms and kissed her goodbye – the other members of her family had discretely gone back into the house giving them a few moments alone. As he brushed her tears away, he whispered goodbye, and as he drove up the street, he continued to wave to her out the window. In his rearview mirror, he watched as she disappeared from view as he rounded the bend.

The drive home was not as wonderful as he'd envisioned, things had changed between Kinsey and himself. He felt the pull to stay with her every bit as strong as a spaceship might find when trying to break away from the gravitational pull of the earth's atmosphere. His heart was empty without her, though his mind was filled with her voice and grace.

Any feelings of being unequal to any of his peers was gone like vapor on a pond under the heat of the morning sun. The horrible secret that had dogged him for years was so deeply buried within his subconscious, that he hardly thought about it. It had been so long ago, that he doubted anyone knew or even remembered anything about the situation. As Grandfather used to say, "it was long gone and forgotten".

As the years went by, as they grew up on the farm, little by little Mother had told them the real reason why their father had gone to jail. After that, they were even more ashamed and, slowly one by one, the past pieces floated forward in their minds of what he'd done to them. Each of them had suffered at his hands in different ways, scarring them for life. For Cal, his father had planted the seeds of self-doubt, worthlessness, unworthiness, useless, abandonment, and being unwanted. When his mother had asked him, if "he'd" ever "hurt them", he and said, "No", not wanting his mother to carry that guilt around for the rest of her life.

In his mind, Kinsey was a gift sent from heaven to make up for all the wrongs that his father had done to him and the kind of life that he had been forced to live. Though, unlike his father, his nature was not to hurt others, especially his children or to ever make them feel worthless and unwanted – he would only show them love and caring.

His family was surprised and happy to see him. Phone calls were made to relatives announcing a get to gather to celebrate his homecoming with a special meal. Later, as they were rejoicing, he told them about Kinsey. They, of course, wanted to meet her and were full of questions about her, so he started planning the details that would make that possible.

A little while after arriving, his Uncle Clyde took him aside and told him that his mother had been beside herself with worry. Cal was confused, and asked his Uncle Clyde why she'd been worried?

Then he'd told him that his paycheck had come, so she knew he must not be far behind. When several days passed and he hadn't shown, she started to worry and, the worry drove her to taking longer and longer walks - walks that took her far from home for hours at a time – no one knew where she'd gone. This was so unlike her, that the whole family was in a state of panic about what had become of him and worried about his mom.

When he put it all together, Cal was irritated and upset with himself for upsetting her. She should have realized, by now, that given his new life, he wasn't someone who liked to be pinned down to a date and time to be somewhere. That, at this point in his life, his only allegiance was to the service. Beyond that, he could be anywhere, at any time in the world.

When he next saw his Mom, he'd thought about the "the talk" he'd had with his Uncle and playfully chided her for her concern, asking her what she would do when he married and didn't live around here anymore? She took it in stride, saying that it would be his wife's turn to worry. That she could take a break from it. It was only then that he realized the depths of his mother's love and concern for him over these past years. As an afterthought, she added, "You know ... I'll always be your mother, and I'll always worry about you – that's what mothers do, you know".

Even so, over the years, he remembered this incident and wished that it could have been otherwise; he didn't mean to worry her to the extent that he had on that occasion or any other, for that matter. Never in his wildest dreams had he calculated that his paycheck arriving at home before he had, would cause such a stir, or his prolonged absence would worry her so much.

His stay at home was punctuated with several phone calls to Kinsey and time taken out to write and read her letters. His thoughts were continually on her and how much he missed her. Her calls and letters were filled with family type news and her love for him. Each letter ended with her promise of eternal love. He knew he could trust her with anything and everything - after all - they were a couple.

After returning to the ship, the following months were filled with work, correspondence courses, letter writing, phone calls and visits to her home, when he wasn't out to sea.

He wanted to go slow this time, to allow the both of them time to really to get to know one another and for her to get to know his family.

One of the most memorable days came when a surprise package arrived from her; it was an 8 x 10 graduation picture of her. He remembered her mentioning having had her Senior picture taken, but was surprised to see that he was one of the recipients. It was the most beautiful picture of her, he'd ever seen. She looked like a movie star or a model. His heart fairly leapt out of his chest with pride, and he was warmed by the knowledge that she loved him.

He taped the frame to the inside of his locker door. From that vantage point, she welcomed him first thing in the morning and the last thing at night and every other time he opened the door - she was always there, her smile warmed his heart and helped him to get through every day that they were apart.

When he was able to make the trip to see her, the hours were spent riding the roads – they rarely parked – he respected her too much to risk getting her into trouble and further, he respected her and her parents who had put their faith in him to behave himself. As long as he lived under their roof, he wouldn't violate that trust. So when others were out parking and making out at the movies, they were discovering new roads, new places to see and just enjoying each other's company, with the strength of their love up most in his mind.

It was time to step up and make a commitment to Kinsey and show her family that his intentions were honorable.

Chapter 18.0

Kinsey's and his love continued to grow stronger by the week. He couldn't imagine that he could love anyone or anything more than he loved her – it was time to make a commitment. He'd known her for over three years. He also knew that they enjoyed each other's company and he felt they had established a deep trust and respect in one another - this time, "*it was right*".

One night, Kinsey gave him directions to the top of a nearby mountain where they could see forever, and she had been right. They loved the view, and he felt close to heaven, and with Kinsey at his side, it just didn't get any better.

He was due to ship out again, and it weighed heavily on his mind. In fact, he felt sick about having to go on another Med Cruise. He knew that it would be months before he'd see her again and he'd not get another chance to ask her to marry him. He was nervous, and when he felt that way, he tended to kid around and this night was no different. Finally, he knew the time had come and had grown silent as he wrestled with how to ask her the most important question of his life.

When he got that way, she knew to be quiet until he was ready to talk again. She was good about that – she understood his moods. She also knew how to pull him out of himself. He remembered the last time; he'd asked a girl to marry him and how that had turned out. Kinsey had told him that she wasn't like Shelley, that she wouldn't and couldn't do that to him. He had, over the months, come to trust her and believed her when she said she was – different and on his faith in her and their love for one another, he was going to build their future.

Finally, taking a hold of her hands, he turned and looked deep into her deep green eyes, he could feel his throat tightening, and his mouth felt dry as talcum powder; he could hardly breathe. Somehow the words came out, "Will you marry me"? He had hardly asked the question when she answered "YES," without the slightest hesitation. She was beaming from ear to ear, and at that moment, she'd made him the happiest man on the face of the earth. He would never forget it – not ever.

Suddenly his mischievous side reared its head as he said, "the ring is somewhere in the car, I've forgotten just where". He tried to sound serious, having to clench his jaws until they hurt so he wouldn't give it away – he'd no sooner said it than she was up on her knees and looking everywhere, begging him to tell her where he thought it might be. After a few minutes, he couldn't resist her pleas and gave in, taking it out of his pocket, saying, "Oh, here it is!" and as he said it, she thrust her hand out and he put it on her finger.

Immediately, she gave him a kiss that seemed to stop time. Her eyes were full of tears as she told him that she wouldn't have believed a year ago, that they'd be engaged to be married. She also said, that "to think she had once wished him luck with Shelley and their continued happiness, and WOW, now – well - they were so much in love. The reality of before, and now, seemed worlds apart as if the former had never happened.

She wanted to rush home to show her family but, she remembered that she'd promised her parents she wouldn't get married until after she graduated from Nurses Training, which meant that they'd have to wait two years. At that moment, two years was a walk in the park to them, and it would give him time to get out of the service and get established in a job and a home. All though as to where the job might be, and where they'd settle was lost in the excitement of the moment.

Kinsey was 18, and within months of graduating; he knew her parents would be very apprehensive about their engagement and he said as much to her. But she assured him they'd get "used to it". They decided, rather than to make a big announcement, that they would wait to see who'd be the first to notice the ring on her finger, then they'd make the announcement.

When they got home, supper was being put on the table. They sat down on the right side of the table with her brother seated beside him and her three sisters on the other side from them and her mother at the head of the table, in her father's absence (he was often away for several days at a time, as he was a postal person on the train between DC and their home).

As usual, there was some idle chatter between her sisters, punctuated by a question or a statement here or there by their mother. The dishes of food had been passed around with each person taking a helping, and the conversation ebbed and flowed. So far, they hadn't said anything, as they were still basking in the glow of their memories of the day.

When Kinsey reached for a dish of food from the middle of the table, one of her sisters noticed the ring and screamed, "Kinsey's engaged"! From that moment on all the decorum of a well laid out meal disappeared along with the proprieties of good manners. Apparently, the sisters had been talking among themselves about this much "anticipated" event and when it might occur and now that it had, everyone wanted to know the details.

Suddenly, everyone was talking all at once, until their Mom, said, "Shush". It became very quiet so

Kinsey could talk. She told them the details and that she and Cal realized, understood, and agreed that they wouldn't marry until after she graduated.

He felt bad that he didn't have a formal education as she would. When he later mentioned it to her, she told him that it didn't matter to her, and with what he was learning in the service, he'd be able to get a very good job. And along the way, he could always take courses and get his degree later. That was another thing that he loved about her, her ability to make him feel like he was much better than he felt he really was and her positive, reassuring attitude.

It was shortly after that that she and her twin sister put their engagement announcements in the paper. Later, when she showed him the newspaper with their announcement, he was so proud he could have busted. Here again was tangible proof of their love for each other, for the whole world to see.

The family had become used to giving them their space during the times he was there and, apparently, Kinsey was excused from her duties to be free to come and go with him. Even so, she always made it a point to ask her mother's permission. As time went on and he was there more and more often, the rule apparently was changed, and she was expected to help out more. So, when it was her turn to wash dishes, he'd help her – why not, maybe in some small way this would show his appreciation to her family for putting up with him. After all, they'd gone out of their way for him so he could stay there. Without realizing it, he'd lost his perception of what was going on around him. His love for Kinsey seemed to blind him to everything; his values, which he held so dear were in tatters and the "real him" was fast disappearing. He was heedless that people around him were going out of their way for him and he forgot about offering to pay his way, something that he should have remembered and heeded.

*   *   *

He later came to learn from Kinsey, that his abrupt arrivals and departures were causing family arguments but she hadn't told him about them until much later, during a moment of reminiscing. His endless drives around the countryside with Kinsey was also grist for much humor. More often than not, when he looked back reflectively, he wondered how Kinsey had ever put up with him during those early years. Even so, she was infinitely patient, kind and as steadfast as a rock. She was his girl, and he couldn't imagine it being any different – not ever.

*   *   *

The house was full of talk of a joint wedding, possibly a joint honeymoon and the girls were putting together hope chests. Kinsey told him that she was not for the joint honeymoon idea, and he assured her, nor was he. They were also talking about the number of children each of them thought was a good size family. These were matters for the women to talk about. He was content to bask in the warmth of his new family.

Now Cal felt that he could start to build a life, to be someone. With Kinsey at his side, he felt that if he could be, and do anything - even to becoming the Mayor of Cumberland.

During their dating, they never saw a movie, or went out to eat, or went to a dance other than her Senior Prom. She seemed content to just drive around. After she'd taken him to the park, they made it one of their favorite spots. As parks go, it was fairly large with a roadway that circled in and out around age-old trees and shrubs. In the evenings they parked, talked, and got to know each other every way possible - but one. They even carved their initials into a large old tree, that already bore the initials of others who'd found love and wanted everyone to know it.

Because of his promise to her folks, they never crossed that line – they came close on several occasions, but close only counts in horseshoes. Maybe it was because, in his mind, he couldn't envision himself ever getting to the point where he'd be making love to her until after they were married.

Time was getting away from him, and Cal knew he had to get back to the base. More than ever he hated to say goodbye. But finally, he did and drove away, with his hand waving at her.

He watched her from his rear view mirror until he turned the corner – her hand out stretched as if reaching for his, still waving, a picture that was burned into his memory forever. Even to this day, he can still see her there. He'd never felt closer or more a part of another human being in his whole life than he did at that moment. He would have given anything to have stayed; it made him sick to be driving away. Somehow he found his way through the despair and sorrow he felt at leaving her behind. He knew that the feelings wouldn't lift until he held her in his arms again.

In the distance, far behind him, another car was traveling in the same direction. There was no sadness or, for that matter, happiness, only a benign attitude about the job they were being paid to do. The older gentleman in the back seat of the black town car was well dressed as was the driver. They had been assigned to a person or persons unknown to them, and were to keep tabs on this particular young man and to record and report his comings and goings – but to never interfere with him or to allow him to know, that he was being watched. They and others had been watching him since child birth and would continue to do so for some years to come, until a time that had, as yet, not been revealed to even them.

Chapter 19.0

H er letters were filled with plans for their future and the things she was doing from day to day, and he savored each and every one, reading them over and over. They were his lifeline from the day-to-day insanity of living on a floating penal colony, as he often referred to this form of life.

In a few days, the ship left Little Creek. Again, the pier was lined with caring wives, loving girlfriends, mischievous children and various relatives of the guys on board. Many were drenched in tears. His heart ached for Kinsey and his need to see her – on the pier among the crowd, waving and throwing kisses. He missed her more than anything, and as the ship left US waters, a terrible feeling came over him. He couldn't have grieved more for her if she'd died.

The ghost of his past relationship with Shelley loomed before him, taunting him, "they're all the same ... "one in the hand, is better than two on board a ship. So you're stuck on this ship far away from her and she's young and pretty, so all kinds of guys hitting on her, she wants to get out and have fun with her friends, so what do you expect that she's going to be doing"?!

There was another feeling that Cal couldn't shake - the feeling of abandonment. His mind again flashed back to Shelley and what had happened between them on the last Med Cruise. He knew as well as any married man, engaged or going steady, that long cruises wreak havoc with relationships – it was the litmus test of a relationship. But, he kept reminding himself, Kinsey was different, he'd known her a lot longer than Shelley, and he and Kinsey had a whole lot more history than he and Shelley ever had.

Again, as before, Cal lived from letter-to-letter; writing her every night and during any spare moments that he could scratch our of a day, even at the neglect of writing his Mom and family. The days, then weeks ticked by, each a milestone toward the date they'd be heading back to home port.

Their first stop, as before, was Nice, France. However, unlike last time, the weather was cold, and there were no girls in bikini's sunbathing on the Côte d'Azur (Riviera).

Because he had recently been promoted to Petty Officer 2nd Class, he often pulled Shore Patrol. As such, in addition to his Dress Blues, he also wore a wide, white belt holding handcuffs, Billy club and a whistle hung around his neck. Around his arm was an SP (Shore Patrol) insignia, black band. In some areas, he'd also have a firearm issued to him, and there were incidences in which he was glad he had it.

Usually, pulling Shore Patrol was pretty much boring. You'd patrol the streets where the bars were, watch for drunken sailors who were making a nuisance of themselves, and see that they got back to the ship. On one occasion, he found a man stabbed to death, lying on the sidewalk in his own blood. He'd called for backup, and they'd reported it to the local law enforcement people. They were dressed in dingy, dark colored clothes that had little resemblance to anything to do with law enforcement. They seemed pretty unconcerned, not asking the usual questions of the neighborhood, as one would see back in the states. A panel truck soon arrived, and they picked him up and, unceremoniously, tossed him into the back and away they went.

One night a ruckus broke out in one of the jewelry shops and the owner sent someone to alert us. The owner was claiming that a sailor had broken his showcase window and he wanted to be paid for the damage. The sailor swore it was already broken when he arrived. In fact, he had noticed it was broken while he was looking at the jewelry in that particular case. We both suspected that the store keeper was lying about when and who did it, but we were stuck between two situations: one, cultural and two, who was telling the truth.

Cal had no experience in this area, so asked his partner, to get the acting CO of the Shore Patrol. Chief Workman showed up, and after hearing Cal's appraisal of the incident, the two sailors account, and then the shop's owner, he took a close look at the glass and asked the shop owner how much for the damage. A hundred and fifty dollars was his quick reply.

He immediately realized this was a scam that he had pulled before, perhaps many times but, Chief Workman was on to him.

He nodded okay and, as he reached for his wallet, he told the shop owner that he wanted the broken glass or no deal. You could have heard the store owner's face hit the floor. None of them expected this move on the Chief's part. But, in and of it, Cal detected the wisdom and experience of their old Chief.

Grudgingly, the shop owner detached the broken glass, put it in a box and then handed the box over to the Chief, who then paid the store owner and asked for a receipt. The store owner was beaten at his own game, and he knew it, as he hastily wrote out a receipt and handed it to the Chief. His days of cheating other sailors was over – at least for the moment.

Back on the ship, mail call was happenimg. All the men lived for mail call and in among the letters from Kinsey, was one from his mother with a short note in it. It had gotten to the point where his mom was now mailing letters to him with blank paper, self-addressed, stamped envelopes - but he still put off writing to her, seemingly never having the time.

Out of the blue, a few days later, he was summoned to the Master at Arm's office and told to write a letter to his Mom - today and to have it in the mail pouch before turning in that night. At first, he had been rocked back on his heels. His mom had figured out how to get a message to the Captain through the Red Cross. The old man wasn't in the least happy about having to remind him to write his Mommy.

"Believe you me", he sent out a note to her, and it read, "Hi, I'm okay, busy as hell, Love your son". He was upset, more than anything else because she'd barged into his world. As time went on, he wrote longer letters and was more considerate about writing more often.

At every port the ship put into, he'd buy something special for Kinsey; he'd planned to ship it to her for Christmas. Uncle Sam paid for the postage, no matter how heavy the package or how many letters he sent and, it always got through.

He had also purchased a tape recorder and extra tapes. He thought that a verbal account of what he saw and did would be more interesting than just writing about it. So he started taping what he saw at each port, first identifying the port, then talking about it. He tried to paint a picture with words, of everything he saw and did. He couldn't help but say how much he loved her and other romantic things. Later he learned from Kinsey when she was playing the tapes for others to hear; she wouldn't always get it turned off in time before he'd pop out with something romantic and she'd get kidded unmercifully.

When Christmas arrived, they were in Athens Greece. Cal had located a large box that everything he'd bought, for Kinsey, would fit. Again, his total concentration was on Kinsey and how surprised she'd be finding things from all over the world in the box. To make it even more fun, he not only taped the box shut, but ran electrical armature wire around it in all directions and then put tape over that. He could just image her trying to get into it.

Cal later learned that it had taken nearly an hour for her and her dad to open it. She couldn't believe all the stuff he'd sent her. Her family kept kidding her, saying that surely some of it must be for them. When he'd heard that, he'd felt guilty for not having bought for not only her family but also his. He'd been so consumed with his relationship with Kinsey that he had thought of little else. He felt like such a clod and again wondered what was wrong with him – *"had he lost his mind"*? He'd never been like this before.

Day by day, and month by month, Cal looked forward to her letters. Christmas had come and gone, and so had New Years. He was remembering their good times, every time he got a letter from her. Her sweet perfume filled his locker. He dreamed about her at night and thought about her during his long days, while far below the waterline working or standing watch. It was a wonder that he could do his job – perhaps it was became the work was so well embedded in his mind that he'd become like a robot – automatic in his movements - requiring little thought.

They'd been out to sea on maneuvers for a couple of weeks, with NATO task forces, practicing war games off Sardinia and Valencia, and morale was reaching a new low. They were all starved for mail - word from loved ones. No matter where they were, whether on duty or off somewhere else on the ship, the department head would hunt them down to give them their mail.

The "old man" decided to have a beer party, hoping to boost their sagging morale. The ship was maneuvered in close to a large, deserted part of the

Libyan coastline and the anchor was dropped. Neither long range spy glasses nor radar could pick up anything for miles. So it was deemed to be safe to go ashore. He didn't want to cause an international situation as he was flying under the radar so to speak. He was sticking his neck out for all of us, knowing how much we all needed a morale boost.

However, the old man, not wanting to take any chances, had a few Marines and sailors who were not predisposed to drinking, armed to accompany them ashore. The word was passed via the ship's silent PA system (scuttlebutt) all over the ship, that we were about to go ashore and have a beer party.

I wondered at the time, where the beer would be coming from and soon learned that cases of it had been stowed behind steel bulkheads, accessed through hatches that led into voids between the inner and outward hulls. Since the hatches had been spot welded, an acetylene torch was brought to bear and the welds cut, allowing for the hatch to be removed, while in the presence of the Master at Arms.

War ships were not supposed to carry and dispense beer to US sailors while at sea or in port, but with it stowed in this manner and being consumed off the ship; it was considered to be acceptable, though it was common knowledge that alcoholic beverages were readily available and consumed in officer's country.

It took several Mike boats to fairy men, beer, hotdogs and rolls to the mainland and, once there, firewood was gathered as men bearing arms took to the high ground to stand guard. The fire had barely been started when, far out in the midday haze, a lone Bedouin was sighted through the waves of shimmering heat. Initially, it was believed there were no other living human beings for a hundred or more miles but, here was this guy with his donkey, barely visible with the naked eye, making his way through a sparse covering of low growing desert-type vegetation, that didn't look like it could support any type of life. From all appearances, he was headed toward us. We watched with muted interest, as many of them found sticks to insert into our weenies and started cooking them while chugging a warm beer. After dispensing a hot dog into a waiting bun, garnished with mustard, Cal passed his stick along to another waiting sailor.

As Cal ate his hot dog and drank a beer, he wandered outside the milling circle of men and climbed up a sand dune to look around. Not far away, he noticed a lone sailor sitting in the sand, head down, with his face in his hands. For a time, he let him have his privacy. With the last bite of his hot dog and bun sliding down his throat, he eased over to where the sailor was and quietly commented about the barrenness of the landscape, adding that he couldn't understand how anyone would want to live in such a place.

The sailor whom he recognized as "Yale", a nick name they'd given him, softly replied, that it reminded him of home. "Where, would that be?" Cal asked aghast. "New Mexico," he answered back. This makes me homesick, he continued, as he gestured with his hand at the landscape.

We stood together in the late afternoon watching as the Bedouin gradually drew closer. We could now make out details in his clothing and could see that he carried an aged rifle that was longer than he was tall. With him was a mite of a boy, who had been walking on the off side of the shaggy old mule, shielding him from their view until now.

Behind us, the sound of men shouting and laughing had intensified as they had stripped down to their jeans and were playing with a makeshift ball made out of a knotted up shirt. Others were content to drink and talk. A couple groups were in a beer drinking contest to and were piling up empty beer cans by the dozens as they spilled most of it over themselves in their hurried attempt at beating one another.

Others of our group, seeing the approaching Bedouin, had gone out to meet him, with much waving and laughter. He was quickly named, Ahab the Arab and, the donkey was called Charlemagne, and the little boy, "Kid". Before long, Kid was wearing a sailor hat and a big grin. A couple of the guys were handing out green backs for a ride on Charlemagne, and everyone was grinning. It was quite a sight - the west meeting the east and communicating with sign language and laughter.

The contrast was notable between the desert garbed old man who was barely five feet tall, sporting a gray mustache that seemed to part his weather-worn face, and our barefooted men in rolled up pants.

He later signaled that he was interested in our empty beer cans, no doubt to be traded off at some remote encampment. So we shook on it, believing that we probably got the better deal since we didn't have to haul them back aboard the ship for later disposal.

With the sun preparing to set, we and the Bedouin parted friends, all waving as we headed back to the ship. All in all, the Captain had succeeded in allowing them to blow off some steam, have a good time and make some new friends. We no longer looked at the Marines and, they at them, as a bunch of swabbies and jarheads, but as fighting men, with families and dreams of things to come. Cal felt that if all the ships in all the Navies were to hold joint beer parties, perhaps the world would be a safer place to live.

When mail call finally came, he could hardly wait for those sweetly scented letters, but as the supply man passed out letter after letter to those around him, Cal realized that there was none for him. The good feelings fostered by the beer party were now smothered into oblivion by this latest development. He was devastated and couldn't understand it. He went back and read the last letters from her, hoping for a clue as to what had happened. He read them over and over, nearly committing them to memory, and still, there wasn't a hint as to why she'd suddenly stopped writing.

Cal started having flashbacks of Shelley and what had happened. He was filled with doubt; had Kinsey, like Shelley, found someone else? He knew his absences must be hard on her, especially with all her friends dating, going to dances and having fun. After all, it was her senior year and so much was happening - it would be so easy to get caught up at the moment and start seeing someone else. His stomach was turning itself wrong side out and upside down, and he hadn't eaten for days. He was becoming physically sick and felt as if he was going to puke at any minute.

He heard they were pulling into a city just south of Rome in a few days. He'd found out from the guys, that they had a phone system where one could call the US and pay them when they were done. He made his mind up that was what he'd do, call Trans-Ocean-Atlantic and find out what was going on. He didn't care if it was the middle of the night back there, he had to know, as not knowing was killing him. He fought to hang on to every shred of sanity he could muster and counted the hours until he could get off the ship and make the call. Finally, the moment came, and he headed straight to the phone center and placed the call. Again he had to wait until the call got through, as one of the international operators pointed to one of the phone booths in a bank of booths across the room. He noted that one of the booths had a light flashing over it. He ran to it hoping the light wouldn't stop, before he got there.

"Hello, hello", he shouted into the phone, his throat was tight, his voice hoarse with emotion. He turned his face toward the back of the booth, as the tears coursed down his cheeks - then he heard one of her sister's answer. Upon hearing his voice, requesting to speak to Kinsey, she immediately said someone has gone to get her. He heard a sound on the other end of the phone, then her voice. Right away, she started apologizing for not writing him; she said she was sorry and it wouldn't happen again. She also said that she and her mother had, had a talk and that she'd already written him several letters and that he should be getting them soon. He needed to hear her say it - that she loved him". Cal listened to her as she continued to reassure him that everything was okay and not to worry. It wasn't so much what she was saying, "*it was what she wasn't saying,*" that tore at his heart. Finally, he said, "I love you more than anything in this world and miss you beyond anything you can imagine".

She softly said, "I love you too, and I'm so sorry that I have worried you". His time was up, and he had to go, so he simply said, "Goodbye Sweetheart". As he retraced his steps, the familiar sound of her voice still echoed in his ear, and he started to feel better ... but that didn't stop the little voice in his mind from still asking the question, "*What happened?*"

The seed of doubt had been sown. Something inside him was telling him not to pressure her, to give her some space and not to worry, that everything was going to be okay.

In looking back over the incident, Cal believed she'd gone out on him; having gotten bored and feeling unsure of their relationship. He also believed that her mother, when she found out what was going on, sat her down and had a long talk – no doubt telling her that now was not the time to be breaking up with a service man and, to at least wait until he got back, and do it face to face - if that was still what she wanted. He was sure her mother reminded her of the commitment she'd made and that she expected her to keep it. Her mom was that kind of person and Kinsey respected her mom and dad, and she had a strong sense of family and honor.

True to her word, the letters came in bunches, five the first time, then in twos and threes, rarely less than one a day. Her first letter again hinted at a problem that she had had and that it had been taken care of and that was all she said about it.

*   *   *

During his time in the Navy, he'd see two Mediterranean and thirteen Caribbean cruises. He calculated that accumulatively, they were in Little Creek, their home base, a total of six months or so out of his total four years and six months on board the Fort Mandan.

*   *   *

When he returned and first saw her, they hugged and kissed. However, he could feel that something else was going on, there was something she was keeping from him. Several times she acted as if she wanted to tell him something, but then she started crying. He tried to encourage her to tell him what was bothering her so that they could work it out, but she'd only shake her head, "No". Continuing, he said, "Whatever it was, he'd forgive her," thinking that perhaps that would help her to stop crying – seeing her this way was tearing him apart.

He was surprised when she snapped at him that she hadn't asked for his forgiveness. He was stunned and puzzled at the change in her voice and demeanor, so he kept silent, thinking about what a strange answer that was, and what it meant. He didn't know what to say after that.

After she wiped her eyes and put her handkerchief away, she took his hand in hers. He could see the diamond in her engagement ring, glimmering brightly in the moonlight, and it comforted him. They kissed and held each other for a long time that night, and he dismissed the issue as so much water under the bridge. He had to, as for him, it was a matter of faith – within her and God. He believed her when she told him that she loved him and that was all that really mattered.

*   *   *

She never did tell him what had happened. Cal started to wonder if he really knew her after all, and how many other secrets she was keeping, secrets that could shake the foundations of their relationship, if they were ever known. Irrespective he felt sure that had he known, he they could work through them and become stronger for it. And upon reflection, the same could be said for him. After all, does one really share "everything"?

*   *   *

Their time together was more hectic now with the prom and her graduation looming. In looking ahead,

Cal saw his time in the Navy was nearing an end, and he could hardly wait. He had asked Kinsey to her prom more as a formality than anything else, after all, they were engaged, and this was something that Cal knew was important to her – so why not? He was excited about the prospect of going with the prettiest and, certainly, the most loved girl, by his account, in Cumberland. He looked forward to it and knew how happy it would make her. He'd purchased a custom made tux out of New York, months before when he had been overseas and he couldn't wait to show it off. It even had his name embroidered on the inside just above his pocket. He'd never owned a custom made suit, let alone a tux. He also bought flowers for her, based on the color of her dress.

The evening of the prom was filled with full tilt activity and unbounded excitement around the house. There was only one bathroom for Kinsey, her sisters and Cal to get ready. Delia, Kinsey's twin, was going with Ernie, her fiancée, and two of her sisters who would be meeting up with their boyfriends. Amazingly enough, they sandwiched getting dressed and his needs in between the others who had to get their make up on. Several times Cal had to look the other way – it was the gentlemanly thing to do. They didn't seem to mind Cal being upstairs with them and paid little attention ... after all, he was like a big brother.

They wouldn't let him see her until she was ready. In a way, Cal could see the same scenario with Kinsey and he, on their wedding day. Again, he was downstairs with Ernie, waiting like an expectant father for that magic moment when Kinsey and Delia would appear.

Cal had only met Ernie, Delia's boyfriend on a couple of occasions. Like her, he was a Senior and college bound. Ernie was very reserved, hardly saying a word, he was also shorter and stocky. If anything, he might have been just a bit shorter than

Delia, so he supposed that Delia might not be wearing heels that night. Ernie also wore glasses that made him look like a Professor. He sat patiently on the couch as Cal paced the floor, as they waited. He and Ernie only exchanged small talk; they didn't seem to be on the same wave length and had little to nothing in common. As he paced the floor, trying to walk off his nervousness, he noted that Ernie seemed to be taking it all in stride as if he'd been through this many times.

Finally, Cal heard her coming down the stairs. He couldn't believe how beautiful she was. Even dressed the same, he could always tell Kinsey from Delia. To a stranger, they appeared alike; to him, there was a subtle difference.

Kinsey and Cal left in his car after the pictures had been taken and arrived at her school along with Ernie and Delia in their car. Several of Kinsey's classmates said, "Hi" to her and paid scant attention to him, as they went into the gym. They made their way to a table where Cal didn't know whether they were going to sit down or stand. He was waiting for his cue from Kinsey. He could sense that she suddenly seemed unsure of what to do with him. Cal had never met any of her friends and had no idea what to talk about. He felt totally out of place.

Quickly, Cal told her that he'd stay there and keep an eye on their stuff, for her to meet with her friends. For the first time, he became keenly aware that this part of her life, was not "theirs". Her life at school and with her friends would always be her life. There would always be this void in their lives, as it would have been if the roles had been switched. Though afterward, he wondered why she had not introduced him to her friends, other than those he'd met earlier while decorating.

Never had Cal felt more out of his element, as he watched her bobbing about between her classmates. Here he was, standing in the middle of a bunch of kids who had no idea who or what they were, all still living at home and having not the slightest idea what it was like to have gone through boot camp, then "A" school and be part of the fleet, a man in charge of men, responsible for millions of dollars in equipment. He was in a word, "from another planet". He knew that most of them didn't have a clue about what they'd be doing once they graduated.

In the course of trying to stimulate conversation, Cal asked a guy who seemed to be stuck watching pocket books and coats the same as he, what he was going to do once he graduated. He shrugged his shoulders, seemingly having no idea what to say to such a deep question. Another only had some vague idea what he was going to do, maybe go to college, he quipped - but only after taking some time off first. Beyond that, they didn't have a clue what the world was really all about, and he'd exhausted the limit of what he had to talk about to them. At least with Kinsey, they seemed to be able to talk about all kinds of stuff. Again, he watched in envy as Kinsey moved among the other girls, talking and kidded, completely at ease. He remembered when he had his senior prom and how he'd been able to move about and visit.

The music finally started, and they danced a few dances. When they were seated at their table, practically no one came by and again Cal felt that he was keeping her from enjoying herself.

If she'd been asked by one of the guys in her class, she would have had more to talk about and more interaction with the others. Cal felt that he was holding her back, he was a liability to her, and that really bothered him - it was the last thing he wanted.

She must have sensed his discomfort, as pretty soon she asked Cal if he wanted to go and he numbly nodded, "yes". He was upset with himself about not being able to fit in and to be a better conversationalist. Cal was not a glib person, able to spin great tales and charm the tail off a dog like some men – he was about as far from being the life of the party as one can get, more like the undertaker.

Cal regretted that he was not up to the challenge and a better date for her. As it turned out, Ernie and Delia were ready to go too. They both agreed to meet at one of their relatives to show off their new duds, then to make the rounds to other relatives. He could tell right away that it was easier for both Ernie and him to relate to smaller groups of people, particularly older people.

Cal's memories of that night, were not those of a total failure, as they enjoyed her relatives and had a lot of fun with them. They also did their share of making out in the car and, when they finally came home, they were both ready for bed. He knew that Delia had come home sometime before they had and had already turned in.

Chapter 20.0

T here were times when he saw Kinsey's father, though he suspected that, at first, her mother and Kinsey tried to keep them apart.

He was a man used to speaking his mind and didn't mince words. He was very protective of his girls and suspicious of any young man's attention toward them, particularly a serviceman. Cal remembered Kinsey telling him that her father had served in the Air force as a crew member on a B-17.

He was slightly taller than Cal, almost completely bald with a razor sharp mind. Cal had heard that he was very good at playing cards and often brought home some very large winnings. He loved sports and had committed to memory all the basketball, football and baseball players names and stats.

He also drank a lot – Cal never saw him without a beer in his hand or, on the side table next to his chair where he'd sit for hours, sorting "mailing route cards". There were piles several inches high, situated all round him that added into the thousands. These cards, he once told Cal, denoted drop points for mail, indicating the villages and towns along the rail system, where the mail was to be routed. Cal had shaken his head in wonder at the enormity of his job and responsibility. Cal was also intrigued that he worked out of both a mail car and a caboose. When asked about his life in the mail car, he said he'd get his work done quickly and spend most of his time playing cards in the caboose.

After they'd visited a couple of times, her dad seemed to mellow toward him, though he still suspected that Kinsey's Mom engineered his coming and goings around her husband's absences.

Kinsey told Cal that her Dad had in the past asked her if she was putting out to him, as he couldn't figure out why he'd be driving so far, just to see her. She had of course told him, "No – that Cal drove this far because he loved her". She had also noted that after that, he'd backed off on the subject.

One evening after returning from driving around they'd parked in front of the house and had been kissing. Suddenly they were startled by a gentle, but insistent knocking sound on their window. By this time, the windows had pretty much fogged over, however, they could see that it was Delia. She was obviously embarrassed to be bothering them and quickly told them that Dad was upset about their parking out front and that they had better get into the house pronto. So he moved the car to the back of the house.

Once in the house, he wasted no time in telling them, in no uncertain terms, that he didn't approve of his daughters' parking out front. He didn't want the neighbors to be talking about them, and moreover, it wasn't good for their reputations, which Cal could fully understand, once he'd been made aware of it.

He directed Kinsey to go to bed and for Cal to sit down on the couch. It was apparent that he'd had a few and this was one of the few times, that Kinsey's mother didn't run interference for them. In fact, she was nowhere to be seen. In the past, she'd always shushed him, telling him that she was taking care of "it". But this time, he was going to say his piece.

Kinsey's dad had been sorting postal shipping cards. They were apparently addressed and had to be put in order of stops from DC to here and back again. Again, He was in awe of his ability to be able to commit thousands of cards to memory and all in order. He started out by telling Cal about what he thought of people who didn't follow the rules and how he'd taken his wife's word that they would behave themselves and not bring dishonor to his house.

Cal was shattered to think that he thought they were doing anything wrong and that he was something less than an honorable man. He let him go on without interrupting and when he finally stopped, Cal asked if he might tell him about where he was from and how he'd been raised.

He nodded and listened as Cal told him how he'd been reared, about his family and their values. He also told him about the service and how hard he'd worked to make his pay grades so that he could buy a car and how Kinsey and he'd met. He didn't get into the part about Shelley, but did tell him how much it meant to him that they had let him stay at their home and how very much he loved and respected his daughter.

He seemed to soften after that, and they talked some more about his job and how hard he worked and the days and nights her dad was forced to be away from his family. He was a night owl, used to working all night, so seeing that he was nowhere near ready to go to bed, Cal finally asked, if he minded if he turned in and thanked him again for their talk and for letting him stay in his home.

After that, they rarely spoke to one another at length. He now understood where her dad was coming from and her father knew that Cal understood his position, but Cal was still a sailor, and as an ex-serviceman, he knew full well what kind of mischief they could get into.

Another time they had come home late, both Kinsey's mother and dad were still up and, as usual, he was working on his postal cards. It was obvious that her mother was worried about what he was going to say, particularly since he'd been drinking a lot.

As soon as he saw them, he launched into telling Cal an off colored joke. Immediately, his wife started shushing him, but he was not going to be deterred. Cal had a feeling, given the way her mother was acting, that it was going to be one of those jokes that was going to embarrass Kinsey and, not wanting to see her embarrassed by her dad, Cal sought to deflect it by shrugging his shoulders and moving on toward the stairs.

It was obvious that he wouldn't be denied his moment, as he continued unabated, as they made their way upstairs, he stole a look at Kinsey, who had flushed two shades of red, and Cal knew she was embarrassed. Kinsey apologized for her father's actions, and Cal told her not to give it another thought. There would be other times that they would be embarrassed by her dad.

During one of his visits, Kinsey mentioned to him, as discretely as possible, that little Jimmy had been sleeping in her parent's bedroom during his visits and that it was severely cutting into her parent's love life, and her dad was getting upset about it. Without hesitation, Cal told her that little Jimmy could sleep with him. That really, it was okay - the last thing he wanted was to put her folks out. If that was not a satisfactory solution, they'd schedule his visits when her Dad wasn't home.

She quickly indicated that, for her, that was not an option, a comment that made him happy to hear, but he was still reticent to be encroaching on her parent's privacy. Upon his next arrival, apparently, the decision had been made that little Jimmy would sleep with him, an idea that not only saved the day, but made his.

Once they were ready for bed, he decided to tell little Jimmy a bedtime story. All the girls, hearing this, came running in and piled on top of their double bed. Just as he went to open his mouth to start the story, the bed suddenly collapsed.

The crash was so loud, that he was sure the neighbors must have heard it. The noise had hardly died when Kinsey's mother appeared at the door. He'd never seen her so upset and she appeared to be the most upset at him. The girls tried to explain that it was not his fault, that the bed had simply given way. No one was rough housing or anything. Even so, she shooed them all to bed and proceeded to relocate the bed on the floor minus the legs and, without missing a beat, swooped little Jimmy up in her arms and was gone.

After she went back downstairs, Kinsey came back to his room and whispered that it would be okay; she'd talk to her mother in the morning and straighten it all out. She was visibly upset and had been crying as there were still tears in her eyes and running down her cheeks.

Cal desperately wanted to hold her and tell her that it was okay, that he understood where her Mom was coming from but, if he was caught embracing Kinsey while only in her night clothes, it would be the end of his staying with them. And he most certainly didn't want to incur any more trouble, feeling terrible that such an innocent thing had been so misinterpreted.

*   *   *

Looking back, it was obvious that he was fast wearing out his welcome and nerves were being frayed left and right. Cal often wondered, had their roles been switched, would he have been so open-minded about having his daughter's suitor sleeping only a door's width away. However, as it is with youth, he was blind to what was usually unaware of that was going on around him and could only see as far as his own immediate needs.

*　　　*　　　*

The way Cal had been raised, was a lot different than Kinsey's Mom had raised her children. Kinsey's Mom was more trusting, and the girls respected that and tried hard to please her. She was soft spoken and smiled continually, always interested in what they were doing and their ideas. It was a two-way street as, in return, they respected her and their dad which was evident in how they talked about them.

In contrast, Cal was raised by his mother, his aunt, a grandmother and grandfather who were firm believers in speaking once and getting out the whip second. Cal had grown up under a much different philosophy - that of having to earn trust and even so, he knew that they loved him and would do anything for him. This difference in their mother's ways of rearing their children would come to be a problem for them as their relationship evolved. He was always amazed at how lenient Kinsey's mom was with her, and he never heard her refuse her daughter, when she asked about going here or there with him. To him, it was like saying "I trust you, now don't let me down". This trust also extended to their home and Cal. Therefore, they had a free rein to come and go as they pleased. Cal had a key to open the door and lock it again for the night. Often, they'd come in late and go upstairs to their separate bedrooms and go directly to bed.

He'd wait in his bedroom, until she was done with the bathroom and then he'd go in and wash up. The doors to all the bedrooms were wide open at night to aid in ventilation, and there was always enough light to see into the rooms, from the bathroom night light. Being a gentleman, he was always careful to avert his eyes and, would be as quiet as possible so as not to wake anyone when using the facilities.

Kinsey slept in the room to the right at the top of the stairs with her twin, his room was dead ahead, and her other two sisters slept in the room to the left of his. He was always careful of their privacy, though, at times, they'd call out to him and then he'd stop outside of the door and visit. He always regarded them as his sisters and brother.

During one of his visits, they decided to meet up with her dad and do some fishing. Kinsey and he'd been somewhere and had arrived back at the house in time to see her father getting some fishing gear together with her brother, Jimmy, helping. Little Jimmy was all excited about going fishing as it and baseball were his passions. He knew a surprising amount about baseball. He would often tell Cal the player's names on each team and who the pitchers and catchers were. It was obvious he had his dad's memory.

It was spring, and the water was high. He was surprised to learn that they were going to be fishing in the Susquehanna, the same river that ran through Binghamton. Their dad was familiar with Binghamton because that was where the Cubs used to play and now the Dusters were the big name in town if you followed hockey and, of course, he'd seen the card come up on his mail routing for that area.

They drove to where they were going fishing and hung around for awhile to watch and hold the pole. Nothing was biting, and he soon lost his patience with it and left with Kinsey. He had noticed that her dad didn't seem to be in a talkative mood – he rarely was unless he had had a few drinks and, even then, it was a toss up what kind of mood he'd be in.

The open road was calling, and he had too few hours to be standing around on that chilly, overcast, spring morning in the mud, watching the dark, cold, brown waters flowing by. It only took one look at each other, as they stood there shivering, to decide it was time to put their poles away and cast off, looking for their next adventure.

Chapter 21.0

During his last leave, he'd stopped off at Kinsey's, as they'd been talking about her meeting his folks - after all, they were engaged, and she still hadn't met them, and it was also Christmas Eve.

After she'd told him that her mom had said, that she could go home with him, he was thrilled at the opportunity for her to at long last meet his family. But there was a catch; Kinsey told him that, first, he had to ask her mom personally for her permission.

Usually, Kinsey had always made the arrangements, and he assumed, this time it would be no different. He'd already stayed at Kinsey's for a few days, prior to his plans to be leaving for home. Kinsey and he were happily anticipating the prospect of going. However, he could also detect that she was conflicted about missing Christmas with her family. Their was an air of sadness about her. The fresh smelling tree was up, and brightly lit. Gifts were piling up under the tree as each family member added theirs from time to time.

After a time, Kinsey whispered to him, that she was packed and ready to go. He'd already put his stuff in the car and was waiting for an opening to approach her mom. He could sense the electricity in the air, as everyone was waiting nervously for him to "*ask the question*", while passing the time with small talk, punctuated with nervous laughter. He watched as her mother hurried about between the kitchen, dinning and living room, preparing for the next day's celebration. It was nearing 8 pm, and he knew if he didn't get going, he'd not make it home by the following morning. Finally, after stalling as long as he dared, he cleared his throat as he got up from the couch, and walked up to her mother.

"Mom," Cal said, "I'd like to take Kinsey home, with me to meet my family," quickly followed up with his promise to have her back Christmas day or that evening depending on the roads.

Her mother visibly stiffened for a moment and he immediately felt terrible as he saw moisture forming in her eyes. You could have heard a pin drop in the whole house.

She finally nodded her head and said, "Okay". Cal couldn't believe it. She was actually going to let Kinsey go. Surprised, he abruptly asked her, how she could do it, and she simply said, "I trust my daughter". He nodded with mixed emotions, he doubted that his mother would have so easily acquiesced and his spirit was also buoyed by her trust in him.

She went on to tell him, that this would be the first Christmas that any of her children would be missing - not having Christmas in their home. Cal told her this would be the first Christmas that he'd be having with his family in over three years, and they all very much wanted to meet their future daughter-in-law. Kinsey's mom nodded her head, understanding what he was saying as a tear ran down her cheek and fell on to her flowered apron. He gave her a hug, and said, "Thanks mom, this means the world to me, and we'll not let you down".

Cal was amazed; he'd never seen anything like it; he couldn't imagine his mother, or anyone else's, allowing their daughter to go off unescorted, with a young man, to someplace hundreds of miles away.

She handed him a present from under the tree; it was from all of Kinsey's family.

He was moved, he hadn't thought to get them anything – it simply hadn't dawned on him. Cal felt unworthy, he didn't deserve this sort of kindness, but to refuse their gift would have seemed even crasser than his forgetting to get them something. He numbly said, "thanks" and gave them all hugs.

There was a strange silence that ran through the house – Cal felt like he was stealing their Christmas. He saw them all standing there around the living room, putting their best face on, as they said their goodbyes and he helped Kinsey carry her bag out of the house. They wished them a safe trip, and Kinsey assured them all that they'd call upon arriving and would keep in touch.

They were both excited about the trip and being together in this special way. As they hit Rte 220 North, all of a sudden Kinsey became very still. Turning his head toward her, Cal saw that her smile had turned to tears.

Was this all a big mistake? Was he being selfish? He was saddened and perplexed, as she'd been such a strong proponent of going. He had no experience in these things, and her tears were upsetting him. "Had she changed her mind?"

"What's the matter, honey"? She only shook her head, her face still looking at her lap as the tears streamed down her cheeks. Cal pulled over, parked the car, and reached over drawing her close, and he waited silently for her to stop crying.

After a time, he gently said, "I'll take you back home – this isn't right, not if it bothers you this much". Cal hated having to do it, but if leaving her family at this special time was causing this much heartache, he would take her back if she wanted. She shook her head, "No," and said in a halting voice, "I'll be okay in a minute, it's just that this is my first Christmas away from home".

Again, Cal felt guilty, the joy of the moment was gone, and he felt sad for her. His only wish was to see her happy and to never be the cause of any unhappiness. He was sure that once she met his family, she'd feel welcome and assured that she was surrounded by people who loved her. After a few minutes, she indicated he should go on, so Cal pulled back out on the road, as she finished mopping up her tears and they continued on north.

Her mood shifted as the miles rolled away; she was seeing country she'd never seen before. He'd made the trip on at least one other occasion, feeling that it was the most direct route he could take from her home to his, although not the fastest. However, during this time of the year, you could run into some pretty severe weather in the mountains.

They were perhaps a couple of hours out of Cumberland when Cal noticed that she was wearing a dress and was struggling to get comfortable in the front seat. The dress was binding on her, so he suggested that she might want to change into something easier to ride in. Apparently, she thought so too as, before he knew it, she'd vaulted over the back of the seat. He was amazed and impressed at her speed and agility. He turned the inside, overhead light on so she could see what she was doing.

The next time Cal glanced at the rear view mirror she was stripped down to her bra and panties. He'd never seen her with so little on except when they'd gone swimming at the Recreation Center pool. This was different, and Cal suddenly felt very protective of her. He quickly looked away as she moved about changing. As they drove along, he kept an eye open for other cars and nearby buildings, but there were none. At this hour of the night, they had the highway all to themselves, and were in a world of their own. Soon she'd completed changing into her jeans and pullover and rejoined him in the front seat. She leaned over and gave him a peck on the cheek and then gently rubbed the lipstick off with her thumb.

The miles continued to roll by and, after a while, she dozed off with her head leaning against Cal. When he stopped for gas, she got a drink and went to the bathroom, and then she snoozed some more. It made him feel good knowing she trusted him and that someday she'd be his wife. After hours of driving, he was starting to get tired and knew he needed to take a nap. He pulled into a service station parking lot, stopped and killed the lights. The service station's lights were out, and the lot was dark as ink.

They curled up in each other's arms and snoozed for awhile; long enough for him to push back the fatigue that threatened to close his eyes, and that was dulling his senses.

After waking up and collecting themselves, Cal backed the car around. As he turned the car to the right and started to move forward, it suddenly stopped with a bang that rocked both of them. Shocked out of their wits, they looked at each other, wondering what had just happened?

In the dark, Cal had failed to see a telephone pole in the middle of the lot. Apparently, it had suffered the same consequences on other occasions, as it had steel brackets installed all around it. They got out and took a look at the damage to the car. There was a sizable dent in the passenger side door, but it wasn't serious enough to keep the door from opening or closing. It made him sick that he'd done such a stupid thing.

Kinsey admitted that she'd not seen it either. Cal knew she realized how badly he felt and was trying to comfort him. He was not prone to cussing just because something went wrong so, after silently feeling bad about it, he managed to put it into perspective. Cal knew he couldn't get it fixed at home as there wouldn't be enough time, and besides, he needed his car to get around. He'd have to wait until after he got back to the base to make an appointment with one of the body shops in Norfolk.

Cal drove until daylight, stopping only for gas. They'd traveled for a couple of hours through some of the most open countries in Pennsylvania when finally another route sign came into sight displaying 120. He'd been thinking that something was wrong; the scenery was not anything like he remembered and, finally seeing another road sign, his suspicions proved correct. Somehow during the night, he got on the wrong Rte. Instead of staying on 220, he was on 120 west. The signs had been few and far between along this lonely old road. He checked the road map and was shocked to see that he had lost at least four hours. They were out in the western part of PA. After examining the map, Cal realized Rte. 6 seemed to be the shortest way back to Rte. 220. As they started out on it, he soon found out that it was really a back woods road that wound through some pretty tough country. The double backs and hairpin curves amazed both of them. When it said 15-miles an hour, you'd better be going 15 or less, or, you'd be leaving the road.

At the top of one mountain, they drove by what looked like a POW camp. There were no signs on it, but there was Constantia wire around the top of the 15–foot tall telephone pole corners that were supporting the chain link fence, complete with guard towers at each corner.

There were guys inside the enclosure dressed in camouflage uniforms, beating the tar out of each other. Cal didn't waste any time getting the hell out of there. He never did see that place again, nor did he ever want to.

Finally, they were back on Rte 220. It was like seeing an old friend again. By noon, they were in Pennsylvania Dutch Country and stopped at a Quaker House that was posing as a restaurant. They were road weary and hungry.

Kinsey was a real trooper, she never complained, always thoughtful, sometimes talkative, sometimes just content to ride and watch the countryside roll by.

He didn't know how she managed to do it, but she always looked good, even after riding for hours in a car. She stopped for a moment before getting out, to run a comb through her hair and to straighten her clothes.

The Quaker restaurant was more of a farm house than an actual Restaurant. As soon as they approached the door, a young girl met them and escorted them in. She wore a huge bonnet on her head and, as they walked in, her full dress made a swishing sound as it brushed against the floor. Every woman they saw wore large bonnets and black plain-looking clothes. The men had beards and black brimmed hats and only nodded at them as they passed.

Cal and Kinsey were seated in two spindle type chairs at an oak table with a white tablecloth in a small room with white curtains and a couple of tapestries on the walls. They were both starved, as they had had no breakfast and it was past 1 pm. In his entire life, Cal had never been served more food, and that had such a vast variety. It appeared they were serving each food group in sevens. They displayed seven types of meat from which to pick, seven vegetables and finally seven cakes and seven different pies.

There were seconds if they wanted them; however, they were so stuffed that they could hardly walk. Kinsey admitted that she'd never heard of, or seen the likes of this before. This was an adventure for them. Cal was sure with all the food they'd consumed, that it was going to cost him a small fortune. There'd been no mention of price, no prices posted anywhere or on anything, when they'd arrived, nor were there any menus. They had just brought each type of food to them. The moment they looked up from eating, they'd rush to bring more food to them.

Finally, Cal told Kinsey, that whatever she did, not to look up or they would both be in trouble.

She thought that was funny and they both laughed. She had a sexy laugh, and Cal enjoyed seeing her happy. She also had a way of lighting up a room when she entered. You could tell she was caring; it showed through her eyes. She had the greenest eyes he'd ever seen; they actually changed shades when she was happy, sad, laughing or was feeling passionate – that was his favorite shade of green.

They both took a long break in the bathroom to freshen up. As he waited for her, he paid the bill. One of the younger girls told him that his wife was very pretty – he didn't bother to correct her, it made him feel good to hear Kinsey referred to as his wife. He nodded, as he smiled, thanking her for the compliment.

After leaving, he told Kinsey about the conversation, and she leaned over and gave him a big kiss as she said, "I like the sound of that too – "husband". A warm, sweet feeling spread all over inside his chest, and he felt as if he was on top of the world.

The road wound through some of the lushest countryside's he'd ever seen, with brightly colored farms, like colorful pins in a green quilt. Then finally, they were crossing the state line and coming into Binghamton. The tone and color of the hills changed. The buildings were dingy and the roads full of grit and salt.

He was anxious to get to where his family lived. He had never been there before, as his Mom and his sisters had moved into a large apartment house just down the street from the hospital where they worked.

Kinsey was silent, taking her lead from him. He always liked to surprise his Mom and sisters with his sudden appearance. When he popped in on her that morning, she went into shock, particularly since he had a special companion with him. He introduced Kinsey on the fly as they hugged, his Mom lamenting that it was crowded there ... but she guessed Kinsey could sleep in Marie's bed with Marie. He'd have to make the best of the couch, which really didn't bother him.

Mom referred to Kinsey as "Dear", which made him feel good. Mom took her under her wing immediately, by scolding him for not taking better care of her and not being more thoughtful. "After all, she could have become sick, being up all hours of the night, driving all over the place. You should have checked into a motel ... of course with your own rooms," she added. He sensed Kinsey stiffening at his mother's comment, but he didn't read into it the message that Kinsey was getting.

They stayed for one night and headed back the next day. During that first day, Cal took her to all the spots where he'd grown up. He showed her the school where he had graduated and the farm where he'd grown up. They stopped off at his Uncle Clyde's and Aunt Anne's. They were glad to see them, and Clyde was his usual self, always flirting. They stayed only long enough to pay his respects to that part of his family and moved on. Night time found them still driving around; they'd stopped off at the farm and shared Christmas with all the relatives. Then it was time to go.

He was getting antsy to do some more driving. He could tell Kinsey was getting fidgety, so thought of the airport as a good place to park. It was his favorite, by far, as he loved watching the planes coming and going, always wondering where all the people were going, and what wonderful places they'd seen. They sat there for awhile; he noticed her shivering and turned the car on so they'd get some heat. They kissed for awhile and held each other close. He felt her responding and wished that it could be more, but he knew that he had given his word.

All the way home, she was in a depressed state of mind, and they talked very infrequently. Cal couldn't figure out what was going on with her and she wouldn't tell him. Later, she told him that she had wished they had had more time to themselves.

On the way back, they ran into a wicked storm at the top of a mountain and had to pull off the road several times, until it let up. Realizing that he couldn't get her home before early morning, Cal pulled off where there was a phone booth, and she called her mom so that they wouldn't worry. Cal asked her what she'd said, and she mumbled something about it being okay, and to be careful.

He had half expected that she would be scolded or something. Again, he was surprised; his mom would have been upset, and showed it by giving all kinds of advice in a tone of voice that would sound harsh – it was only her way of showing him that she cared and he didn't mind, as he'd heard it all before.

Carefully, so as not to have an accident, he came down off the mountain to dryer roads. In fact, the landscape changed so much, that one would never have known they'd just come through a blizzard.

Finally, they'd arrived at her home, tired and road worn. It was early morning, the day after Christmas when they let themselves in. Kinsey, without hardly a look at him, headed straight to bed. He stayed behind long enough to tell her Mom thanks and to explain that they'd come through a really bad storm. She just nodded and smiled.

He could tell from the wrapping paper, and boxes strew about, that they had missed Christmas with her family. Maybe that was why Kinsey was so distant.

Later that day they all got up and came down for lunch. They were all full of questions about his family and Kinsey seemed to be full of life again and excitedly told them all about what they'd seen and done. Even to the part where they had gone to the airport to watch airplanes come and go in the freezing cold. Her sister piped up and said you could do that here too. Cal hadn't realized they had an airport and immediately suggested going. Kinsey nodded and said, "okay," as she smiled over at Cal.

Later that day, he did find out part of what was bothering Kinsey. One, she had hoped to spend more quality time with him; two, she had not expected to be sleeping with his sister, but with him, after all, they were engaged to be married (the implication was that she thought they would have their own place to stay while visiting) and third; she was sure his mother didn't like her.

Cal was surprised that she'd preferred to have stayed in a motel. If only he'd known, he would have arranged it in a minute, as that would have been his preference, also. He was only trying to be respectful of her reputation as they had spent a lot of quality time together, but he guessed what she had in mind was more intimacy. He tried to convince her that his mother really did care for her; she was just different about how she showed it. In the end, it would come back to haunt him. As for the quality time, he told her she should have told him how she felt so he could have done something about it.

She just shook her head from side to side with a sad look on her face, saying that it was something he should have felt - the same as she did. Her comment often echoed in his mind, and he thought about it a lot, but he could only think that his actions were motivated by years of training to be a gentleman.

In the next few days, everything seemed to have returned to normal and he no longer felt like he was about to be grilled for supper. Kinsey was back to being her old self, and they were having a good time, walking, driving or whatever else that they decided to do.

Chapter 22.0

Time has a way of marching on, and so it did with them. Their time together in Cumberland was nearing an end. Cal was to make another cruise to the Caribbean and upon returning, pick up his discharge papers on December 27th, 1966. In the meantime, Kinsey graduated from High School and moved to DC to start her Nurses Training.

However, upon returning from leave, Cal was ordered to report to the Yeoman's Office and sign papers extending his active full-time service from December 27th to April 17th.

The war in Viet Nam was heating up, and they needed time to draft more men and get them trained. So a freeze was put on all personnel getting out of the service, with the exception of the reserves. This ruling created a bit of hostility toward the reserves. Admittedly, in general, the reserves within their ranks were not highly thought of. Perhaps it was because they were not "full timers", i.e., not having the same length training period in boot camp and shortened active duty hitches. The feeling was that they were "skaters". Although he respected them on an individual basis, he was of the mind, if they did good work, let well enough alone. His motto was, "live and let live".

After being extended, he bought a standby to do his duties every weekend. He had a short timer's attitude, and no one could blame him; by rights, he should have been already discharged. Everyone thought he got a bum deal. The rest of his time was spent in a state of limbo. Kinsey seemed to take his active duty extension in stride. She was currently involved in her preparations of moving to Washington, DC to start her nurse's training and her letters were full of her excitement for that and for her new freedom to be with him.

Also, she was happy to be closer to him and to where he would be getting his job, once he got out of the Navy. Now, instead of driving over four hours to see her in Cumberland, Cal would only have to drive approximately two and, once she was in DC, they would be less than an hour apart. They would also be on their own for the first time, with no parents to answer to.

During his almost-every-weekend trips up to DC, Cal would get a room at Howard Johnson's in Cheverly. After several trips, the manager started giving Cal a discount and a sly wink. At first Kinsey and he would just hang out there watching TV and catching up on their sleep but, as time went by, it became harder to keep his promise to her folks. He wanted to wait until they were married.

During this time, there was never any doubt that they would marry and he was willing to wait. He felt that was the glue that brought them closer.

It was during these frequent trips to DC and back that his good old friend, the 59-Chevy gave up the ghost. He had had the dent fixed in the door by a body shop in Norfolk and the car repainted with every intention of keeping it. But, she began to use oil and smoked when he drove it anywhere. It needed a valve and ring job, and eventually, Leroy, Larry's brother consented to do the job. The deal they struck, was that Cal would buy the parts and Leroy would put them in. During this time, Leroy would get the use of the car while Cal was at sea and, by the time he got back, the rebuild would be finished. He could hardly wait – counting each day until he'd be back and could enjoy the freedom of the open road.

Finally, at the end of the cruise, he came back looking forward to a completely rebuilt engine and to his disappointment, the car's rebuild hadn't even been started. So, having returned, he pressured Leroy into getting started on the job as he had promised, so the following weekend, they jacked it up and tore it down. As usual, something always gets forgotten, so it couldn't be completed until the following weekend.

Cal hated not having his car and felt bitter that Leroy had not followed through on their agreement. They finally got it done and then discovered, when they went to turn it over that it was too tight, and they had to back off on most of the bearings. Leroy hadn't torque the main bearing on the crankshaft correctly, and Cal was starting to worry about the quality of work being done on his car in general and, Leroy's so called mechanical abilities.

This feeling was further supported by the amount of smoke pouring out of the exhaust pipe. It now smoked worse than ever, and Cal had to keep adding oil as often as he bought gas. Later he had a garage give it a compression test, and his suspicions were further born out. The compression test revealed that it had broken rings in two of its eight cylinders. Cal felt sick about all the money he'd put into it and, the substandard job he got for of his efforts. Because Cal needed his car for his trip north, he ended up driving it all the way home and then up to Kinsey's home.

The smoke did decrease a lot after the other rings wore in, but never completely. Each time he shut it off, it wouldn't start until it had time to cool off. He knew that it was time for a new car.

After returning to Little Creek, he went from lot to lot and finally found a bright red 1964 Chevy Malibu. It had low miles, looked as clean as a new one and ran like a dream. He negotiated the trade and held his breath when the guy went to start his old car. It belched a little smoke, and he explained to the salesman that it had just gotten a new ring job and would be a little stiff for a time. He went on to show him the new dual antennas he'd just installed. The car looked super clean, and he got a good price for it as a trade in, almost as much as he'd paid for it a couple of years back. He only needed a little more money to swing the deal, so he went across the street to House Hold Finance (HFC) and picked up another 800-dollars.

He rushed back across the street and paid the man, grabbed the keys and was gone before he had time to restart the old Chevy. He found out later that when they went to start it, it wouldn't start and they had to have it towed. Later they wholesaled it to a lot in South Carolina.

He was proud as punch of his new car; he kept thinking about how surprised and pleased Kinsey would be. He could hardly wait to pick her up. They had decided that she would take the train down as it was less expensive and probably safer than a bus.

When he finally met her at the train station, she was surprised when he pointed out the new car, but not in the way he'd expected. She was upset that he'd not included her in on the decision of buying it. She immediately told him how she felt. It had never occurred to Cal to include her in the process of getting the new car. He could see where it would have been nice for her to be involved, now that she had brought it up, but he had never considered her involvement in his rush to get rid of the other car and its problems. There were time limitations – he was afraid that had he waited around, he was sure he would have lost the deal. He was so happy about it, and all he wanted was to share his happiness with her. It was apparent, that he was having a hard time with the "they, them and we concept" of doing things. It wasn't that he didn't like the "together" concept of doing things, it was that he had, for so many years, acted independently – he had never had anyone in his life to have to consider in his decisions - up until now. In retrospect, Cal had to agree with her, and he admitted to her that she should have been involved. He apologized for not involving her in the decision and told her that, in the future, he would, and she could count on it.

Thankfully, her hurt feelings were short lived, and soon she was exploring the car as he had. He showed her the new engine and all the storage places it had. For being a used car, it had very low mileage and still smelled brand new. They were looking forward to it lasting them for many years.

They had been listening to the conversation through a shotgun mike and recording it.

"Well, he's learning, the older man said to the driver. Given how he was raised, I'm surprised that he's lasted this long with her. She must really love him, to be so patient."

"Do you remember what it was like when you were his age?" The driver queried the older man.

"Yeah and that's why he's having such a hard time."

"How's that?" asked the driver.

"Well, his grandfather was a lot like my grandfather, and he had a lot of influence on him, along with his two daughters and, they were raised at the far end of a bullwhip. So I can appreciate where this young man is coming from, you know it was a whole different world than what you were raised in."

"Kind of like coming through a generational time warp, isn't it?"

"Yeah, it's like your damn if you do and damn if you don't."

"It will be interesting to see how this all plays out – two bits, that they don't make it," the old man said.

"I'll take that bet, cause I think she loves him enough to stick it out, no matter what," said the younger man.

Chapter 23.0

Finally, his discharge day had arrived. They'd just returned from the Caribbean and, ironically, had tied up to the same tender at the same pier that the ship had been when he had first come aboard. How well Cal remembered that day – it was like yesterday.

The night before his release, several "boots" came aboard and, as they entered the department, Cal turned and asked the first man when he was due to be released.

He popped it off the top of his head as if it'd been burned there. "That sounds like a life's sentence," Cal shouted at the top of his lungs, "God if I had that long to go, I'd kill myself". The boot looked at him as if he'd just taken leave of his senses.

"Ask me how long I have", Cal shouted, and the boot did as he was asked. It felt so good to be able to say – "One day and a wake-up, and I'll be out of here so fast you'll hear the sound barrier being broken as I haul ass off this sorry ship".

In fact, he was already packed and signed out all over the ship, all that was needed was to pick up his discharge papers tomorrow morning on the way off the ship. He had even gone as far as to check with the yeoman to be sure his discharge papers were signed and ready. There would be no slip-ups, mix ups or anything else if he had anything to do with it.

He was up and showered long before reveille, the happy day finally had arrived; he had said his goodbyes and was ready to leave – to be a civilian again, to reclaim his life, to be with Kinsey. The

Navy, the ship, and its men had been an alien way of life to him.

On several occasions, the officers had come from "God's Country", to see him in the Starboard Pump Room, and had offered him a shipping over bonus of 1,200-dollars and a 1,000-dollars a year on each anniversary of that date.

He appeared to be interested only so far as to get them out of his face. He had no intentions of shipping over, particularly on that ship. As far as he was concerned, it was a floating penal colony and he didn't trust any of them to keep their word.

Just as he was about to leave the ship for good, he was called back to the Yeoman's office – wasn't he just down there yesterday and at the time had been assured that everything was a "go"?

"Now what – was it another extension?"

His stomach was in a knot, and he was thoroughly pissed off, as he rushed headlong down the ladder one deck and then to the Yeoman's Office.

As he came around the corner, he saw a man in a dark civilian suit standing next to the Yeoman. He had never seen this man before, but he looked important as he stood there with a briefcase in hand and a very stern look on his face as he stared at him.

As soon as they saw him, the man in the suit, motioned for him to come in and, as he did, he reached into his brief case and produced a set of papers, then he explained that Cal must read these closely and sign them.

The letter head was stamped with the seal of the United States Department of Defense. It also was stamped "TOP SECRET". In essence, it said that he would be prosecuted should he reveal the substance of his special training as a diver in the experimental program or even mentioned its existence.

He saw no reason that this would be a problem, as most of what he'd been through in the Navy, was something he'd just as soon forget. He was restarting his new life as soon as he hit the pier.

Then the man asked him if he wanted to delete "this part of his training" from his "Jacket"[56]. He thought about it for a moment, wondering what he had to gain by deleting it?

The man as if reading his mind explained that should he ever have an altercation in his civilian life which resulted in injury to or death of his opponent, this information could be used against him in a court of law. He went on to explain that his special training involving hand to hand combat, both defensive and offensive would be considered in a court of law that as such he was considered to be a deadly weapon and he could very well lose his case and be charged with murder. He strongly recommended that this information be deleted from his record.

After giving it some thought and remembering that part of his training, he had to agree. So nodding to the Yeoman, he retyped that page of his record and reinserted it back into his Navy file and a new copy back in his record's jacket. And just like that, there was no longer any record of his ever having taken any special defensive or offensive training or of ever having ever been a diver. He and the plain clothed man shook hands, and he left.

Cal was given a large check containing his severance pay, back pay and travel pay. Some of it, he later used to buy things for the apartment, which he knew he would be getting near his new job in Dumphries, Va. He remembered going to the on base Navy store and buying a toaster oven, salt and pepper shakers, sheets, towels, pillowcases, broom, mop and more. It seemed like he spent a small fortune setting up house keeping.

He'd solicited several places for work and had been hired by Virginia Electric and Power Company

---

[56] Personnel US Naval File

before he was even out of the Navy. He was scheduled to work a weekly swing shift at their Virginia, Dumfries plant. He was particularly pleased since this was within 45-minutes of DC. As soon as he was off the base, he called Kinsey to tell her the good news, that he was finally out of the Navy and had been hired by VEPCO.

He remembered that moment like it was yesterday - he was standing on the corner of Granby and Virginia Beach Blvd, across from the main gate to the Base on a clear sunny morning feeling free of the burden of his duties aboard ship, free to do what he wanted – to come and go at will, to finally start living HIS life.

He stopped to see Kinsey on the way up through to see his Mom and family. She was somewhat more her old self and interested in the things he'd bought. She felt that he'd spent too much money and should have been more careful. She was still upset that he hadn't involved her in the purchases. Once again he'd left her out of the decisions that would affect not only him but her. His only excuse was that by buying them from the ship's store, they were so much less expensive, than at any civilian store.

Looking back, she was right, but he had no experience in being "domestic". Cal could see where he hadn't considered her feelings in the decisions that also affected her. He was terribly naive about a lot of things, and this was one of the biggest. He had lived since he was 14 as a person who did things for himself, it was a survival mechanism. He had never observed his mother and father collaborating on a purchase or his Granddad and Grandmother. She saw it as leaving her out, not allowing her to have a say in the very items she'd have to use when they setup housing keeping.

Youth is blind and unfeeling, so it has been said, and having been there Cal can honestly say that often he was blind and unfeeling about those around him as well as "them".

He hated her feeling like this as he knew she was sad again, and he felt her pulling back from him as they parted and he drove home. He didn't really want to leave things that way, but he felt the pull of home and the open road.

He called daily, and they talked about what she was doing and what he was doing. They both expressed their love for each other and talked about his coming back down to DC.

He had been informed about his starting date with VEPCO and was so excited he could hardly contain himself and called her right away. It was then that Kinsey asked him if he was sure if this was what he wanted – he was incredulous, how could she think otherwise - of course this was what he wanted – it was the start of their life together. Her question baffled him.

The day finally came when he drove south with all his earthly belongings. As soon as he got there, Kinsey and he started house hunting, she had already made up a list of prospects that were located between where she went to school and where he had to go to work. He was pleased at her foresight and it felt good that she was a part of their working together to find a home.

They finally settled on a one-bedroom apartment in Alexandra, Virginia located a short distance from Mt Vernon. It was a large colonial brick, and the apartment was on the second floor, right-hand side. Parking was on the street, and the sidewalk was long and the steps high.

Even though it was a furnished apartment (bed, couch, some chairs, and a lamp), it lacked a lot of the amenities that they'd hoped would be there. Even so, Kinsey unloaded all the boxes, dispersing the house keeping items where she would be using them

288 | Three Squares and a Rack

and put his civilian clothes away in the dresser and hug his shirts and pants on hangers in the closet.

He was running short on food and would soon be out of money too. They had talked about his situation and Kinsey started bringing him boxes of cereal from the cafeteria to help tide him out until he got paid.

Trying to stretch his last few dollars, Cal bought cans of Campbell's Cream of Chicken soup, mixed boiled rice with it and ate it day after day as he waited for that first paycheck.

Cal was also alarmed as he had been watching his gas gauge dropping lower and lower. He was to the point where he was ready to park the car in the back lot at the power plant and live out of it until he got paid. Returning home and picking his mail out of the mail box, a miracle happened. Out of the clear blue he got a letter from his Mom with two twenty dollar bills enclosed. It was a Godsend! He immediately went next door and called his mom and thanked her. He'd earlier made an arrangement with the elderly lady to use her phone to receive calls from his job until he could afford his own phone. In return, Cal agreed to take her grocery shopping and carry the groceries up to her 2nd-floor apartment. Also, he would reimburse her for any long distance calls that were on her bill.

With the forty dollars, he was able to buy gas and something more to eat, and it would be enough to tide him over until that first paycheck came in three weeks, from the time he'd started. He only had a couple of more days to go.

In the meantime, Kinsey asked if it would be okay if she invited a friend, Bailey, and her boy friend, Tom, to come and stay over at their place. This meant they would have to make up a bed for them selves on the living room floor – camping out style, Kinsey said with a smile.

He felt odd about the arrangement, but deferred to Kinsey as it seemed to be important to her.

The following evening, they arrived, and Kinsey introduced Cal to them. Tom was slender and dressed in a suit that seemed to be a size too big and was extremely nervous, where Bailey was quiet and reserved and wore a permanent smile. Kinsey showed them around the apartment and to the bedroom where they put their over night bags and came back out, thanking them for their hospitality.

After some discussion, they ended up ordering in a super sized pizza with all the trimmings, some soft drink, and rolls. In no time it all arrived, and Tom paid the delivery man.

While they ate, Cal found a deck of cards, that the last tenant had left behind and they started playing Hearts. It was one of the few card games Cal knew.

Before long, Tom started yawning, and Cal knew it was time for all of them to turn in and said, "Well, I think it's been a long day for all of us, so how about we all turn in for the night." There was no doubt that they were all in agreement, as the cards were put away; the girls swiped up what was left of the pizza, buns and soft drink bottles, disposing of them in the kitchen, and put what was left of the pizza in the refrigerator while Tom and he made small talk.

Once they had turned in, Kinsey and he put together a camping type bed on the floor between the living room and kitchen. He'd been watching her move as her night shirt was playing peek-a-boo with the rest of her body. As she walked past him, she snuggled up close and whispered in his ear, "Thanks for having my girl friend over and her boy friend, it means a lot to her and me.

He just shrugged, "always glad to make you happy, Hon," he whispered in her ear.

She drew the drapes, flicked the light switch and whispered, "well … what are you waiting for"?

The following day, they all arose, got their showers and dressed. Kinsey was beaming as our guests had had a good time and were all smiles when they came out for breakfast.

The job at the power plant was easier than anything he'd ever done onboard the ship. It was a huge coal burning plant with six gas turbine standby units. In the plant, they had 120, 160, 80 and 30-megawatt generators. His job was to take readings on all the machines and take the main circulating pumps on or off line, as he was directed from the control room. He also had to clean screen washes and condensers on occasion. Each shift was eight hours and ran five days, at which time he would be off two days and swing forward to the next shift, which was eight hours later than the one he'd been on and do it all over again.

Cal's boss was a huge Irishman named Fitzpatrick and Fitzpatrick's boss was a man called Mr. Fisher. Fitzpatrick was a jolly, good natured, huge man who wore bib overalls just like his grandfather had. He always had a smile on his ruddy face and always had a good word for each of his men. Mr. Fisher, as he knew him, was hardly ever seen. When he caught a glimpse of him, he wore a dark blue, three-piece suit, never smiled and was all business. He kept to himself in an office several stories above the two level plant. The office appeared to have windows around its periphery, no doubt they enabled a view of the workings of the plant.

They all got along well, and the biweekly paycheck was good if you put in extra hours, otherwise, as a starting pay, it was not enough to get by on. Often he was called upon to work extra shifts due to someone calling in sick at the last minute – too late to get a substitute.

It was his first taste of having a full-time civilian job, a home, furniture payments, car payments, car insurance, utilities, food, gas for the car and other miscellaneous expenses to manage. He couldn't afford a phone, TV, newspaper or magazines, or even pictures for the wall. It was a real struggle to keep up with the maintenance on his car. He was broke most of the time and hanging on by the skin of his teeth from paycheck to paycheck. It wasn't a fun time and to balance work, eating, sleeping and then trying to balance all that with Kinsey's schedule was putting additional pressure on their already fragile relationship.

Working sometimes 16-straight hours, and then driving an hour to get home, shower, sleep and find time to eat and see Kinsey, stretched his ability to concentrate to the limit and beyond.

He reached the point where he didn't know if he was coming or going. Kinsey was also showing the stress as they didn't see as much of each other as they wanted and she was having a hard time getting from DC General Hospital down to his apartment in Alexandra. Something had to give. After some discussion, they decided that he should move closer to the hospital where she was taking her training.

She knew someone who knew someone who managed the apartments across the parking lot from the hospital. The only way to get one was to know this person and get the address and to go downtown in person for an interview. She had told him that they were very careful about who they rented to.

With the new apartment, she'd be in walking distance to the hospital training facility. The consensus was that she could come over anytime, study and enjoy piece and quiet from the dorm.

He welcomed anything that meant they'd be closer and that would eventually lead to their marriage.

The transition went smoothly and in no time, with Kinsey's help, he was living in the new apartment only steps away from Kinsey's hospital training center and trainee's residence.

292 | *Three Squares and a Rack*

Often upon returning home from work, she'd be there fixing supper for him and studying. Life was good and they were happy.

He had joined the Navy to see the world, and had for the moment satisfied his desire to see what was over the next hill and around the next corner. He had come to the conclusion that he was fortunate to have been born in the US. He had visited many countries whose civilization were hundreds of not thousands of years older than his and along his journey of discovery he had absorbed the best of their cultures, realizing that older does not necessarily mean better. He had left home a naive young man and had returned a cultured world traveler. He was self assured and knew what he wanted out of life and in time, his aspirations of helping others would lead to "paying it forward" in ways that he had yet to discover – but he would with God's guidance.

Out on the shady, tree lined street, parked not far from Cal's red 1964 Chevy Malibu, was a large black Cadillac Eldorado. Again, as before, a man dressed in black, had been sitting, watching the young man and Kinsey come and go from their apartment and monitoring where they went during the week. There were also others who were checking in to all aspects of their lives. The current Manila folder had grown in size, even after having been divided many times, each housed, in order, in his brief case. Finally after their last sighting of Cal and his fiancé; Kinsey, he smiled as he said in an English accent, "it rather seems that our young man has adapted quite well from his years on the farm and his time in the Navy and seems to be getting a sense of what life is all about. I quite admire how he thinks and his ability to adapt, no matter what the obstacles he encounters. This certainly bodes well for him in respect for our plans for him.

"When do you expert that you will tell him, the younger man asked?"

"Soon, very soon," he said as he rubbed his chin whiskers with one hand as he finished making some notes in the binder.

END

Operations

ROUTINE DATE/TIME GROUP ₂31430Z MESSAGE

FROM:
U.S.S. NEOSHO (AO 143)

TO:
U.S.S. FORT MANDAN (LSD-21)

NAVAL MESSAGE

Operations

On 3 October 1962 in a heavy fog, FORT MAN-
DAN went alongside the USS NEOSHO. The rigs
were passed and fueling commenced. It was then
a contact was sighted by radar approaching on a
collision course. The only solution was an emergency breakaway in the quickest time possible to
avoid the contact. The following messages tell the
results:

U N C L A S

YOUR SKILL AND SPEED IN RIGGING AND UNRIGGING OUTSTANDING.
PLEASURE TO HAVE YOU ALONGSIDE.
FORT MANDAN EXECUTED EMERGENCY BREAK AWAY SMARTLY WITH NO
DAMAGE TO RIG

U N C L A S

HOLIDAY CHEER

1. THE USS FORT MANDAN WISHES ALL SHIPS A
MERRY CHRISTMAS AND A VERY HAPPY NEW YEAR.

SMOOTH SAILING

DRAFTED BY:

FROM:
CTF 61

TO:

INFO:
U.S.S. FORT MANDAN (LSD 21)

U.S.S. HYADES (AF 28)

U.S.S. FORT MANDAN (LSD 21)

U N C L A S

THANK YOU VERY MUCH.

U N C L A S   A VERY FINE JOB MY FAITH IN LSD'S IS REVIVED.

CONGATULATIONS, SWIFT TURTLE.
THE RABBITS CONCEED. YOUR ENGINEERS
DESERVE A HEARTY WELL DONE

TO:
CTF 61   U.S.S. FREMONT (APA 44)

INFO:
U.S.S. MULIPHEN (AKA 61)

U N C L A S
THE TURTLE WILL SLOW DOWN FOR THE RABBITS IN ORDER
THAT THE WALTZ OF THE PACHYDERM'S MAY CONTINUE IF
...SIRE.

*Picture taken from the USS Fort Mandan LSD-21 Mediterranean
Cruise Book (1962 to 63)*

Cruise Fact Sheet

Fact   *Sheet*

Believe it or not!

It has been an arduous and extended Med. cruise: The "FORT MANDAN" has met every commitment adeptness, alacrity, and supreme competence. To do this all hands participated in an exemplary fashion, utilizing arts and skills that the Mandan has always been famed for.

The following is a compilation of facts and figures that enabled this cruise to come to a successful conclusion. This ship has:

1. Distilled 2,906,690 gallons of water utilizing 11,625 watch hours.
2. Purchased an additional 944,680 gallons of water.
3. Received 1,218,475 gallons of Black oil.
4. Steamed over 18,000 Engine miles making 15,941 nautical miles good.
5. Used AVGAS to keep a helo airborne 270 working days.
6. Anchored 39 times and moored to a buoy once.
7. Handled 1,736 people at sick call and gave 1447 immunizations. They further distributed 11,500 APC's, 15 gallons of cough syrup, 1150 seasick pills, 3,000 band aids, and untold hangover cures.
8. CIC plotted 722 skunks.
9. Laundered 2,050 shirts, 1,520 trousers and over 900 bags of unmentionables.
10. Soda Fountain sold over 10,000 ice cream cones, 7,000 ice cream cups, 7,706 assorted juices, 1,548 assorted nuts, 57,000 vending machine drinks and 56,254 assorted candy bars.
11. Ships store sold over 2,227,000 cigarettes, 45 radios, 65 tape recorders, 572 bottles of perfume, realizing $54,355.66 total sales.
12. Barber shop butchered 3,920 heads.
13. The "FORT MANDAN" cafeteria doled out over 200,000 hot meals using 16,000 loaves of bread, 4,000 pounds of fresh vegetables, 26,425 pounds of potatoes and 17,254 pounds of beef (12% was steak). Since so many people have asked for the recipe for MANDIES MACARONI LUNCHEON LOAF (L-47):

Luncheon meat 13½#	Milk pwd. 1½#
Vienna sausage 7½#	Eggs pwd. 12 oz.
Macaroni 2½#	Bread 3#
Salt 1 oz.	Cheese 1½#
Flour 1½#	Water 3 qts.

Grind meat and mix cooked macaroni, flour, milk, eggs, bread, and cheese. Place or throw in pan, warm slightly or burn, put on chow line and run for cover.
14. Communications handled 6,664 messages.
15. Gunnery (never in anger) expended 191 rounds of 40MM ammo.
16. Deck distributed over 3,400 rolls of toilet tissues, 672 lbs. of scouring powder, and 864 lbs. of alkaline soap.
17. HME 262 had over 1100 carrier landings, flew 1500 hours (weather permitting) and hoisted aircraft 536 times. This was all accident free. A record for LSD operations on a 6th fleet deployment.
18. A total of 364 lamps are used for Med lights and 320 had to be replaced.
19. Total charges for port facilities were $1,469.23.
20. Rewound motors for TELFAIR, POCONO, MULIPHEN, FREMONT, CHUCKAWAN, and WALDO COUNTY using over 14 miles of wire.
21. Aside from rewinding motors, we made over 35 emergency issues to various units of 6th fleet, keeping them in fighting trim.
22. Used 1488 wood pencils, 276 ball point pens, 117 reams of mimeo paper, 840 lined tablets, 1900 pounds of wiping rags, 123 swabs, 79 brooms, and 102 cans of snuff.
23. Pathfinders made 308 jumps.
24. Finally, a tape-deck system, ships newspaper, and telephone services to the states were also available.

Picture taken from the USS Fort Mandan LSD-21 Mediterranean Cruise Book (1962 to 63)

ABOUT THE AUTHOR

P hilip R Morehouse was born in upstate New York. Among his many jobs, he worked as a writer for over 50-years and he was also a professional photographer. Now retired, he pursues his interest in writing true-to-life, survival, and adventure-type stories.

Other books written by the author are:

- *The Wanderer*
- *The Recluse*
- *Retribution*
- *Flash Back*
- *The Benton Harbor File*
- *The Man Without a Country*
- *Ten Dollars a Week – Room and Board*

Made in the USA
Middletown, DE
19 December 2019